SINGLE MOTHERS AND THE STATE'S EMBRACE

Single Mothers and the State's Embrace

Reproductive Agency in Vietnam

HARRIET M. PHINNEY

UNIVERSITY OF WASHINGTON PRESS
Seattle

Single Mothers and the State's Embrace was made possible in part by a grant from the Charles and Jane Keyes Endowment for Books on Southeast Asia, established through the generosity of Charles and Jane Keyes.

Design by Katrina Noble
Composed in Alegreya, typeface designed by Juan Pablo del Peral

25 24 23 22 21   5 4 3 2 1

Printed and bound in the United States of America

UNIVERSITY OF WASHINGTON PRESS
uwapress.uw.edu

LIBRARY OF CONGRESS CATALOGING-IN-PUBLICATION DATA

Names: Phinney, Harriet M., author.
Title: Single mothers and the state's embrace : reproductive agency in Vietnam / Harriet M. Phinney.
Description: Seattle : University of Washington Press, [2021] | Includes bibliographical references and index.
Identifiers: LCCN 2021006505 (print) | LCCN 2021006506 (ebook) | ISBN 9780295749426 (hardcover) | ISBN 9780295749433 (paperback) | ISBN 9780295749440 (ebook)
Subjects: LCSH: Single mothers—Vietnam. | Motherhood—Social aspects—Vietnam. | Reproductive rights—Vietnam. | Motherhood—Government policy—Vietnam.
Classification: LCC HQ759.45 .P56 2021 (print) | LCC HQ759.45 (ebook) | DDC 306.874/3209597—dc23
LC record available at https://lccn.loc.gov/2021006505
LC ebook record available at https://lccn.loc.gov/2021006506

The paper used in this publication is acid free and meets the minimum requirements of American National Standard for Information Sciences—Permanence of Paper for Printed Library Materials, ANSI Z39.48–1984.∞

"The Unwed Mother"

No husband, but pregnant, that's skillful.
Husband and pregnant, that's pretty ordinary.

—HO XUAN HUONG, 1772–1822 , trans. Balaban

CONTENTS

PREFACE

This book is based on many years of ethnographic fieldwork. I first went to Vietnam in 1993 to study the Vietnamese language. It was then that I became interested in "older" single women who had decided to get pregnant out of wedlock: women who had "asked for a child." I conducted the initial study from 1995 to 1996 in northern Vietnam, in the capital city of Hà Nội; in a village on the outskirts of Hà Nội; in rural villages in Sóc Sơn District, thirty-two kilometers due north of Hà Nội; and in rural villages in the Phú Lương District of Bắc Thái Province, ninety-three kilometers north of Hà Nội. I returned to Hà Nội and Sóc Sơn a number of times from 2004 to 2017 to conduct follow-up research along five tracks: to clarify historical details about the postwar era that had been murky in the mid-1990s, to gather a more robust understanding of adoption practices, to visit with the women who had asked for a child and continue to learn from them, to discuss new policies and concerns with social scientists and governmental authorities and catch up on contemporary media discourses, and to talk to single women and single mothers of the next generation about their marital and reproductive decisions—in essence to develop a long-term understanding of *xin con* (the practice of asking for a child).

I also returned to Hà Nội for other purposes. In 2004, I conducted fieldwork on love, marriage, and HIV in Hà Nội, examining married women's risk for contracting HIV from their husbands and men's extramarital relations (Hirsch et al. 2010; Phinney 2010). From 2007 to 2012 I served as a consultant for Columbia University's Star Partnership Project, a training program in ethnographic research methods. I worked with Vietnamese scholars at the Institute for Social Development Studies (ISDS) researching the intersection between HIV, antiretroviral therapies, and the government's Population Quality Campaign (Phinney et al. 2014). As a result, the analyses I provide in this book derive from three different, but overlapping, research projects.[1]

Throughout this twenty-year span, my research on *xin con* has been shaped by Đổi Mới policies and the extent to which governmental reforms and Vietnam's integration into the global market economy affected the lives of my research participants, as well as my access to and interactions with them.

1993–1996

When I first arrived in Hà Nội in 1993 to study Vietnamese there were so few Americans that children riding by on their bicycles would call out "Liên Xô! Liên Xô!" (Soviet Union! Soviet Union!). Two giggling young girls' breathless exclamation that "just a few years ago we would have needed a permission card to even talk to you on the street!" signified the changing Hà Nội landscape: Westerners from non–Eastern bloc countries had begun to tour the country, study the Vietnamese language, conduct research, and explore business opportunities. When I returned to Hà Nội in 1995 to conduct research, I was one among many Americans living in Hà Nội. However, the ground rules for foreign scholars, particularly Americans, were unclear, tenuous, and slippery—especially those of us who wanted to live in rural areas.

Gaining permission as an American to conduct ethnographic research outside Hà Nội in the mid-1990s was a test of patience. Although the government had opened up Vietnam to the West in 1986, the state sought to maintain control over "foreign access, the traffic of information and the representation of 'the people' and 'the nation'" (Craig 2002, 24). The sociologist David Craig (2002, 25) aptly described the situation for many Western scholars:

> Foreigners conducting research crossed an ill-defined border into the subtle, highly formalized and managed domain of official information, where the power of representation and knowledge was all too well known and respected. They crossed this line without being organizationally or culturally locked into the formal and informal constraints of official management of information, and were thus potentially something of a loose cannon. The absence of clear guidelines and past experience created strong suspicion about foreign researchers among officials at all levels— about their methods of research and what they should be allowed to see and raised fears about who would assume responsibility if anything went wrong.

As a result, anthropological research was "circumscribed, at times heavily, because of direct and indirect surveillance by Vietnamese state agents and fieldwork restrictions as a result of Vietnamese war time legacy" (Luong 2006, 2). It took the efforts and ingenuity of the anthropologist Dương Bích Hạnh and the sociologist Phùng Tố Hạnh, who had the requisite cultural capital to establish the contacts and secure governmental permissions at the commune, district, and provincial levels necessary for me to complete my research.[2]

In 1995 and 1996, I was able to interview women on my own in Hà Nội because I had met them through friends. But in Sóc Sơn and Phú Lương, where I had been introduced to single mothers through the local Women's Union, I was accompanied everywhere I went; all of my interviews were observed by Women's Union officials (i.e., agents of the state). Sometimes the Women's Union official would participate in the interview, sometimes she would remove herself from where we were sitting and otherwise occupy herself, and other times she might wander in and out of the house to keep onlookers at bay. The respondent and I were rarely alone for the duration of an interview but occasionally did have moments for private interactions. Neighbors or relatives who had clued into the news that a foreigner was visiting would slip in the door and sit down to listen; I don't recall anyone ever knocking or asking to come in. Visitors would stay for a spell and be on their way. Men who ventured in were quickly asked to leave and did so once they understood I was asking about "women's issues." Women, on the other hand, were not as easy to get rid of; if it was one woman's business, it was every woman's business.

Through the course of my research, I came to understand the extent to which women's reproductive lives in Vietnam were not simply private or public but shaped by the confluence of personal, domestic, and international concerns. This was evident at a basic level by the manner in which children, women, and men wandered (without hesitation) in and out of the women's houses. It was evident by the fact that the local Women's Union officials who accompanied me on my interviews already knew the basic outline of the "private lives" of many of the women I interviewed. It was also apparent by the fact that many of the women I interviewed were participants in microcredit programs for single female–headed households, the funding of which came from international development agencies. And then, of course, there I was, a curious anthropologist. Thus, though some of the women were happy to speak with me and all of them had formally agreed to do so, others may have felt pressure not to refuse. I never directly pressured anyone and actively sought to avoid talking with women who seemed unwilling.

By the time I left Vietnam in the autumn of 1996, I had gathered personal accounts from thirty-five single women who had asked for a child: twenty in Sóc Sơn,[3] six in Thanh Liệt,[4] five in Phú Lương District of Bắc Thái Province,[5] and four in Hà Nội.[6] All women were of the Kinh ethnic majority. I also conducted dozens of formal interviews with single women without children, women who had adopted a child, women who had unintentionally become pregnant, war widows, social scientists, Women's Union officials, journalists, lawyers, public health professionals, and anyone else willing to talk to me about the practice of *xin con*.

While waiting for permission to travel outside Hà Nội, I collected and analyzed newspaper articles, Vietnamese social science journal articles, and literature relevant to single mothers, reproduction, adoption, marriage, and family law circulating for a twelve-year period, from 1984 to 1996—all of which were subject to government censorship.[7] I also watched television programs and movies. Because media was censored, they provide insight into the "limits and forms of the *sayable*," what was possible "to speak" (Foucault 1991a, 59) during this time period. As such, the texts are evidence of Communist Party discourse, valuable insight into the pedagogical aims of Vietnamese state actors.

It is not possible to fully ascertain how my being an American shaped my fieldwork. Everyone with whom I spoke had suffered as a result of the "American War," as Vietnamese refer to it. None of the single mothers raised the topic unless prompted; it was the elephant in the room. I shied away from it as well. It was other people who drew attention to my nationality: a cadre from the Sóc Sơn People's Committee who, pointing to a pregnant woman whose fetus was known to be deformed due to her husband being exposed to chemical warfare down south during the American military's Operation Ranch Hand, wanted to know what I was going to do about it; a lawyer at the Ministry of Justice who wanted a legal dictionary from California to get information on welfare law; an elderly man in Trân Dù Town who took both of my hands in his and asked me if I knew Jane Fonda; and my host in Sóc Sơn who broke into tears while telling me about the American bombs that had killed her father and some of her brothers there in Sóc Sơn.

2004

When I returned to Vietnam eight years later, I found Hà Nội transformed. Families had turned single-story homes into three- or four-level houses.

Foreign companies had demolished entire neighborhoods to construct shiny new office towers complete with luxury apartments, restaurants, parking, and swimming pools. In contrast to the early 1990s, when bicycles dominated the roads, Hà Nội was congested with motorbikes imported from China and cars. Hà Nội traffic felt hazardous; I no longer risked riding a bicycle and instead chose a *xe ôm* ("hug vehicle," or motorbike taxi) or car taxi. Large, cumbersome objects once carted on *cyclo* (pedicabs) were now being transported on motorbikes: couches, large panes of glass, pigs, and of course, whole families. Increased mobility and access to the internet were changing how people met new people and connected with the rest of the world. Đổi Mới (economic reforms instituted in 1986) had transformed Hà Nội from a quiet city with little commercial activity to a city bursting with commodities, opportunity, and new levels of inequality.

Sóc Sơn had also undergone significant changes. The new airport road from Hà Nội to Sóc Sơn, the Thăng Long–Nội Bài Freeway, a broad six-lane highway, had replaced the old two-lane road. Phương, a Women's Union official with whom I had lived in 1996, now had a cell phone; she no longer needed to use a neighbor's landline. The street where she lived had become noisy, busy, and dangerous with fast-moving cars, trucks, vans, and motorcycles. Đổi Mới had enabled improvements in infrastructure, higher incomes, new employment opportunities, increased rural-urban mobility, and ubiquitous building construction and renovation. Sóc Sơn, once a village, was on the verge of becoming an exurb of Hà Nội.

I had returned to Sóc Sơn to see if I could reconnect with women I had met in 1996. I felt fortunate that I was able to do so. My repeated attempts to maintain contact with women in Phú Lương had proved unsuccessful due to administrative and personnel changes at the People's Committee and Women's Union. Despite relaxed restrictions on domestic and international mobility, the Vietnamese government continued to require all researchers, foreign and Vietnamese, to obtain permission to conduct formal research. And once again, I was not able to simply meet women on my own in Sóc Sơn without an official representative. As was the case in the mid-1990s, I was keenly aware that the structure of the situation meant that, more likely than not, women were providing me with narratives that a Women's Union official would consider acceptable.

On the way back to Hà Nội from Sóc Sơn, I realized that contrary to my previous experiences in 1995–96, I had not worried about my nationality. At the same time, having become a mother myself, I shared a new context of intelligibility with women. The focus of our conversations had shifted from war and the decision to get pregnant to something shared: our children.

2010, 2013, 2015, 2017

By 2010, the effects of Đổi Mới were in full swing. In 2010, 2013, 2015, and 2017, I returned to Vietnam to visit with the single mothers in Sóc Sơn whom I had last seen in 2004 and to conduct follow-up research on *xin con*. One of the principal questions the 1995–96 research had generated was whether *xin con* was solely a response to the postwar demographic imbalance or whether it presaged a long-term shift in reproductive strategy. And so, I set out to find younger women who had intentionally chosen to get pregnant out of wedlock.

To find these single women, I relied on old friends and acquaintances willing to locate and reach out to them on my behalf. Because people don't tend to ask single women how they got pregnant, and single women are not often inclined to tell, the women I met were perhaps unusual in their bravery, willingness, and hope that somehow sharing their stories with me might one day prove beneficial for Vietnamese single mothers in general. In Sóc Sơn, Phương from the Women's Union was present during repeated visits with women I had previously met. But in Hà Nội I met with women on my own and in some cases corresponded via email after I had left Vietnam.[8] In addition, I conducted internet searches for news and discussion pertaining to single women and intentional single motherhood for the years 2004–17.[9]

I continue to hear about many more such single mothers in Vietnam who asked for a child; adopted because they feared social opinion; traveled to other countries to be inseminated; or wanted to get pregnant with a Western man to have a mixed-race child. Their circumstances hinted at new research trajectories, paths that began to diverge too far from *xin con* to include here. It is time to finish the book.

ACKNOWLEDGMENTS

It is perhaps a truism to state that it takes a village to conduct ethnographic research, an intersubjective process requiring the interest, cooperation, and participation of many different kinds of people over an extended period of time. Unfortunately, it is not possible to thank each and every person who contributed to my ethnographic endeavors. But I do want to call out a few individuals.

First and foremost, I am deeply indebted and grateful to the single women who asked for a child who agreed to share their lives and thoughts with me off and on over the past two decades. I dedicate this book to them. I am especially thankful for Trần Thị Ngợi, who invited me to stay with her family and welcomed me back numerous times to visit with her family and with the single mothers I first met in the mid-1990s, and later to meet new women. I also owe a debt of gratitude to the Vietnamese social scientists who, in the mid-1980s, brought attention to the lives of single mothers and their children. I cite many of these scholars in the text but want to especially thank Lê Thi, Lê Thị Nhâm Tuyết, and Nguyễn Thị Hoài Đức, who told me stories and talked to me about their research.

My research would not have been possible without the assistance of Đoàn Thị Tuyến, Dương Bích Hạnh, and Phùng Tố Hạnh, each of whom went out of their way to make research contacts for me and facilitate my travel outside Hà Nội. In 2013 and 2017, worried about my rusty Vietnamese speaking skills, I asked Tuyến to accompany me during interviews; she helped me understand and see nuance when I had not. Over the years, numerous other individuals also shared their wisdom, for which I am ever thankful: Carole Beaulieu, Holly Barker, Danièle Bélanger, Leslie Butt, Bùi Thế Cường, Đào Thế Đức, Dương Đình Giao, Thị Khánh Hoà, Đỗ Lan Phương, Lisa Drummond, Debra Efroymson, Tine Gammeltoft, Pamina Gorbach, Hanna Griff, Caroline Grillot, Lyanda Haupt, Judith Henchy, Hồ Anh Thái, Hue-Tam Ho Tai, Palmer T. Jones, Khuất Thu Hồng, Lynn Kwiatkowski, Lê Bạch Dương, Lương Thị Chắt, David

Marr, Nguyễn Hữu Minh, Nguyễn Thị Văn, Loralee Newman, Natalie Newton, Jodi O'Brien, Melissa Pashigian, Phan Thanh Hảo, Helle Rydström, Merav Shohet, Christina Schwenkel, Daniel J. Smith, Jane Sullivan, Janelle Taylor, Eric Thompson, Michele Thompson, Trần Quốc Vương, Bich Ngoc Turner, Trần Thị Vân Anh, Allison Truitt, Janet Upton, Mark VanLandingham, Vũ Mạnh Lợi, and Vũ Phạm Nguyên Thanh.

I would especially like to thank Ann Anagnost for upending my understanding of the politics of reproduction, Tani Barlow for teaching me the skills to do critical analysis, Stevan Harrell for his stimulating conversations about kinship, Laurie Sears for encouraging me to have confidence in my own ideas, and Charles Keyes for his keen advice, wisdom, and friendship. I am also deeply grateful for the intellectual engagement and support of my ingenious and joyful LMHIV colleagues Jennifer S. Hirsch, Constance Nathanson, Shanti Parikh, Daniel J. Smith, and Holly Wardlow.

A number of people provided valuable feedback on the manuscript. In particular, I would like to thank Alana Berger, Maureen Emerson-Feit, Jennifer S. Hirsch, Joanna Phinney, Holly Wardlow, and my anonymous reviewers for their incredibly helpful comments. A very special thanks goes to Adam Berger for his enduring interest and countless insights, and to S. Chris Brown for his creative visions. When I could not see what was in front of me, Chris proposed intriguing paths of light for moving forward. He is a wizard. All mistakes are mine.

I am thankful to the Blakemore Foundation for providing funds enabling me to study Vietnamese for a year in Hà Nội. Since the ideas expressed in this book derive from a few different research projects, I have many people and institutions to thank for their support: Professor Phan Huy Lê (Center for Cooperation in Vietnamese Studies), Trịnh Duy Luân (Vietnamese Academy of Social Sciences), Khuất Thu Hồng (Institute for Social Development Studies), and Nguyễn Phương Thị Cham (Institute of Cultural Studies). Research was made possible by funding from a Fulbright-Hays Scholarship, the Social Science Research Council, and National Institutes of Health (NIH). I am thankful to be part of a supportive and collegial community at Seattle University, in particular the Department of Anthropology and Sociology. Many thanks also go to Michael Ames for believing in this book from the beginning, to Lorri Hagman at the University of Washington Press for her interest, kindness, insights, and patience and to Elizabeth Berg, Jennifer Cullis, Eileen Allen, and Joeth Zucco for helping me cross the finish line

Finally, I could not have conducted this research over the years or written this ethnography without Adam, Elijah, and Alana Berger's love and support.

SINGLE MOTHERS AND THE STATE'S EMBRACE

Introduction

IN THE EARLY 1990S MAI DECIDED SHE DID NOT NEED TO BE MARRIED TO HAVE a child.[1] Born in 1952 in a rural village in Sóc Sơn District, forty-five kilometers west of Hà Nội, she had wanted to marry, but her love was thwarted by war and circumstance. Mai was not interested in loving again, or marrying for the sake of getting married, but she did want a child. After eighteen years of living away from home in government housing while working for various state enterprises, and later for the war effort against the Americans, Mai decided at age thirty-nine to *xin con* (ask for a child). In 1991 Mai built herself a tiny house on a small parcel of land back in her home village. A year later, at age forty, she retired from her job as an electrical switch operator and returned home to give birth to a healthy baby boy.

I met Mai in 1995 to talk about her decision to "ask for a child." When I first arrived in Hà Nội in 1993 to study Vietnamese, I had planned to research population policies. But it quickly became clear that few Hanoians I spoke with found family planning a particularly compelling topic. "Chán quá" (So boring), said my elder male Vietnamese language teacher as he swept his hand through the air. Had I heard of *xin con*? he asked. No, I hadn't. "It is quite remarkable," he said. "You should research that." The woman who sold *phở* in the alley where I ate breakfast each morning also told me I should look into women who had *xin con*. So did a Vietnamese social scientist, the woman at the photocopy shop, and a journalist. Was this a new reproductive strategy or had women been "asking for a child" for some time, I wanted to know. Yes, it was new, each replied, since the war.

I was intrigued. The idea of a single woman asking a man she did not intend to marry to get her pregnant ran counter to everything I had read about Vietnamese kinship values and practices. Scholars describe Vietnamese kinship as based in a Confucian-oriented patriarchal patrilineal ideology. Assertions that ancient Vietnam had once been a matrilineal society (Lê Thị Nhâm Tuyết 1975), and recognition that northern Vietnamese also engage in bilateral,

3

non-male-oriented kinship practices (Luong 1989) notwithstanding, most contemporary women reproduce descendants for their husband's lineage. From this perspective, bearing a child out of wedlock was a serious breach of filial piety, resulting in a loss of status for the woman and her family. According to historians and social scientists and a few of my research participants, in the "feudal times" well before reunification, a woman who became pregnant out of wedlock had her nape shaved and smeared with lime (gọt gáy bôi vôi). Or she was forced to walk around the village with a bucket on her head and be publicly insulted. In extreme cases, a woman could be bound naked to a banana palm raft and set adrift on a river (Nguyễn Thị Khoa 1993; Lê Nhâm 1994). If she lived, she was supposed to "nourish her fault" by looking upon her child with disgrace. She was not permitted to argue her case. Some women took their own lives; others left home. According to the social scientist Nguyễn Thị Khoa (1993, 47), the woman's family, despite having to pay a heavy fine, approved of the severity of this punishment because it was "indispensable for maintaining social morality" and the "purity of the family bloodline."[2] In the 1990s social scientists and Women's Union officials used such accounts to call attention to how socialist policies had improved women's lives.[3] By 1993, clearly something had changed; the people urging me to investigate *xin con* did not view women who asked for a child with opprobrium. If anything, they expressed understanding and approval.

Social scientists and journalists used the terms *xin con* and *kiếm con* (literally "find a child") interchangeably when writing about such women, translating both in English as "ask for a child." However, *kiếm con* was more typically used to refer to infertile married women finding an infant to adopt. Over the course of the 1980s and 1990s, the term *xin con* became not just a literal description of a reproductive event but also a category of social action, a discursive formation that referred to a specific reproductive strategy undertaken by single women considered past marriageable age.

This book is about single women in northern Vietnam who, finding themselves without suitable marital prospects after the Indochina wars, decided to "ask for a child," and about how *xin con* became recognized as a "socially intelligible kinship" practice (Dorow and Swiffen 2009, 564). This book is also about revolutionary transformations, the way in which "older" single women—amid a significantly altered political, economic, and social reality—drew upon existing values and practices to chart an alternative future for themselves. I focus especially on the politics of their reproduction, the ways in which women's individual reproductive desires were embraced rather than rejected by the Vietnamese state as a means for producing a new female subjectivity as Vietnam entered the global market economy. This book explores what women who asked for a child have to say about agency, governmentality, and subjectivity.

Concepts pertaining to social phenomena are contingent and open. The ability to make effective decisions, of governments to address whole populations, and for people to locate their social selves comes into view in Vietnam in different ways at different historical moments. This book elucidates how they do so in relation to *xin con*. As such the book is a theoretical exploration of different ways to think about women's actions as "empirical realities and as analytic categories" (Biehl, Good, and Kleinman 2007, 15). I treat agency, governmentality, and subjectivity as key nodes for conceptualizing *xin con*; each node provides a progression of different kinds of explanations, tracked in the progression of chapters below.

The circumstances surrounding Ngọc, another woman born in 1952, shed light on the complex, and sometimes contradictory, gender and kinship ideologies that propel women to "ask for a child." Born with a facial disfigurement that left her with poor vision, Ngọc had a hard time finding a husband in her village of Thanh Liệt on the outskirts of Hà Nội. Nonetheless, she rejected her parents' attempt to arrange a marriage for her by returning the traditional *trầu cau* (betel nut and areca nut) offering to the intended groom because, she said, she believed that "real love is voluntary." At age forty she fell in love with a married man with four daughters whose wife sent him "out into the world" to *xin con trai* (ask for a boy). Having always "dreamed of love and of having a baby," Ngọc agreed to "become his second wife" (*làm vợ lẽ*). Then he changed his mind. Nevertheless, Ngọc decided to ask him for a child because of the "magnetism" between them. A year later, when he and his wife realized that Ngọc had given birth to a boy, the wife invited her to come live with them. Ngọc was not interested. She wanted to raise her child on her own.

Xin con thus combines old and new patterns of social action that coexist. Ngọc's refusal to accept an arranged marriage reflects her desire for a "modern" notion of marriage in which love must be mutual and voluntary, a requirement the socialist state instituted into law in 1959. Yet she was willing to engage in the "feudal" and illegal social practice of polygyny that had accommodated many older single women's desires to become a mother in the past. A man, with his wife's encouragement, asked Ngọc to become his second wife in the hope that she would bear him a son. When that arrangement fell through, however, she did not abandon her desire to become a mother but pressed ahead to assert herself in a way that was the opposite of feudal. Ngọc's decision to "ask for a child" demonstrates the innovation of *xin con*, a novel Vietnamese reproductive strategy that offers an alternative to the patriarchal family. While it is new, it is nonetheless rooted in both pre- and postwar values, practices, and notions of gender, kinship, love, and sexuality. Viewing *xin con* through a historical lens demonstrates how contemporary Vietnamese patterns of social action, often explained in terms of Đổi Mới (Renovation; a series of economic reforms instituted in 1986) or neoliberal policies, are rooted in social practices that predate Đổi Mới, and as such exemplify both continuity and change (Kerkvliet 2005; Gainsborough 2010).

Although established patriarchal practices and socialist collective ideology inform *xin con*, it is nevertheless an expression of agency and individual will. In the 1920s, "popular wisdom" portrayed women as "entirely at the mercy of their fate, their happiness dependent on the men in their life." By contrast, men "had the power to exert control over their destiny by making use of whatever talents they possessed and were therefore not supposed to 'fold their arms and accept defeat'" (Tai 1992, 18). And yet, in the mid-1990s Ngọc was unwilling to let others—her parents, the biological father of her child—decide her future.

On the other hand, some women's stories do not portray *xin con* as a brazen and unconstrained expression of individual will and agency. Born in 1944 in Sóc Sơn, Nam was widowed shortly after getting married; her husband died in the south fighting the Americans. Nam remained in her husband's home to care for her mother-in-law, who in turn advised Nam to *xin con*. Since Nam did not want to remarry but did want a child, she decided in 1980, at age thirty-six, to ask for a child from a man she met at the nearby army base. In Nam's case, her decision to ask for a child was an accommodation to marital and wartime misfortunes. The war took her husband. If it hadn't, she would have borne and raised a child with him. *Xin con* provided Nam with a means to become a mother. Nam's narrative raises an interesting question: Was her decision to *xin con* an expression of individual desire or was it more a means of fulfilling her duty as a daughter-in-law?

Most social scientists attribute *xin con* to the high male mortality inflicted during the war with the Americans; there were not enough men for women to marry (Lê Thi 1990, 2005; Lê Thị Nhâm Tuyết 1995). Some social scientists also attribute *xin con* to social change resulting from revolutionary efforts and socialist policies enacted since the mid-1950s that provided women with opportunities for autonomy from their families (Bélanger and Khuất 2002). I expand upon these sociological accounts by following the women's lead and approaching *xin con* as an intentional reproductive strategy, rather than a default act of circumstance. Women attributed transformational significance to bearing a biological child as a fundamental determinant for not pursuing alternative routes to motherhood. In their pursuit of maternal love, single mothers drew upon discourses of romantic and socialist love—generated, discussed, and debated by intellectuals, revolutionaries, and policy makers—to explain their decisions not to marry and to ask for a child (Phinney 2008). And remarkably, single women were able to navigate their local moral worlds without appearing to threaten normative values of marriage and reproduction. Attention to the culturally informed and socially strategic aspects of *xin con* reveals an intricate relationship among larger social structures, reproductive desire, and individual agency.

Familial and social responses to women asking for a child varied. Thắm, a college-educated woman born to a well-established Hà Nội family in 1959, said she did not tell her parents she had asked for a child because their "feudal ideology" would prohibit them from being sympathetic. However, her friends supported her, and she had secured permission to ask for a child from the state office where she worked and that provided her housing. Yet, wary that one day her rights to the child might be challenged, Thắm wrote a formal contract stipulating that the biological father relinquish all rights to the child.

In 1986, at age nineteen, Chi agreed to a marriage her parents had arranged. She had married "without thinking of love." Two years later, when she discovered her husband was "lazy and unfaithful," she divorced him. In 1991, at age twenty-three, Chi asked for a child. When her father learned she was pregnant, he refused to help. But when it was time to give birth, Chi's mother took her in and hired a midwife. After a few months Chi went to live with her brother, and a few years later she built her own house on communal land given to her by the Sóc Sơn People's Committee.

Hà, also from Sóc Sơn, came of marital age just when she went "to the front, to the firing line" for a few years; she was eighteen. After being a soldier, she went to work in a new economic zone. At age twenty-five, upon her return home, Hà refused an offer to become a second wife. Her parents, realizing that her quiet and shy demeanor and age made marriage unlikely for her, encouraged her to *xin con*. Hà asked for a child from the man who had wanted her to be his second wife. "I wanted it to be uncomplicated and to be free. I did not want to negatively impact his wife or child," she said.

The support that Thắm, Chi, and Hà received indicates that *xin con* as a form of agency is not only individual but also relational, because it is inherently embedded in relations of power. Essentially, women *asked* men for their sperm and, because they chose to bear children out of wedlock, they were not in a position to expect social or familial support. Support given was not rooted in official kinship etiquette and practices but consisted of acts of kindness and of acknowledgment.

Older single women's decision to *xin con* did not go unnoticed by the Vietnamese state.[4] In the early 1980s, the Vietnam Women's Union commune and cadre leaders became aware that among the thousands of women raising children by themselves were single women who had asked for a child. The state dealt with this new reality by sending out social scientists to conduct research. In 1986, the government passed a new Law on Marriage and the Family that recognized all women's right to have their own biological child regardless of marital status. At the local level, Women's Union district and commune leaders such as Phương, who was born in Sóc Sơn and lost three brothers to the American War (the Second Indochina War), worked with international aid organizations and local People's Committees to provide credit programs for single female–headed households. With a twinkle in her eye, yet a fierce stickler for rules, Phương pushed and prodded single mothers to learn new skills, voice their thoughts in public, and advocate for themselves.

Xin con, a personal decision agreed upon quietly by two people, became a subject of national interest and legal concern. The state created policies and laws to support the practice, and worked with foreign nongovernmental agencies (NGOs) to implement development programs specifically for single female–headed households. But why? For what reasons did the state care about single mothers? State rhetoric and practice centered on women's bodies became grounds for working out new modes of governmentality, productive sites launching a new type of subject at the advent of Đổi Mới. The uniqueness of the Vietnamese state's response to *xin con* is notable. Rather than condemning or trying to restrict single women's reproductive agency, government officials followed their lead to enact a population policy that would accommodate both the women and the state.

The state's reaction to *xin con* can be attributed, in part, to Đổi Mới and the way in which its socioeconomic reforms have been rolled out and by whom. In 1986, the Vietnamese government launched a series of reforms to transition from a centrally planned to a market-based economy with a socialist direction (market-based socialism). In addition to dismantling agriculture-based cooperatives in favor of household production, the state removed most welfare subsidies. This resulted in the eradication of social safety nets, including health, childcare, and care for the infirm, as well as reductions in educational support. The state began to downsize and close state factories, promote private enterprise, and enable the expansion of import and export markets. It also shifted responsibility for the welfare of citizens and the economic progress of the nation from the state to the family. The state's recognition of *xin con* served this shift and, with the leadership of female social scientists and Women's Union state officials, helped incorporate single women–headed households into the Đổi Mới economic and social order. The actors concerned with and invested in improving the lives of single mothers illustrate an intriguing alignment of Confucian heritage, Communist ideology, and governmentality, and as such broaden our understanding of governmentality in non-Western societies.

The first generation of women who asked for a child did so prior to the promulgation of Đổi Mới. While their reproductive innovation ultimately prompted the state to legislate on their behalf, many had already suffered from the stigma of being single and pregnant. Single women who asked for a child in the early stages of Đổi Mới reforms were more readily accepted than their predecessors, but they still struggled. Two decades later, single women who asked for a child did so in a markedly improved economic context and in quite different social circumstances (e.g., widening employment and educational opportunities, increased mobility, access to domestic and foreign consumer goods, and broadening awareness of different gendered ways of being and living in the world—to say nothing of a more balanced sex distribution). And the women I had met in the mid-1990s who had long ago asked for a child were enjoying improved economic independence and living conditions as part of their greater integration into society and the market economy.

Having the privilege of keeping in touch with women from Sóc Sơn over a twenty-year time span provides long-term insight and thus a more complex understanding of their reproductive agency than a synchronic research project offers. For example, it becomes clear that, as their children reached marriageable age, the women's intentions were not just about having a child for themselves but also about reproducing orthodox familial values and social structures. The same may not be true of the next generation of single women who intentionally choose to get pregnant out of wedlock. Tracking the practice of "asking for a child" across generations enables me to compare how *xin con* has both changed and stayed the same, and how government policies have struggled to keep up with both women and their reproductive agency.

CONCEPTUAL FRAMEWORK

This book is structured in terms of what different analytic lenses can tell us about *xin con*, and how cultural change takes place. It is divided into parts that begin with vignettes setting the stage for the following chapters.

Part 1 delineates the sociocultural and political milieu of the 1980s and 1990s within which single women asked for a child. Chapter 1 explores single women's reasons for asking for a child rather than pursuing conventional strategies for raising a child. Because most research on reproduction in Vietnam focuses on married women, our comprehension of maternal desire has been almost entirely framed in terms of the patrilineal family and women's role in maintaining it. Single women who asked for a child draw our attention away from men's patrilineal concerns to women's own maternal desires and subjectivities. They also demonstrate how elements of the same kinship ideologies can be used to justify an unconventional family form.

Chapter 2 describes how war and governmental efforts to create a modern socialist society altered the familial, marital landscape, making it difficult for women to marry. Examining the shifting marital terrain demonstrates how global politics (the American War) and northern Vietnamese governmental efforts to create a socialist society intersected at a most intimate level. I explore cultural notions of marriageability, paying close attention to how single women drew on dominant kinship ideologies and gendered social practices to explain why they did not marry or chose not to do so. By highlighting women's voices, I complicate accounts that depict all such women as unmarriageable.

Part 2 examines *xin con* in terms of agency and governmentality. At a fundamental level *xin con* can be understood in terms of the larger sociocultural and demographic context. But because social forms mediate but do not determine behavior, they cannot fully explain *xin con*. Focusing on agency is useful for examining how people envision and make effective decisions. Chapter 3 analyzes *xin con* as a "cultural project" (Ortner 2006a, 139), a clear demonstration of sexual and reproductive agency bound by culturally informed gendered mores and practices. It describes what asking for a child entailed and how women sidestepped conventional routes to childbearing and motherhood to perform a valued social role.

Chapter 4 explores *xin con* in terms of governmentality. Governmentality, in broad strokes, is an exercise of power whose purpose is the management, welfare, and improvement of the population (Foucault 1991b). The government's goal is to shape the conduct of its citizens such that they act in ways beneficial to the state. This chapter explicates how and why the government came to embrace single women's right to bear children and how *xin con* became not just a literal description of a social action but also a discursive social category signifying a socially intelligible reproductive strategy. It also elucidates how state actors (social scientists, in particular) discursively constructed a new subject position that would be embraced by the women it was intended to signify. Attention to how the state governed *xin con* in the post–Đổi Mới era provides ethnographic insight into a culturally distinct instance of governmentality in which management of the population was informed by Vietnam's Confucian heritage, its single-party socialist ideology, and Đổi Mới policies.

Part 3 assesses what we learn about *xin con* by analyzing the intersection among reproductive agency, governmentality, and subjectivity over the long term. Chapter 5 focuses on the subjectivities of contemporary women who asked for a child from 2000 to 2017. Subjectivity refers to both a person's subject position—a political designation—and to their felt interior experiences: their modes of being in the world. I analyze how contemporary women spoke about marriage and their experiences with love, their reproductive strategies, and how they framed their decision to get pregnant out of wedlock. I situate their actions in relation to government policy and their voices in relation to the prevailing public discourse about single mothers at the time—a discourse that reflects shifting ideas about love, sex, gender, and marriage. It is apparent that as much as *xin con* was a novel social practice at the end of the twentieth century, at the beginning of the twenty-first century it shifted to accomplish similar, yet also new and different, ends and to embody new values. Subjectivity is a useful lens through which to analyze this shift, revealing how subjects reflect on and respond to their lived experiences in ways that lead to cultural change.

The concluding chapter provides a focused discussion on what we have learned about and from *xin con* through the three analytic lenses of agency, governmentality, and subjectivity. While each chapter uses a different analytic node to analyze *xin con*, it is clear that agency, governmentality, and subjectivity are intimately intertwined; they inform and shape one another in specific ways at particular moments in time. But just because these empirical realities are mutually interdependent does not mean they are stable; instead it is a dynamic relationship, each changing in response to the other. Agency, governmentality, and subjectivity bump up against one another in productive ways. The book concludes with a return to Mai, who is featured in the vignette that opens part 1.

PART 1

MATERNAL DESIRE AND THE POSTWAR MARITAL TERRAIN

MAI

MAI, TUYẾN, AND I SAT HUDDLED TOGETHER DRINKING TEA ON THE THIN straw mat Mai had pulled out for us to sit on while we talked.[1] She had a new black patent leather couch, but we chose the mat; it was more intimate. The last time I visited her, in 1996, she lived in a tiny one-room house with her four-year-old son. This new house, built in 2010, felt palatial. She now had a refrigerator, running water, a bathroom with a water-saving toilet, a polished wooden armoire, and a relatively new TV and DVD player. Upstairs she had two spacious bedrooms, one for sleeping and the other for praying to the "god of the land," off of which was a covered outdoor porch for hanging laundry.

Once we settled in, Mai began to recount the trajectory of her life and why she had decided to ask for a child. It was a lot easier for her to talk this time— seventeen years later—about her work, her relationships with men, her struggles as a single woman and mother, her neighbors, and her family. In 1996 her answers had been short and to the point. In 2010, at age fifty-eight, wounds had healed, experiences were not as raw, social attitudes had changed; she was at ease sharing her personal stories and details of her life. Mai could now look back and see that she had clearly made a number of wise decisions.

Mai was born in Tân Minh Commune in 1952. Her father fought against the French and subsequently became the village leader (làm lãnh đạo ở xã). Mai finished grade 10 and then studied electrical engineering at the Ministry of Energy (Bộ Năng Lượng) for three and a half years. At about age nineteen she left home and for the next eighteen years lived in housing provided by the government enterprise where she worked. Her first work assignment (phân công tác) was for the Vĩnh Phú Department of Construction (Ban kiến thiết xây dựng Vĩnh Phú). When that department dissolved she moved to the Xuân Hoà bicycle factory, which had recently opened, but later transferred to a car factory. In 1979, when the car factory relocated south, she chose not to follow, instead joining the Military Engineering Department (Cục quân khí) working on national defense. In 1982, single and unmarried at age thirty, she transferred to Army Enterprises (Xí nghiệp quân đội)

418, where she was a laborer on the railroad's electric line (*công nhân điện ngành đường sắt*).

Mai never married, but she had fallen in love with a fellow engineering student at school. They were separated when she was assigned to work in Vĩnh Phú, and he went into the army and was later sent to the border when China invaded in 1979. They eventually lost track of one another when he was transferred to another location. After the war, when she knew he had left his unit, she went to find him but learned he had another lover. "I did love once, but he betrayed [*phản bội*] me, so I did not want to love again. . . . I focused on work in order to forget him. Other men showed interest in me, but I did not like men anymore, so they stopped coming around. I was too old. I was too busy to think about men anyway."

At the factory where Mai worked and lived (in employee housing), a few female *thanh niên xung phong* (youth brigade volunteers) who were a generation older than Mai had decided to become second wives. One was pregnant and the other had a baby at home, so Mai often had to work the night shift. After a man tried to force himself on her at night when she was working alone, Mai thought it might be a good idea to develop a closer friendship with a male friend of hers who also worked at the factory; perhaps he could protect her from untrustworthy men. (Unmarried women and unmarried mothers were often targets of thieves and sexual assault.) Her friend had already expressed interest in her, but she had not wanted to become a second wife or ruin his family's happiness. However, she did want a child.

Mai saved money and with a little help from her parents and her brother eventually acquired a small parcel of land in her home village and built a small house (*nhà nhỏ nhỏ*) near her parents in the late 1980s. In 1992, at age forty, five months into her pregnancy, she retired and moved from government housing into her house in time to give birth to a son. She was able to retain her entire six-month maternity leave benefits and collect the three-month one-time payment allocated to all retiring employees. In addition, her office (*cơ quan*) owed her a pension of 996,000 Vietnamese *đồng* for her work over the past fourteen years. Because they didn't have all the money, they paid her 300 *đồng* and 1,000 cement bricks (then worth 1 million *đồng* (US$83). She did not need the bricks since she had already built her house, so she sold them. She used the money to pay the laborers who had built her house. At that time the government was engaging in land reorganization. As a result, the commune allocated her two *sào* to farm: one *sào* (360 square meters) for her and one for her son. In 1996, ten years after Đổi Mới, Mai signed up to become a member of a new joint venture between the local Women's Union and the nongovernmental organization NAV (Nordic Services). Because her engineering skills were limited and she was not able to make any money farming two *sào*, Mai enrolled in the new credit program and skills training for single mothers to learn about animal husbandry. I met Mai in the spring of that first year of the credit program.

CHAPTER 1

Maternal Desire

The "Thirst" for a Biological Child

"ALL VIETNAMESE WOMEN WANT TO HAVE A CHILD," VIETNAMESE FRIENDS, acquaintances, married and single women have told me repeatedly since the early 1990s. In 1993, I was newly married at the age of thirty-five, long past the age at which most Vietnamese women gave birth. I was often asked, "Chị bao nhiêu tuổi?" (How old are you?), "Chị lấy chồng chưa?" (Have you married yet?), "Chị có con chưa?" (Do you have a child yet?). "Yet" was the operative word in these common grammatical constructions. In this context, "yet" signaled not just expectation but also an appropriate sequence of events in which all women's life course was to unfold. Newly married women and men alike were often subjected to relentless questions and advice about their reproductive status. "Có con đi!" (Have a child!), an elder relative might exclaim. "Có mất gì không?" (Are you missing something?), a friend might gently taunt.

Mai, like other single women, suffered through the first two questions about age and marriage for some time before friends and relatives finally conceded that she would not marry. She was not asked the last question, "Do you have a child yet?" Nor was she told, "Có con đi!" Mai's life, disrupted by war and revolution, had not followed the normative marital trajectory she had assumed it would when she was young. This did not mean Mai didn't still desire a biological child; after all, she too had been interpellated (hailed) by the same reproductive ideology as had her married friends. The primary difference was that Mai was not supposed to act on her biological desire; if she

18

really wanted a child, she should adopt one from a relative, as had previous generations of single women. But Mai was not interested in adopting. She, like other single women past marriageable age, eschewed adoption in favor of asking for a child.

This chapter elucidates the significance of childbearing for women in Vietnam in general and single women's maternal desires and reproductive reasoning in particular. Single women's reasons for asking for a child drew from two narratives, both with long histories, that circulated after the American War. The first narrative extolled the values of gestating, birthing, and raising one's own biological child—an embodied experience considered to be socially, psychologically, and physically transformative. The second narrative warned of the dangers of adoption—a narrative of risk that had intensified during the postwar era. The way in which single women drew from both narratives to chart their own futures is instructive for what it tells us about their reproductive agency and how social change takes place. Their reproductive agency is informed by existing cultural values and practices, which the women then configure in new ways.

THE PATRILINEAL FRAMING OF MATERNAL DESIRE

Vietnamese historians and social scientists frame childbearing in terms of the Vietnamese Confucian patrilineal tradition, in which having children, like getting married, is a moral imperative and a "'natural vocation' [thiên chức] or 'Heavenly mandate'" for women and men (Rydström 2004, 78). According to this tradition, bearing and raising children is a sacred act, one that links the living to the dead and to those not yet born. Women demonstrate "filial piety" (hiếu) by producing heirs who will take care of their husband's elderly parents, continue the patrilineage, worship ancestors, and tend to their graves in order to create harmony among family members and between the living and the dead. Prescribed patrilineal inheritance and patrilocal residence practices create a preference for sons. For a woman who marries the eldest son, producing a male heir secures her a place in her husband's household. My married research participants, such as Tiên (one of my Vietnamese teachers) and Phương (a Women's Union official), said that one way a woman expresses love for her husband is by birthing his children; they reiterated the common assertion that children are the "thread" (sợi dây) that binds a married couple together. A woman who bears and raises her children well acquires familial and social status. Women who are unable to birth children suffer; it puts their marriage at risk, creates tension with in-laws, and raises the specter of being a bad person or having bad karma.

This narrative of how a woman's reproductive life should proceed, and for what reasons, glosses over the variety of ways that women experience relatedness in Vietnam. Essentially, it only speaks to married women. This is largely due to the fact that, despite socialist efforts to eradicate "feudal" vestiges of the "traditional Vietnamese family," social life remains principally organized around the paternal bloodline. Most women did and do reproduce within a marital context in Vietnam. Older single women who asked for a child did not. Because they chose to bear and raise children outside marriage, women who asked for a child, like infertile women, reveal not only "the diversity of reproductive experiences among women in Vietnamese society" (Pashigian 2009a, 39) but also how certain reproductive norms are sustained while others are transformed. Intentional single mothers shift our focus away from men's patrilineal reproductive concerns to women's own maternal desires and subjectivities.

TRANSFORMATIONAL VIRTUES OF MOTHERHOOD

Single women who asked for a child, like married women, wanted a child because children are transformative. Bearing and raising a child transform a woman psychologically, physically, and socially.

Childless Women: Lonely and Difficult?

During the mid-1980s to mid-1990s in Vietnam, as a single woman reached and passed marriageable age, her social life began to shift if not shrink. Her married friends who were raising children no longer had as much leisure time—if they had any to begin with. Tiên, my Vietnamese teacher, who had married her boyfriend, felt fortunate that she did not have to live with her in-laws, but nonetheless sadly reflected, "I no longer have time to *đi chơi* [go out, have fun] with my friends. After work, I go to the market, pick up my son from school, go home, and cook dinner. And I help my child with his homework. My husband, he might either come directly home after work or he might go out to a *bia hơi* [beer hall] with his friends, returning home for dinner when he wants." As a married woman, Tiên's social life had shifted significantly, whereas her husband's had not. She and her husband embodied an ideologically Confucian gendered division of marital labor that oriented men to the public sphere and women to the domestic sphere. When she did *đi chơi*, she did so either alone with her child, with her child and husband, or with family members. "I rarely get to see my school friends anymore. And I can't đi chơi with my male school friends because my husband will get jealous," she added. "We used to have so much fun." Women in both rural and urban areas who resided with their husband's family confronted similar family obligations but were likely to find their free time further diminished by the need to take on household responsibilities such as cooking and caring for elderly in-laws. Her married friends increasingly pulled in other directions, Tiên also found her nonfamilial social interactions curtailed.

Despite socialist success in drawing women out of the home to participate in the revolution and the war, and become part of the labor force, women I knew in Hà Nội, Phú Lương, and Sóc Sơn in the mid-1990s and early 2000s did not venture out alone to đi chơi or spend time in certain kinds of leisure establishments: karaoke bars, restaurants, cafes, or bia hơi (beer gardens). Women were certainly free to go where they pleased, but that did not mean they wanted to do so alone. Dr. Nhơn in Phú Lương, a married, well-known, and respected member of the community, preferred to eat at the office or go home for lunch rather than eat alone at one of the restaurants in Phú Lương town. In Hà Nội, Tiên would not đi chơi alone because it "isn't vui [fun]. It is not normal" (cf. Bélanger and Khuất 2002). In the early to mid-1990s, I rarely saw women hanging out alone in public spaces unless they were at the market, exercising (in Hà Nội), or eating a quick meal, such as phở, bún chả, miến, or bánh cuốn.

The situation was more acute for childless women (Bélanger and Khuất 2002). Based on her experience, Dr. Nhơn in Phú Lương said childless single women over the age of thirty-five were reluctant to engage socially with other people. "They don't want contact with anyone; it is difficult for them to mix with others because of their situation, although they very much love and value young children." She confided that she advised childless patients and friends over the age of thirty-five, single or married, to raise a child because "when a woman has a child, she can go out more. It makes her life vui vẻ [happier] because she is not lonely." Dr. Nhơn's comment calls attention to the way in which a child facilitates single women's navigation of social spaces outside the home. Indeed, "the symbolic dimensions of space—in particular, how places are morally defined vis-à-vis kinship and gender" are "powerful factors shaping behavior" (Hirsch et al. 2010, 17). I would add that this is in part because of how people *feel* being in those spaces. Nga had a child "because it was too sad to đi chơi alone. Even though having children is very difficult, it is happier— they cheer me up [cổ vũ mình]."

The media often portrayed women without husbands as "lonely women" (độc thân) because they had not yet married (Nguyễn Thanh Tâm 1992). However, Nguyễn Thị Khoa (1993) contends that most of the single women she interviewed defined loneliness not in terms of being unmarried but by being childless. This was also the case for the single mothers I interviewed from Sóc Sơn, Phú Lương, Thanh Liệt, and Hà Nội. Single women of marriageable age defined loneliness in terms of having to đi chơi by oneself, coming home to an empty apartment (for those living in government housing) after visiting friends or relatives who had children, not being able to talk with other women about the childbearing experience, and listening to other women talk about their children. Nor would they have the joy of the physical contact a child necessarily requires and brings: young children need to be fed, bathed, dressed, cradled, picked up, hugged. Thắm had difficulty describing her feelings during such situations: "I was always overcome with this sadness. . . . It lingered." Dr. Nhơn used the aphorism "A dead tree is not a tree, a wicked person has no children" (Cây khô không lộc, người độc không con) to describe how some people perceived childless women and how the women might think of themselves. Having internalized the stigma of childlessness, older single women "đi chơi very little," Dr. Nhơn added.

A few of my research participants said childlessness also affects women's mental health. Hào (born 1952), who had asked for a child, explained, "Many women who are 'old' [lớn tuổi], who don't have a child—their personality changes. For example, their disposition [is such that] they are not at ease [thoải mái], they fret [bực bội], they are alone and lack sympathy [tình cảm] for others. They are sad and worried [buồn phiền]. . . . Whether a woman marries or not, she should have a child—it is much better to have a child." Nhân (born 1959) said that because it is a woman's physiology to have a child, if she does not then "her thoughts will become scattered, unhappy." Indeed, Nhân had been very unhappy. "Single life is sad," she said. In Hà Nội, Thắm's doctor told her that a woman can become "khó tính" (difficult) if she does not have "intimate sex" with a man. Thắm continued, "My doctor said a woman without a man becomes thinner [gầy đi], wilted [khô héo], and her yin and yang [âm dương] will get out of balance." Hiền, who had not yet had a child or a husband, rejected this association of one's sexual experience with one's emotional state: "People say that at age thirty if you have not yet married a husband then you will have a problem with your psychology, but I feel that my social psychological life is very normal."

Tô Thị Anh, a psychologist who was interviewed in 1988 about the recent spate of older single women choosing to get pregnant, concurred with Hiền's assessment.[1] She asserted that it was not marriage per se that balanced a woman's character, but the experience of having a child. Tô Thị Anh explained that a woman's character is not stable over time. If she is not married by age thirty-five, "her psychological make-up will become a problem. . . . A woman's character changes; it becomes excessive and intolerable, *khó tính.*" *Khó tính*, a slur used to refer to someone with a difficult character, was often used to describe unmarried childless women. Other terms included *hâm hấp* (slightly crack-brained), *nghiêm khắc* (strict or severe), or *khắt khe* (too severe and too strict). More pointedly, Tô Thị Anh added, "To realize the right to become a mother is to realize a woman's function." A woman became unbalanced because she was not fulfilling her natural biological function, which was to be a mother.

In 1996, in response to my query about *khó tính*, an obstetrician from the Center for Reproductive Family Health (Trung Tâm sức khỏe Phụ nữ và Gia đình) in Hà Nội said, "Many people think that a female is not a woman if she does not have a child: she does not know how to give birth or how to breastfeed; she does not have the sentimentality or the emotion of a mother; she does not know how to love—and by extension, [does not have] the capacity to care for others. She does not know how to be a mother." According to the obstetrician, lack of personal knowledge and experience with birthing, along with the scorn heaped upon her because of her lack of experience, makes a woman *khó tính.*[2] "Society looks down on women who don't have children. As a result, they won't have good friends or good relations with the community," she asserted.

Becoming a Woman

The women I interviewed largely confirmed the assertions of these experts, and many of them suggested that the physical processes of gestation, giving birth, and breastfeeding not only make a female a mother but make her truly a woman. Nga said, "To be a woman you must have a child." Thắm's remark, "When I had a child, I felt very happy, exceedingly happy because I saw myself at that moment really as a woman," epitomized many women's perceptions of the importance of childbearing. Phương (born 1925), who came of marital age in the early 1950s, did not agree that a woman needed to have a child to become a woman, but she still thinks that all women should have a child. Bích Thủy (born in 1953) equated childbearing with becoming a woman and was "elated" (*phấn khởi*) at having done so.

Arguably, *khó tính*, a temperamental trait ascribed to childless women, was socially produced. Childless women were marginalized and stigmatized because they were not fulfilling their "natural" function, and thus withdrew socially. Lonely and devalued, it is not surprising that some might have become "difficult." In contrast, women who did bear and raise children achieved the symbolic capital necessary for venturing out into the world, had more expansive and valued social lives, were happier, and were consequently less "difficult."

Giving birth to a healthy child demonstrated to others that one was not only fertile but also desirable. Pregnancy also makes a woman more beautiful as a result of blood being exchanged between mother and fetus. "She has a radiant glow," said Ngọc Anh, my landlord's daughter-in-law. Research participants, Tiên, and friends told me many times I should get pregnant because I would become more beautiful and younger looking. Ngọc Anh said that a woman with a child is more charming and more beautiful than a woman without a child. Tiên cited the aphorism "A woman with a child is so beautiful that when you look at her you cannot take your eyes off her," and then elaborated, "You gaze and gaze until your eyes become so tired that they are as thin and smooth as a stone that the sea has washed over and over and over again." However, she warned that a woman who has too many children will age quickly. A Hà Nội social scientist pointed out to me that in Vietnam being visibly pregnant is an indirect way of showing that one is attractive; it advertises that one has had sexual relations without speaking about it.

The women I interviewed also asserted that bearing and raising children changed women psychologically. Having had sex and become a mother, a woman is no longer at risk of becoming *khó tính*, but rather develops a maternal disposition enabling her to embody an appropriate maternal subjectivity. Hương, who had unintentionally gotten pregnant with her boyfriend, said, "In the past I spoke coarsely [*cục cằn*], rudely [*mất dạy lắm*]. Now even if I am angry I speak sweetly and softly [*ngọt ngào và dịu dàng*] to my child." Thị Hòa, who adopted a child because her infertile husband would not let her get pregnant by sleeping with another man, said that before she had a child she was full of sorrow and self-pity. "Since having the child my mind has become at ease, at peace, and happy because I have someone."

Lý (born in 1956), who asked for a child when she was thirty years old, said that before she had a child she was often cross with people. After giving birth her temperament changed. She said, "I am almost never cross or furious. . . . My behavior toward everyone is more soft-spoken. I work at everything because of my child. I behave very well and show sympathy for other people. . . . I must be more modest and courteous, soft-mannered with everyone so people will love [*yêu quí*] and esteem [*quí mến*] my child." Lý attributes her change in mood and disposition to finally having something of her own to love. At the same time, by behaving in a manner expected of mothers, Lý is transforming herself. It is not for me to question the origin of Lý's change in demeanor, but it is important to consider the "mutually constitutive relationship between body learning and body sense" (Mahmood 2005, 157) instigated by raising a child. By caring for a child and interacting with other mothers who have definite ideas about how mothers should behave, Lý has learned how to embody a socially appropriate maternal demeanor. And in the process, through her performance—or subjection to a particular kind of maternal subject—Lý creates symbolic capital for herself and her child.

Maternal love enables women to "demonstrate and acquire moral value" (Gammeltoft 2014, 142; Pashigian 2009a). According to the psychologist Nguyễn Thị Khoa (1996, 134), "A woman who has a child or a son will prove to others that they are not lonely due to fate [*số phận*] or position. They have vitality [*sức sống*] that comes from their children." Minh, who was living with her relatives, said, "Now that I have a child, I no longer have to live such a lonely and solitary life." The child also facilitated Minh's social mobility.

Caring for a child enabled a degree of autonomy and freedom of movement not readily available to childless women. For example, having children created opportunities for new social interactions, such as visits to the doctor and conversations with teachers, attending Women's Union child-rearing educational meetings, and sharing stories and advice with other mothers. Childbearing creates and facilitates belonging (Gammeltoft 2014). This suggests that it is not a husband who provides daily mobility through social spaces for a woman, but rather her child. For women like San, who asked for a child in the early 1990s, having a child was a means to become independent from her natal family, to establish her own home, and to be more mobile. Like Hạnh, who had adopted outside the family, a woman who asked for a child created a family for herself. Indeed, one of the reasons single women living with their brothers wanted their own child was so they could set up a separate residence. As San said, "I want to do things myself. I haven't yet asked anyone for help, including my family. I want to be independent [*độc lập*] and not rely on my parents." And Hà said, "Since having a baby, I have been at ease [*thoải mái*] and have peace of mind [*yên tâm*]. Here is my child, my joy [*niềm vui*], and my hope [*hy vọng*] for the future. At the same time, my child will be my support [*chỗ dựa*] when I am old." Bearing and raising children enable single women, in addition to married women, to create a new future.

Happy (Vui vẻ)

Xin con was clearly an incentivized pragmatic choice: women gained social approval, status, and inclusion by having a child. But the social benefits do not fully explain older single women's desire for a child. A solely pragmatic orientation ignores the fact that sharing *tình cảm* (sympathy, shared understanding) with a child is itself desirable.[3] As Thắm said, "A house with children is more fun. . . . Children bring joy and love, they are silly [*ngớ ngẩn*], and mine is mischievous [*nghịch ngợm*]." Quỳnh admitted that raising a child on her own was very difficult because she was responsible for everything, from cooking and cleaning, to making money, to fixing the roof. But "at home with a child I feel happier. When I come home from work, my son often does something silly that makes me burst out laughing." The amusement that Quỳnh got from her son I witnessed again and again among my Vietnamese friends living in Vietnam and in Seattle. In Seattle, when Adam and I brought our infant son to parties in the late 1990s, Vietnamese friends—both men and women—scooped him up the moment we entered a party, passed him around, were amused by him, played with him, and kept him until we were ready to leave, often hours later. When we didn't bring him to parties, they asked why not. We had numerous similar experiences in Vietnam. Our Euro-American friends in Seattle, on the other hand, looked at him, said, "Oh isn't he cute," and in the same breath asked why it was we couldn't get a babysitter. After the quick hello, they turned their attention elsewhere. "A child is joyful," exclaimed Dân. "Since having a child, I no longer think about getting married. . . . It is too lonely for a woman to live alone; she should have a child." Nga said, "If you don't marry and don't have a child, then it is very difficult, difficult being at home alone [*một mình thui thủi*]."

SOMEONE TO LEAN ON

The importance of bearing a child for the psychological, physical, and social transformation it enables cannot be overstated. Yet in 1996 people said that the first and foremost reason <u>women need a child</u> is <u>so they will have someone to lean on</u> (*có người nương tựa*) <u>as they age</u> and become too <u>frail to care for themselves</u>. "Taking a husband is something you are compelled to do, must do," said Nga (born 1949). "But having a child is more important, much more important. Women really take a husband to have a child, in order to have someone to lean on."

During the 1980s and 1990s, despite the disruptions of war, population migration, and provision of state employment and housing, most of the elderly lived with or were cared for by their children—on whom they were entirely dependent. Few received pensions or welfare payments as a main source of income.[4]

Parents' expectations that they could rely on their children were based on the Confucian ideology that sharing common blood creates collective responsibility, mutual sentiment, and obligations. Parents taught children that they were duty bound to care for their elderly parents; doing so was a demonstration of "filial piety" (hiếu). Based on Confucian teachings, filial piety, a sacred virtue, is the fulcrum of Vietnamese family relations. It is a "moral debt" (ơn nghĩa) with both spiritual and physical dimensions that obligates children to love, respect, and care for their parents, worship ancestors and tend to their graves, and ensure continuation of the paternal ancestral line. Vietnamese historians and social scientists describe filial piety as a "boundless debt that can never be repaid" to "those already dead and those not yet born" (Jamieson 1986, 130).[5]

Married couples' old-age support was structured by patrilocal practices and patrilineal concerns. In rural areas, patrilineal concerns meant that parents passed down their land and inheritance to their sons, not their daughters. The practice of patrilocality meant that a married son, preferably the eldest son, resided with his parents after marrying and assumed primary responsibility for their economic and physical well-being as they aged and for their spiritual care after they died. Preference for endogamy meant that while daughters left home to live with their husbands upon marriage, they were geographically close enough to return to their natal home to observe annual family rituals (Luong 1984, 1989). Couples without a male heir might adopt a nephew or transfer filial responsibilities to the eldest daughter and her husband. In urban Hà Nội, family household fission and formation patterns as well as filial responsibilities were similar. Limited housing meant that some families divided their houses to provide separate living quarters for each son when he married, often creating multigenerational households in cramped living conditions (T. L. Hoang 1999). In some cases, a son-in-law lived with his wife's natal family (O'Harrow 1995). The growth of state-sponsored housing in Hà Nội beginning in the 1980s offered an alternative residential option for those who worked for the government—and who were lucky enough to access the limited official housing.

Given the ubiquity of marriage and the preferred practices of patrilineal inheritance and patrilocal residence, one might wonder where single women lived and who took care of them as they aged. For the most part, such women needed to create a "living strategy" (*chiến lược sống*) for themselves. In both urban and rural areas, single women who did not have access to state housing lived with their parents in exchange for helping care for them as they aged. A survey conducted between 1997 and 1998 revealed that "a significant number of daughters" were supporting their parents—an indication of the "diversity of living arrangements between married children and aging parents" that had emerged as a result of increased geographic mobility (Barbieri 2009, 159–60). Living with parents was feasible for single women until their parents died, at which point, "their role and status then begins to be problematic. No longer part of their parental unit, unmarried women become extensions of their brothers' families. These women become anomalous and peculiar. . . . The idea of depending on a married brother was not acceptable, and most likely, economically impossible" (Bélanger and Khuất 2002, 106).

Prior to the 1959 Law on Marriage and the Family, which outlawed polygamy, older single women were more likely to become second wives than remain at home. Single women who remained in a brother's home may have needed to demonstrate their value to the household. They could do so by helping out with domestic chores, contributing to household income, or developing a close relationship with and taking care of his children—care that they hoped would be reciprocated when they were old.[6] But this option for old-age support had its drawbacks. First, there was no guarantee that their nieces or nephews would care for them when they aged (Bélanger and Khuât 2002). Second, a man's competing obligations to his spouse and to his sister could incite conflict, not unlike the tension experienced between mothers and daughters-in-law. Tiên, my Vietnamese teacher, suggested that these tensions were rooted in the differential value historically accorded to blood ties versus marital ties.[7] If feasible, a common solution to sibling tension was to build a separate house nearby for the sister. But this solution also had its problems because, in general, "in the eyes of the community, this degree of independence . . . was not well regarded. . . . The idea of a one-person, self-sufficient household [was] not very acceptable—it [was] perceived as a selfish, undesirable, and lonely lifestyle" (Bélanger and Khuất 2002, 107).

Old-age support did not end at death. The social scientist Lan Phương from the Institute of Cultural Studies in Hà Nội, after hearing a talk I gave on *xin con* in 2013, pointed out that I had neglected the importance of having someone pray for a single woman after she died. Quoting the Buddhist phrase "Sống gửi thác về" (This life is temporary, death is eternity), she said, "Most important is the afterlife; this life is a trial . . . so you want someone to care for you in the afterlife." When Lan Phương conducted research in the northern countryside years ago at a younger but past marriageable age, villagers at different times and locations told her to *xin con* so that she would have someone to take care of her and to pray for her when she died. "Having someone pray for you is still very important in the countryside," she said. "But I am not sure about the cities," she remarked in 2017.

In 2017, I asked women in Sóc Sơn this question. Yes, having a child to pray for you after you die is important, they responded, but it is just one reason among many to have a child. Phương, a Women's Union official, pointed out that women don't tend to ponder death when they are young and thinking about bearing children. An elderly couple noted that there are many other means for ensuring a single woman is worshiped: the family could designate a nephew to take responsibility, a single woman could give land to a nephew in exchange for praying for her, or a woman could contribute money or land to the local pagoda so that the monks would pray for her when she died.[8] In Hà Nội, some families erected a *tục thờ cô tổ*, an altar for a grown family member who did not marry, next to their ancestral altar. If the woman was chaste, family members could pray to her to ask for help in their daily lives. These living strategies, both physical and spiritual, eased single women's concerns about remaining childless.

At the same time, it would be remiss to assert that *all* Vietnamese women desire a biological child. Single women in Hà Nội who were close to their nieces and nephews reported not missing having their own biological children. "These surrogate children fulfilled their desire for a child. Some informally adopted one in particular by contributing economically to his or her schooling, for instance, and expected returns in old age in the form of emotional or financial support." Notably, older single women's decision to have a child out of wedlock was considered more "socially acceptable and responsible" than single women who chose not to raise a child (Bélanger 2004, 108).

WHY NOT ADOPT?

Until the 1980s, adoption (*nhận nuôi*) was the principal route single women took to have a child of their own to raise, love, care for, and secure old-age support. Two options were available to single women: either they could adopt a child from inside the family or they could adopt from outside the family. While each strategy provided its own benefits, the challenges and risks they presented help explain why single women in the 1980s eschewed adoption in favor of asking for a child in order to fully satisfy their maternal desires.

Adoption Strategies

Two women—Bốn, who was born in 1953 and is from Phú Lương, and Hạnh, who was born in 1957 and is from Thanh Liệt—illustrate the two different adoption strategies undertaken by single women. Bốn, a schoolteacher, chose the most accepted and common practice, which was to adopt the child of a relative, usually a brother's daughter or son (see also Bousquet 2016, 108–9). She informally adopted her youngest brother's youngest daughter, his fourth child.[9] (An informal adoption, as opposed to a formal legal adoption, is one in which there is no legal transference of rights regarding parentage.) Bốn's brother built her and her daughter a small house on his land with the expectation that the girl would treat Bốn as her mother and would take on the responsibility of caring for Bốn in her old age.

Adopting the child of a relative was consonant with existing family strategies. It was not uncommon for a family to request the assistance of a niece or nephew for a period of time or for a poorer relative to send a child to a wealthier relative to be raised.[10] Bốn herself had been sent away when she was young to live with a relative because her mother could not care for her. "People liked having lots of children around; it was *vui* [happy]," she recalled. When Bốn was young, people had more children. In the mid-1960s the Vietnamese government, concerned with population growth, began to promote a two- to three-child family norm but had few resources to allocate to this goal. Tactics to reduce fertility rates intensified over the next two decades.[11] The total fertility rate dropped from 5.9 in 1979 to 3.8 in 1989 and to 3.2 in 1993, largely the result of high rates of contraceptive use and induced abortion (Haughton 1997). The drop in the number of children suggests that over time brothers may have had fewer children to give to their single childless sisters, limiting the availability of this route to motherhood.[12]

In contrast to Bốn, Hạnh chose an alternative adoption strategy: to look outside the family, a far less common and less acceptable route to adopting a child. Having rejected offers to become a second wife, Hạnh decided to adopt when she was thirty-five (in 1991) with advice and monetary help from friends. But the importance of shared blood rendered unacceptable her decision to adopt an unrelated two-month-old girl from the hospital. Hạnh's brother was furious; he said she should have helped raise one of his children, not a stranger's child. Hạnh clearly remembered the cutting remark he shouted at the time. "He tried to shame me; he said I had *rước voi về giày mả tổ!*," which roughly translates as bringing a procession of elephants to trample on one's ancestors' graves—a Vietnamese idiom used to accuse someone of committing an unforgivable offense, akin to treason.[13] Letters published in newspapers between the late 1980s and mid-1990s indicate that people also had legal concerns about relatives who had adopted outside the family.[14]

Hạnh preferred to have a child with no loyalty or filial responsibility to her brothers. While adopting a niece or nephew sounds like the perfect solution because of shared family blood, my research participants spoke of the frustrations that arose for single women who adopted the child of a relative. The first pertained to whether the child would know who the real biological mother was. Children adopted as infants were not told who the biological mother was. They referred to their adoptive mother as *mẹ* (mother) and their biological mother as *cô* (aunt).[15] Children who were adopted at later ages referred to their biological mother as *mẹ* and their adoptive mother as *cô*. In the latter case, being referred to as aunt was a daily reminder that the child ultimately belonged to the sister-in-law.[16] Second, biological mothers were said to keep a watchful eye over their sister-in-law to ensure that she raised the child properly. Even though all mothers were frequently subject to unsolicited advice from other mothers—relatives, acquaintances, and strangers—advice and admonitions from one's sister-in-law constituted another reminder that the adoptive mother did not birth the child. Third, even if a child recognized a filial responsibility to the aunt, the child's emotional loyalties risked becoming divided upon growing up and learning the identity of her or his biological family.[17] It was hard to keep the truth of a child's birth secret. Although Hạnh's strategy of adopting outside the family avoided these complications, her family's hostile reaction illustrates why other single women would be reluctant to follow Hạnh's approach.

Signe Howell (2009, 152) contends, "Adoption both challenges and confirms explicit and implicit notions about relatedness and sociality." Comparing the differential treatment of Bốn, who adopted her brother's child, and Hạnh, who adopted outside her bloodline, is instructive for what it reveals about normative constructions of Vietnamese families at the time. Why did Hạnh's adoption of an unrelated child incite anger? I did not meet Hạnh's brother and cannot speak for him, but I surmise that Hạnh's decision drew ire principally for two reasons. The first is based on the fact that a brother benefited from giving a sister a child of his own because it enabled him to retain the family land after his sister died. He did not benefit when she adopted from outside the family because, in doing so, Hạnh had created a family of her own. Once it was legally sanctioned in 1986 for single women to have children, single mothers were considered "a family," and by 1988 they were given their own plot of land to live on by the cooperative (hợp tác xã).[18]

Second, Hạnh's decision to adopt outside the family was an implicit rejection of the value of shared ancestry and a failure to demonstrate filial piety. Her act could be viewed as a breach of the Confucian precept of Three Submissions (Tam tòng) that stipulated women's position in society. The Three Submissions called for a daughter to obey her father, a wife to obey her husband, and a widow to obey her son (Tại gia tòng phụ, xuất giá tòng phu, phu tử tòng tử). Hạnh, an unmarried daughter whose parents had died, became her brother's responsibility and should obey him. By acting on her own without the consent of her family, Hạnh challenged her brother's patriarchal authority. Individuals who acted "irresponsibly" could bring shame to their family, as Hạnh's brother claimed she had. Similarly, when Bốn's younger sister became pregnant out of wedlock, her mother beat her severely for bringing shame.[19] Many of my research participants learned from a young age to think of themselves in relational terms—as a younger sister or brother, a niece or nephew, as part of a large extended family network, and as a link between past and future generations—rather than as an autonomous individual. (This relational thinking is reinforced by the language; pronouns are virtually all kinship terms.) Hạnh's behavior therefore reflected not just on herself but also, and more importantly, on other family members, dead and alive.[20] By adopting outside the family, Hạnh achieved a kind of independence from familial obligations similar to women who asked for a child, but at the cost of alienating her natal family, losing their social and economic support, and assuming the risk of adopting a child of unknown parentage.

Adopting from outside the family, from a hospital or an orphanage, also may not have been feasible for other single women for a variety of reasons. Adopting cost money that few women had. Nam (born 1944), for instance, said she was too poor to adopt a child. Not all children in orphanages were available for adoption. Parents and grandparents unable to care for children, often for health reasons, sometimes brought them to orphanages with the intent to retrieve them when they could. And the staff at orphanages preferred to give orphans to married couples, who, they said, provided better homes than single women.

More significant than the problem of logistics, I sensed among a few of my research participants a general dislike of the idea of adopting from an orphanage. Phương said, "No one likes the idea of paying money for a child—it is distasteful." An elderly man whose wife had secondary infertility and who had adopted a boy through an acquaintance said, "What kind of parents would abandon their child at an orphanage?" According to him, parents should find someone to take care of their child, either a relative or another family who wanted to adopt. The worry, he and his wife explained, was that an orphaned child would share traits similar to their parents, who evidently lacked good character. In point of fact, when I asked their daughter-in-law if she had been hesitant to marry their son, who had been adopted, she said no because she actually knew who his biological family was, and she also knew that he had been raised by his adoptive family since he was an infant. They had raised him well, and he is of good character.

Fear of adopting a child of poor character was one reason married couples chose to use the services of an intermediary, a village midwife (bà đỡ), to find a child. The value of using a midwife was that the two families could gather information about one another in secrecy. This arrangement benefited both families; the sending family could make sure their child would be raised well, and the adopting family could make sure the child came from a family of good character and would therefore be a good person.

Advice columnist Chị Thanh Tâm, responding to letters asking about adoption, advised couples to adopt an infant rather than a young child and to tell children when they turned three or four years old that they were adopted.[21] Chị Thanh Tâm reasoned that it is extremely complicated and difficult to instill the right ethics and duty, as well as tình cảm, in a child who has already been living with other people. This was particularly important for an adopted child, she wrote, since children will always find out that they are adopted. Hạnh said she was raising her adopted child to have compassion and felt that as long as she taught him "good habits" he would continue to respect her. "My child loves me. At the moment he is very well behaved," she added. Bốn fully expected her niece to fulfill her filial obligation to take care of her in her old age and saw no reason a niece or nephew couldn't develop tình cảm for their adoptive parents. But, she stressed, it was necessary to instill correct habits at a young age.[22]

The focus on cultivating a good moral disposition in adopted children responds to fears that a child of unknown heritage might develop a bad character or that absence of a biological bond would undermine the development of *tình cảm* between mother and child. For each story of an adopted child turning "bad," there was another account of a child who, even if she sought out her birth parents, maintained her filial duty to her adoptive parents.[23] Women who chose to adopt did not draw a distinction between adopted and biological children and rejected the notion that adoption was risky because it was not possible to develop true *tình cảm* with an adopted child. Denying the necessity or efficacy of shared blood for instilling *tình cảm* or ensuring filial piety, Hạnh, who had adopted from the hospital, considered the distinction between an adopted child and a biological child "a disgrace" because "all children are equally precious."

While adoption remains a strategy for achieving motherhood, ideas about who and how to adopt and how to ensure a strong filial bond reveal an underlying apprehension about the practice. Concerns regarding an adopted child's divided fidelity, women's independence, and worries about the nature of a child adopted from outside the family help explain why single women asked for a child rather than adopting a child.[24]

Biological Tình Cảm

Forgoing conventional strategies, all the women who asked for a child told me that they sought to secure old-age support by giving birth to their own child, a desire clearly articulated in their rejection of adoption. The crux of the issue lay in being able to ensure there was *tình cảm* between mother and child. *Tình cảm*, a mutual bond of sympathy and true understanding, is also the emotional glue integral to filial piety.

According to women who asked for a child, the surest way to instill *tình cảm* with a child is through gestating, sharing blood, birthing, and breastfeeding. The women's beliefs regarding *tình cảm* derived from the value families placed on shared blood inherent in patrilineal family ideology and in local beliefs about the biological and physical components of birthing and nurturing an infant. Women put the concept of shared blood to work in three ways. First, they attributed a higher value to their own blood, differentiating it from others. Second, women asserted that sharing blood provides the biological and symbolic foundation of *tình cảm*, ensuring that children will fulfill their filial duties. Third, based on the strength of blood relations, women construed nonblood relationships as less stable, and therefore risky. As such, women used blood in different ways: as a conveyor of one's ancestry and as a vehicle for transformation.

Foreign Blood Smells Fishy

Hồng (born in 1951) told me, "An adopted child would not be as valuable [quý] as a child I give birth to. When I gave birth to my child, I realized how happy I was; there was *tình cảm* between mother and child." In a similar vein, Chung (born in 1948) said, "Adoption would have been unavoidable if I couldn't give birth. . . . I only wanted a child of my own, to pass down my bloodline [*truyền lại dòng máu của mình*] and so that I can have a more perfect [*hoàn thiện hơn*] child." Chung's sister, brother, and parents agreed. Hương (born in 1973), who had unintentionally gotten pregnant with a boyfriend, who left her upon learning she was pregnant, decided—against the admonishments of her parents and relatives— not to abort the child. "I thought about it a lot. One hundred people, ninety-nine people advised me to abort, but I did not listen. I decided to give birth. This is a drop of my own blood [*một giọt máu của mình*]—I cannot destroy it." Hồng, Chung, and Hương's attribution of value to their own blood echoes Vietnamese idioms reminding children that blood relations are more important and enduring than other relationships. One such idiom was "One drop of red blood is better than a pond of water" (*Một giọt máu đào hơn ao nước lã*). Vietnamese historians characterize Vietnamese families as being united and linked together by a common "blood" male ancestor (Nguyen Khac Vien 1993). Imbued with filial duty and obligation, shared blood is intrinsically valuable.

The evocative phrase "*Khác máu tanh lòng,*" and its English translation, "Foreign blood smells fishy," were both cited to me in 1996 by Tiên, my Vietnamese teacher, to explain why people prefer to raise their own children rather than adopt, why stepmothers don't love and care for their stepchildren, and why a woman would not want to marry a man who was not the father of her children.[25] Recent media references to the term are used to explain tension between mothers-in-law and daughters-in-law.[26] The phrase is used to evoke a negative situation so displeasing it is difficult to overcome.[27] Here blood works to define boundaries and to explain the tenor of different social relations.

Given these narratives on blood, it is perhaps not surprising that Lý felt that a child of her own blood, as opposed to an adopted child, would be closer to her because of the strength of their biological relationship. "It will have more *tình cảm,*" she explained. "If an adopted child discovers its adoptive mother [*mẹ nuôi*] is not its biological mother [*mẹ đẻ*], their relationship will become strained." Hiền wouldn't consider adoption because mother and child would lack *tình cảm*; the child would not be capable of truly understanding her.

Hiền's beliefs echoed the proverb "One will not regret the tree one has not planted; one will not love the child one did not bear" (*Cây không trồng không tiếc. Con không đẻ không thương*).

Physiological Tình Cảm

Single women who asked for a child had been unwilling to adopt the child of a relative. Why? On the surface, there appears to be a contradiction. A single woman should be willing to adopt the child of a brother or sister because, as siblings, members of the same *họ* (family or patrilineage), they share "'blood' and 'pus' [*máu mủ*]" (Luong 1984, 302). (This was certainly Hạnh's brother's assumption.) And as we have learned, shared blood engenders *tình cảm*. But Chung and Hiền, as well as other women who asked for a child, wanted to birth their own child so they could pass down their own blood. According to them, *tình cảm* derives from gestating, birthing, and breastfeeding a child. Nga explained, "There is an exchange of blood between mother and child," and as a result "your blood changes when you have a child." The symbiotic transformation that takes place during pregnancy creates a close connection between mother and child. The blood they spoke of was that of their *họ*, but also symbolically and materially something new, something they created. As anthropologist Janet Carsten (2013, 16) has pointed out, "Blood has the capacity and the resilience to absorb and acquire new meaning."

Medical anthropologist Melissa Pashigian (2009a, 2009b), who has done extensive research on infertility and in vitro fertilization as well as on surrogacy in northern Vietnam, makes this point clearly with regard to what she refers to as "gestational *tình cảm*" (2009a, 43). Pashigian's informant, Tuyết, "explained that during gestation the mother and fetus shared nutrients and blood, and it was through these shared substances, physical closeness and a mutually sympathetic relationship that *tình cảm* grew between a mother and her baby" (45). Expounding upon Tuyết's explanation, Pashigian argues that "in locating the initial development of *tình cảm* in the uterus and in gestation, Tuyết starkly exposes the importance of the development of emotion—and in this case sentiment—believed to occur between a mother and a baby during pregnancy" (46). Sharing "nutritive and emotive substances in the womb engenders a 'uterine identity'" that Pashigian—developing Margery Wolf's (1972) concept of the "uterine family"—asserts "reflects an essential meaning of gestation in Vietnamese culture" (44).[28]

It is this uterine identity that women who asked for a child sought in order to secure a strong, sympathetic, and compassionate relationship with their child. Getting pregnant years before the introduction of in vitro fertilization or surrogacy, they too spoke of the relationship among being pregnant, sharing blood, and *tình cảm*. It was one of the main reasons they wanted to give birth. Uyên (born in 1964) said, "I dreamed of giving birth to a child. . . . I take care of my brother's children, but the relationship is tense, strained [*căng thẳng*]. I thought that if I have my own child, then it would have more *tình cảm* with me." Women who asked for a child redirect our analytic focus away from the meaning typically attributed to gestation (its role in maintaining the patrilineal family) to the mother-child relationship.

Giving birth also enabled women to further develop *tình cảm* through breastfeeding, a practice doctors and public health campaigns promoted over feeding babies the Nestlé's infant formula marketed since the 1930s (Dutton 2012; T. L. Nguyen 2016).[29] Dr. Nhơn in Phú Lương, who introduced me to a number of women who had asked for a child, said she always encouraged new mothers to breastfeed so that they would bond with their child, in part because "breastfeeding increases the *tình cảm* between mother and child. It is friendlier and brings a woman more physically close to her child because she can nurse it when it cries and when it is hungry. It is related to instinct." And she added, "Breastfeeding makes a female feel like a woman."

The value women attributed to shared blood and to breastfeeding that arises from being pregnant—the basis of *tình cảm*—created its converse; the symbolic meaning attributed to shared blood rendered nonblood mother-child relationships less strong and less significant. Lý and Hiền, among other single women who had asked for a child, felt that without a blood bond an adopted child would not "naturally" feel a sense of responsibility and duty toward the adoptive parents. Adoption is risky. A biological child is more reliable. This was clearly articulated by Nam:

> Many women are afraid to raise an adopted child because when the child is older it will want to find its mother and father. I also feared this. If I give birth to a boy or a girl, either one must take responsibility for me. Certainly if I raised an adopted child, when they are grown they will go find their mother and father—they won't be with me. Therefore I must give birth to be certain. When the child is grown, it will build a family here.

This lure of blood, the almost instinctual pull of a child toward the biological parents, was portrayed in films such as *Cô gái mang tên một dòng sông* (A girl called by the name of a river), which played as a television serial for three weeks in April 1996. The film tells the story of a young girl, Nhật Lệ, who reluctantly leaves her unwed mother in the countryside to seek employment in the city. In the city, Nhật Lệ meets an older man, the director of a factory, who, curiously drawn to Nhật Lệ, gives her a job. She likewise is drawn to him. As the story unfolds, it becomes clear that they share *tình cảm*. It is strange, this pull between an older man from the city and a young woman from the countryside, until Nhật Lệ's mother visits, gets a glimpse of the director, and realizes he is her long-lost love, the man who got her pregnant before he went off to the war—Nhật Lệ's father.[30] This lure of blood was also used to explain why adopted children would abandon their adoptive parents to seek their natal parents.

Where did this concern with abandonment come from? In part, it appears to have arisen from stories circulating about people who adopted children. When I queried friends and acquaintances about adoption, someone inevitably recounted the tale of a relative or friend who had a bad experience adopting a child. Either the children, though raised with love, eventually turned "bad" (*bị hư hỏng*), or they went off seeking their biological parents. Or birth parents sought the child they had given up for adoption. Alternatively, parents ceased paying attention to their adopted child once they were able to give birth to a biological child.

The newspapers printed letters to the editor and adoption stories that served as a vehicle for people to express concerns or ask questions. One person wrote to inquire whether they could return their adopted child.[31] There were also letters by adopted children who, though they loved their adoptive parents, wanted to find their biological parents.[32] Chị Tâm Giao, the advice columnist at *Báo Phụ nữ Thủ đô*, described letters and phone calls from children who had grown up without a father, asking such questions as "Why am I this way? Who is my father? I looked for my father and he admitted that he was my father but told me to keep silent. He worries it will break apart his family. What should I do?"

I heard about a number of strategies parents used to forestall being abandoned by their adopted children. One couple paid the birth mother and drew up a written contract requesting that the birth mother relinquish her place as mother and pledge not to search for the child in the future. In exchange, the adopting couples agreed to care for the children and raise them well. The midwife (*bà đỡ*) handled the transaction. Another couple changed the adopted son's name and filed legal adoption papers specifying parental rights. Additionally, single mothers like Hạnh tried to raise their children well, to instill the correct ethics and filial piety.

It would be tempting to conclude that the major difference between women who adopted and those who asked for a child was simply whether they believed in the power of nurture or the power of nature in securing old-age support. Yet, as we have seen, women who asked for a child were also concerned with the value of their own blood, with the kind of *tình cảm* they shared with their child, and in the physical transformation that women's bodies undergo when they become pregnant, give birth, and breastfeed. They were seeking a different kind of relatedness than that offered through adoption. Relatedness through blood not only linked women with their children; it provided a biological link to the mother's extended family—living, dead, and not yet born.

Perhaps most salient is the unspoken moral understanding that giving "life" (*sinh*), bearing and raising a child, is one of the greatest "sacrifices" (*hy sinh*) a person can make (Shohet 2013, 205). Because filial piety entails respect and care for one's parents in this life as well as in the afterlife, when a woman bears a child she ensures that the living will continue to care for the dead. Shohet suggests, "We may view hy sinh as providing the *raison d'etre* for acting toward parents in a filial manner: it is parents' sacrifices for their children that engenders debts and obligations, especially those related to devotion, of children to their parents" (205). Giving life itself provided the moral weight that older single women sought when they asked for a child in order to secure old-age support for this life and the next.

CONCLUSION

Hà (born in 1957) pointed out that "at the end of the wars we were twenty-five, twenty-six years old. So the women of my age group asked for a child [*xin con*] in order to be able to have our own child to lean on and take care of us when we become old."

In the past, adoption had been the route to raise a child, but by the mid-1990s, *xin con* had become an acceptable, and for many preferable, route to becoming a single mother. Women who asked for a child asserted that adoption is problematic and risky. Single women's decision to ask for a child in lieu of adoption was prompted by popular belief that giving the gift of life transforms a woman physically, psychologically, socially, and symbolically. It facilitates social connections and geographic mobility that fosters women's independence. Gestating, birthing, breastfeeding, and nurturing a child enabled women to experience the kind of love they and society felt surpassed all other loves: the love of a child. The desire for motherhood turns on the promise of transformation, the social acceptance that having a child brings. Women are told that they will not be the same person they were before, but it is impossible to know that prior to actually raising children. The promise of transformation is what is projected onto those women, who had not yet undergone childbearing. The assumption of a "yet" in "Do you have a child yet?" is the projection of a sense of inadequacy, lack, and incompleteness that only a child can remedy, but also the promise of something different.

The power of this narrative that a woman without a child is incomplete was driven home to me during an interview I had with a well-known graphic artist in 2004. He spoke of a new public health message, produced by an international family planning agency, that encouraged condom use to prevent the spread of HIV. The video showed a woman sitting in a chair with her back to the screen, her head down. She was alone on the screen. The caption warned married women that they could contract HIV from their husbands and advised couples to use condoms. The graphic artist found the message problematic: "Of course she isn't going to use a condom," he said. "She doesn't have a child yet." For him, the image of a woman alone, by herself, meant one thing: she was childless. It was telling that an artist who had designed posters during the war and in the postreunification period found images of women without children problematic. This was a particular lack he noticed, one that was not present during the war years, when women were predominantly portrayed with guns, or with children and guns, or working to build the new socialist society. His assessment was consistent with the Đổi Mới state's efforts to resituate women back in the home.

It is not just that a woman becomes a true woman upon bearing a child; there is a whole host of emotions, attitudes, and appropriate bodily behaviors that women learn as part of the child-rearing process. And yet, because women who asked for a child challenged existing parameters for bearing children, they were not simply mimicking but creating something new. Children create new social connections, and they expand women's horizons and possibilities for the future: land eligibility, independence, and opportunities to join education programs for mothers.

In 2017, Phương declared, "There is no reason for a woman to adopt if she can bear a child. A woman will first try to have her own child." It is notable that Phương made this assertion; her bold statement represents an attitudinal shift regarding *xin con*. Even though the women I met who had asked for a child two decades earlier had been granted the legal right to bear a child, they would not have made such a declaration. When they explained why they preferred a biological child rather than an adopted child, giving reasons that resonated with "all women," they had spoken softly and cautiously. They knew they had borne children outside the normative and socially acceptable route to motherhood. And they were well aware that family members, neighbors, acquaintances, and strangers had varying opinions of their decision to do so. How did these women come to be in a position to decide to ask for a child? The next chapter examines the sociopolitical and economic factors that created the context in which single women would act upon their desires to have a biological child.

CHAPTER 2

"When Will You Give Out Sweets?"

Sacrificing Youth, Forgoing Marriage

MARRIAGE WAS AND REMAINS THE NORMATIVE ROUTE FOR WOMEN TO BEAR A child in Vietnam, which is, as Phương told me in 1996, the reason "all Vietnamese women want to marry." Most of the women who asked for a child had never married. Why not? Many of the reasons are illustrated by noting how strikingly different Mai's world was from the one in which her mother had come of marital age. Unlike her mother, Mai (born in 1952) left home as an unmarried woman to gain technical skills in engineering that would enable her to obtain salaried work off the farm. Unlike her mother, Mai lived in government housing with people who were not immediate family or relatives and worked for state enterprises where she met people from other communes and provinces. Unlike her mother, Mai's family was not able to ensure Mai married before she was too old to do so. Moreover, Mai held firm to the notion that marriage should be voluntary and based on mutual respect and love, rather than grounded in familial connections and obligations. And unlike her mother, Mai decided she did not need to be married to bear and raise a child of her own.

In all probability, Mai's mother and her contemporaries would have considered marriage an obligation as well as a desirable stage in one's life. According to the sociologist Lê Thi (2005, 19), "Traditionally, marriage was considered so important" that it was not until parents had "organized the weddings of all their children" that parents considered their duties completed and their obligation to their ancestors fulfilled. "Only then" would they "feel confident departing this world." Families with unmarried children "blame[d] themselves for living an unrighteous life" and were said to be "haunted by the guilt before their ancestors." Until women began to ask for a child, marriage was the only socially acceptable arrangement for getting pregnant and giving birth to children in this patrilineal society.

Mai grew up with patriarchal family values similar to her mother; however, cracks had begun to emerge in this Confucian-based ideology that tied women to the home and rendered women largely subservient to men. Anticolonial revolutionaries from the late 1920s on had enticed young women to join the resistance, offering them new opportunities and alternative communities in order to liberate them from their families (Tai 1992, 2010; K. Werner 2017). In 1945, after the Geneva Accords, the Democratic Republic of Vietnam (DRV) began to create a new socialist society north of the seventeenth parallel. The Women's Union worked to eliminate Confucian-based precepts, which they considered oppressive, backward (lạc hậu), and feudal (phong kiến), obstacles to reorganizing society and creating equality between men and women. These efforts paved the way for the People's Army, like the Việt Minh before them, to encourage women to leave their families and exchange one type of guidance for another: the Communist Party for the patriarchal family. While Mai's mother was certainly influenced by revolutionary activities (her husband was a commune leader), her ability to marry had not been obstructed by larger political, economic, and social factors. By the time Mai came of marital age, however, these factors converged to create a radically different social world than the one her mother navigated when she contemplated marriage and childbearing. Mai's technical training, employment, love, and ultimate decision to bear and raise a child out of wedlock provide evidence of this history.

Larger structural factors confounded Mai and numerous other single women's opportunities and desire to marry. In the shifting marital terrain from the early 1960s to the 1980s, global politics (the Cold War) and North Vietnamese governmentality (efforts to create a socialist society) intersected at a most intimate level.

MOBILIZING FOR WAR (1960–1975)

> When I came of marital age we were fighting against the Americans. Then, like now, we had few men in the countryside; they had all gone to the south, and later, north. Everyone had gone to war.

There were only older people and infirm people at home. During
the war years everyone else went into the army.

NGA

The war against the United States and the DRV's efforts to reunite the country (early 1960s to April 1975) had dire consequences for single women's opportunities to find a suitable spouse (Lê Thi 2005). Mobilizing for war entailed
rallying men and women to fight, summoning women to support the war
effort, and evacuating families from urban areas at risk of being bombed.

Rallying to Fight

In 1960, prior to official American deployment in Vietnam, the DRV implemented a universal draft law formalizing men's induction into the Vietnamese People's Army (VPA). Initially, men eighteen to twenty-seven were subject
to an annual draft. Later, during the escalation of the American bombing in
the north, the VPA expanded the draft age to include men sixteen to forty-five
and extended the tour of duty from two to four years, and later to an indefinite
time period (Teerawichitchainan 2009; Bradley 2009).[1] Because of the vast
numbers of young men who joined the army, few able-bodied men remained
in the villages during the war. As Lập from Sóc Sơn said, "I did have some male
friends, but they all went south."

From 1960 to the early 1970s, the North Vietnamese government conducted
a series of mobilization waves to encourage all young and able people to
engage in revolutionary activity. Two "emulation campaigns" specifically
sought to ensure that youth would be ready and willing to join the war effort.
The Three Delays Campaign, launched in 1960, exhorted young people to delay
love, marriage, and children so they could fully devote themselves to the war
effort and to building socialism.[2] "If you have not yet loved, delay love; if you
have not yet married, delay marriage; if you have not yet borne children, delay
bearing children" (Le Thanh quoted in Chanoff and Doan 1996, 6). The 1964
Three Readies Movement (Ba sẵn sàng) "aimed at all of the country's youth,
exhorting them to be ready to (1) join the armed forces in battle, (2) tackle all
problems and intensify production, work, and study, and (3) go where the
country needed them" (Guillemot 2009, 23).

Summoning Women

On March 19, 1965, the Women's Union launched the Three Responsibilities
Movement (Ba đảm đang) to recruit women to join the war effort. The Three

Responsibilities Movement called upon women to (1) take responsibility for agricultural and industrial production, as well as other tasks and jobs men vacated to join the war; (2) take control over household management and encourage husbands, sons, and brothers to join the army; and (3) support soldiers who were at the front and go to battle if necessary (Guillemot 2009). This "emulation campaign" was initiated in response to President Hồ Chí Minh's appeal for all "patriotic Vietnamese" to take up their "sacred task" to "resist US aggression and save the country." Propaganda messages called upon young women to follow in the footsteps of their forebears—such as the Hai Bà Trưng sisters—but more pointedly, to emulate women of their mothers' generation who had joined the *thanh niên xung phong* (youth brigade: youth who volunteered for the war effort), to oust the French colonial regime.[3] Indeed, in the 1950s, the DRV had issued a decree to eradicate regulations that "forced women to live within the confines of their families" and abolished laws that forbade women from participating in activities "not considered compatible with their roles as wives in feudal terms" (Mai and Lê 1978, 171).

Many of the women I spoke with felt that since their brothers, husbands, and children had gone to the battlefront, they too should shoulder some responsibility for the war effort. Women who stayed home made up the "rear guard," protecting homes, tending crops, and taking care of the elderly and young children. Women who left home participated in the war effort in numerous ways, such as working on the Hồ Chì Minh Trail in the Trường Sơn Mountains,[4] joining teams to build roads and create military defenses in their home provinces, working at state enterprises to produce goods needed for the war effort, and nursing sick and wounded soldiers.[5] Young single women volunteered more than married women because they typically had fewer familial obligations.

While Vietnamese war propaganda portrayed valiant women carrying rifles or capturing Americans, many women who volunteered for the war effort worked in remote state enterprises far from the battlefield. From 1967 to 1970, the government created forestry farms as part of the state's industrial investment programs (Fforde 1987) in order to "speed up the Vietnamese march toward a socialist economy."[6] Considered to be a "production front" (*mặt trận sản xuất*), forestry farms were initially organized to provide war revenue. Later, they became part of the government's long-term sustainable rural development income-generating projects. The wood, traded in-country or exported, was harvested for paper, building houses, and firewood. The work force was mostly women. A Military Service Law enacted in 1958 had limited

"Work Well, Train Well." Government propaganda poster. Artist Quốc Thái, 1972.

the proportion of men working in state enterprises to 50 percent so local village authorities could meet the village's military service requirement (Liljeström, Fforde, and Ohlsson 1987, 23). During the war, the DRV conducted campaigns recruiting women from villages in the Red River Delta to work on the farms because the work was considered "suitable work for women" and the men were not available.

Many poor women, along with the *thanh niên xung phong*, sought employment at the state forestry farms located in Phú Tho, Tuyên Quang, Yên Bái, and Hà Giang provinces.[7] According to Lê Thi, the women were "living according to the motto, 'Men go to battle, and women to the forests'" (Lê Thi 1995, 10). A journalist at *Báo Phụ nữ Việt Nam* (Vietnamese women's newspaper) with whom I spoke in 1996 attributed women's willingness or desire to head to the state forestry farms to low education levels and limited skills: "They were only capable of doing simple work. Men on the other hand had more skills and had more opportunity to move about freely to find employment with a higher income." The few men who worked at these locations were typically in management; few women were able to obtain managerial positions (Lê Thi 1995).

Conflating low-skilled work with women, management of state enterprises followed a "common pattern of a gender-based division of labor" (N. A. Trần 2002, 59). The absence of men created a heavily skewed work force (Nguyễn Thị Khoa 1993; Vũ Mạnh Lợi 1991). Within a few years, the forestry farms became crowded with women. When Lê Thi and a team of researchers conducted research at the forestry farms in 1987 and 1988, they found that the production teams consisted of 60 to 70 percent women, the majority of them single.[8] In 1994, Nguyễn Thị Bạch Tuyết, the head of the Forestry Ministry's Women's Committee, told *Far East Economic Review* journalist Murray Hiebert that 70 percent of the country's 52,000 forestry workers were women, and 28 percent were single women, 90 percent of whom were over age thirty.[9] When the war was over, they decided not to return home; they were still single and their parents had died, or they did not think they had a home to which to return (Nguyễn Hữu Minh 2009; Lê Thi 2005). After the war, female veterans became known as the "'five withouts' (*năm số không*)—'without husband, without children, without a house, without social status, without next of kin'" (Guillemot 2009, 44).

Women working at state forestry farms were not the only women who decided not to return home after the war. Other *thanh niên xung phong*, having participated in the resistance since they were eighteen or twenty years old—some as young as thirteen (Guillemot 2009, 27)—and having been independent from their families all those years, decided to remain with their fellow cadres rather than go home. Having dedicated their youth and marriageable years to the war effort, a number eventually decided to *xin con* (Lê Thi 2005).

Not all women had to travel far from home to work at state enterprises. Like Mai, Bích managed to secure work not too far from home in Phú Lương. She bicycled approximately fifteen kilometers to a state-run cement factory and back for eighteen years. According to Bích, because the work required a low skill level considered suitable for women, most employees were women. The management, however, was male. In 1996, when I met Bích, she was one of sixty women who worked at the factory, which had been built in 1971 as part of the war effort. Prior to 1978, the ratio of women to men had been 80:20, but by 1996 the ratio was closer to 60:40. In 1996, most workers were thirty-five or older; few women were under thirty. Retirement age was fifty-five. The majority of the women workers, like Bích, had only studied through third or fourth grade. Women with higher levels of education had moved on to other jobs. The implications of this skewed sex ratio eventually became evident: by 1996, ten of the sixty women working at the factory had chosen to *xin con*.

Gendered notions of work suitable for women, combined with class issues (women's low educational and skill levels), created employment situations where men were effectively absent. Women working in the state enterprises, whether they were near home or located in remote highland areas, highlight the dilemma of many older single women. Not only was it extremely difficult to find men to marry, but many of them, having devoted their youth to fighting for the nation, were now considered too old to find a husband.[10]

Evacuating Families

Responding to the escalation of the American bombing campaign in the north, the DRV evacuated residents from urban areas and from economic production zones. The government dispersed children, their parents, and their grandparents, often sending the children and the elderly to rural villages while their mothers and fathers were dispatched to other locations to continue their work. For example, during the American bombing campaigns of 1965 to 1975, the Thăng Long cigarette factory in Hà Nội was forced to scatter its production and its workers. One worker, Trung, "was assigned to go up northeast to the production center in Lạng Sơn while her husband had to follow his officemates who were evacuating up northwest to Yên Bái. They sent their four-year-old daughter to Thái Bình in the care of Trung's mother. From Lạng Sơn, Trung went to Hà Bắc where she stayed for two years" (Kerkvliet and Le 1997, 5). Family separations were extremely difficult, "but parents reluctant to send their children away were confronted with the prospect of losing their wartime rice rations" (Bradley 2009, 129).

It was not until 1973 that many families had the opportunity to return from evacuation centers and were able to reunite. Though American bombing had stopped by 1973, the fighting was not yet over. Cambodian incursions at Vietnam's southwestern border between 1976 and 1978 prompted the Vietnamese government to deploy large numbers of soldiers to the Cambodian border. Vietnam's subsequent ten-year occupation of Cambodia spurred additional fighting, keeping many young men away from home. In February 1979, in response to Vietnam's invasion and occupation of Cambodia, Chinese armed forces invaded northern Vietnam in what came to be known as the Sino-Vietnamese War or the Third Indochina War. "The Chinese invasion [compelled] Hà Nội to maintain a large portion of its army in the northern part of Việt Nam. . . . The threat of a second Chinese invasion meant that Việt Nam had to continue to keep a large proportion of its forces in this location indefinitely" (Morris 1999, 221; c.f. Thayer 2019). Many men from Sóc Sơn (such as

Mai's boyfriend) and Phú Lương went north to fight, and many remained there to protect the border. Though some women were recruited to participate in combat and to defend the country from the Chinese, there was a larger proportion of men in the army, leaving a shortage of men at home. In 1982, the Vietnamese began a gradual withdrawal from Cambodia, but it was not until January 1990 that the last Vietnamese troops left the country (Young 1991).

MALE MORTALITY

> After the war with the French there were still a lot of men, but after the American War there were only a few men scattered about. Before the American War, we did not have this situation of single women asking for a child; there were many, many young men, but after the war they were all gone, all of them.
>
> NAM, born 1945

Unlike Mai, who refused to marry just for the sake of getting married, women such as Nga and Hào were unable to marry for the simple reason that there were few if any suitable men around for them to choose from. By the time Nga and Hào and the other single women I met came of marital age (at about twenty-three), three decades of almost continual warfare (with the Americans, Cambodians, and Chinese) had created a skewed sex ratio. High male mortality during the American War was the principal cause of this imbalance. From 1965 to 1975 the risk of dying for young men fifteen to twenty-nine is estimated to have been more than seven times higher than the normal level of nonwar mortality; for men thirty to forty-four the comparable figure was about 2.5 times greater. During these years, mortality among all Vietnamese men over fifteen was twice as great as would have been expected in the absence of war.

For young women during the American War, mortality rates were 35–39 percent higher than would have been expected in the absence of war (Hirschman, Preston, and Vu 1995, 805). Estimates of war deaths range from 966,000 (Hirschman, Preston, and Vu 1995, 805) to 1.7 million (Obermeyer, Murray, and Gakidou 2008). Using population statistics from a single province in the Red River Delta, the sociologist Maria-Giovanna Merli found that "in relation to men, women's survival chances were not diminished greatly by the war. Among young women, the risk of death during the American War was only 50% higher than in the absence of war," though there was a greater degree of underreporting for female deaths than for male deaths in Vietnam's census (Merli 2000, 9, 8n11). As for total civilian deaths in both north and south Vietnam, the data are uncertain, ranging from an estimate of one million to four million (Bradley 2009, 144). The bottom line is that during the American War male mortality was significantly higher than female mortality.

The Vietnamese government has not officially confirmed the casualties of the Cambodian conflict, but one estimate suggests that thirty thousand Vietnamese troops were killed, almost all men.[11] Though there were only three weeks of heavy fighting during the Sino-Vietnamese War, it is estimated that around fifty thousand Vietnamese died.[12] Population data from the 1989 census indicate that an imbalance in the sex ratio still existed fifteen years after the end of the American War. In 1989, "between the ages of 20 and 34 years" (born 1945–69), "women in Vietnam exceeded their male counterparts by about 10 percent" (Goodkind 1997, 111).[13] Most of the women I interviewed fell into this age group. Gender imbalances were not evenly distributed geographically, with rural areas, particularly those that had been bombed, exhibiting a more severe sex imbalance (Mizoguchi 2010). "In many rural areas, males only accounted for 42 percent to 44 percent of the population. The percentage of women in the 20–24 and 25–29 age group was as high as 65–67 percent in some areas" (Khuất 1998, 35). Sóc Sơn, one of the two rural areas where I conducted my research, was heavily bombed: it had an international airport and a sizable army base.

According to Women's Union statistics, in both North and South Vietnam, 1.4 million women were classified as unmarried or widowed solely as a result of mortality during the American War (Turner 1998, 156). Nam is one such widow. Before Nam and her husband managed to get pregnant, her husband "went south to fight against the Americans. He sacrificed [hy sinh] his life there." A young widow, Nam remained in her husband's family's house to take care of her mother-in-law and did not take another husband. When she got older she decided to ask for a child. She eventually met a man who agreed to help her get pregnant. In 1980, at age thirty-six, Nam gave birth.

In the 1970s and 1980s, male emigration and high male mortality, combined with a growing population in which men married later than women, contributed to a marriage squeeze (Goodkind 1997; Mizoguchi 2010; Nguyễn Hữu Minh 2009), dramatically reducing single women's chances of marrying. A marriage squeeze is common in a growing population where women marry at younger ages than men: "As each successive birth cohort of females grows, they must seek a mate from the smaller pool of older males born just before them" (Goodkind 1997, 111). Rapid population growth "accelerated sharply" in northern Vietnam during the late 1950s and 1960s. As a result, "birth cohorts contributing to that growth reached their peak marital ages in the 1970s and 1980s" (Goodkind 1997, 111).

Vietnamese women marry men who are a few years older. For the women in Thanh Liệt, who came of marital age in the late 1960s, the majority of men were conscripted just at the time the women would have been getting married. For the women in Sóc Sơn and Phú Lương who came of marital age around 1975, the men they might have married had either died or were still in the army, deployed to the northern border with China or the Cambodian front. Women in Hà Nội who came of marital age in the mid-1980s faced a skewed sex ratio and had difficulty finding a suitable spouse. Betrothed women and married women, too, suffered from high male mortality, leaving them unmarried or widows with few chances of remarrying should they wish (Jellema 2007).

In 1996, the effects of the American War remained evident. The Women's Union official who welcomed me into her home was in tears as she told me about her brothers dying in an American bombing raid. Many widows I met wished to show me a sketch of their martyred husbands. For the single women who asked for a child, it was in their gestures when I asked why they had not married. Time and again, different women in their own way would wave their hands through the air, gesturing to empty spaces, to men who should or could have been there but weren't.

POSTWAR EFFORTS TO BUILD THE NATION: POPULATION MANAGEMENT (1975–1986)

In 1975, with the war against the United States over and the country reunited, the DRV was now able to focus its attention on building the nation and advancing socialism. Most germane to the emergence of the practice of *xin con* were government population and labor management policies, in particular *phân công* (assigning work) and the *hộ khẩu* (household registration system). *Phân công* channeled people into designated professions and determined where state employees would work. The *hộ khẩu* restricted domestic population movement. As a result, the choice of where to live and how to secure one's livelihood was shaped by the state and by family obligations.

Assigning Work

To manage labor, the DRV continued its wartime policy of assigning work (*phân công*). A key component of administering a planned economy, *phân công* was designed to ensure that there would be adequate numbers of people with the appropriate skills working in different economic sectors. This entailed managing international and domestic labor. Directing overseas population movement, the Vietnamese government sent contract workers, students, and professionals to Vietnam's communist allies. "In the 1980s close to 300,000 mostly unskilled workers were sent to work in Bulgaria, Czechoslovakia, East Germany, and the Soviet Union" (Schwenkel 2014, 239). Others were sent to Libya, other countries in Africa, and Iraq. According to my friends from Hà Nội who were sent to Communist bloc countries to study in the 1980s, students did not necessarily get to choose what subject they would study; it was assigned to them. The Vietnamese government designated what kind of training and education the country needed to advance socialism, sending students off to study subjects such as demography, engineering, mathematics, foreign languages, ethnology, and medicine.

The policy of *phân công* also entailed sending people to different communes and provinces within Vietnam where they would best contribute, according to their educational levels, professional training, and skill sets. Throughout the 1970s until the first half of the 1980s, a majority of people worked for the state, either in collective agriculture, in state bureaucracy, or for state-owned enterprises. Employees working in a state bureaucracy or in a state-owned enterprise automatically belonged to a government office or state company (*cơ quan nhà nước*) that provided the coupons necessary for obtaining food and clothing, housing, health care (including subsidies for maternity leave), retirement benefits, and other public services, such as schooling for children and continuing education for adults. Employment in a government office guaranteed work and support for life, unless an employee found work elsewhere, broke the law, or was expelled from the party. Working for the government was a path to economic security, a ticket off the farm, and a means to broaden one's horizons. Poor young country girls, in particular, sought work in state enterprises for these reasons.

Because so many people wanted to and did work for the state, the policy of *phân công* continued the wartime trend of dispersing family members.[14] Few contract workers, professionals, or students living abroad were allowed to bring their loved ones with them, leading to "painful, long-term separations"

(Schwenkel 2014, 244). The government also delegated domestic work assignments irrespective of people's personal concerns: lovers were separated, sons and daughters left their parents, husbands and wives were frequently sent to different provinces for a period of time. Such separations proved advantageous for older single women, such as Quỳnh (born in 1952) from Thanh Liệt, who developed a relationship and got pregnant with a man whose wife worked in Germany.

Hùng, one of my Vietnamese language teachers, who was a doctor during the war, recalled,

> Although the state did not force people to go, there was the belief that you should do what the state asked of you because everyone was busy building the homeland. If you did not go, your village leader would receive a letter saying that perhaps you were not a good worker, and they would look down on you for not supporting your country. But in general, people wanted to go work for the state because they did not want to go back to working on the farms—that work is very difficult, a poor and difficult life. Men were not allowed to bring their wives because someone needed to stay home to take care of the old people and the children, and to watch the land. And there was not necessarily work for the men's wives.

The Household Registration System

A key factor contributing to both men and women's restricted mobility was the household registration system, referred to as one's *hộ khẩu*. Everyone had a *hộ khẩu* that listed name, place and date of birth, place of residence, change of residence, profession, and geographic movement. One's *hộ khẩu* "establish[ed] land use rights, the right of residence, [and] access for social entitlements" (Le Bach Duong et al. 2014, 88). Until the early 1990s, "one's *hộ khẩu* was one's form of social insurance; it was the means through which one accessed public services, education and health care, obtained employment, and secured a livelihood" (Rigg 2016, 33). Lê Bạch Dương described the rights one's *hộ khẩu* entailed:

> Almost all the civil rights of an individual can be guaranteed only with the presence of *ho khau*. Other benefits and rights including rations for food and almost all necessary consumer items, ranging from cooking oil to the "rights" to be on the waiting list for purchasing a bicycle or

government house assignments, even summer vacation, all were bound to and determined by his specific position under the administration of a specific employer within the state sectors (in the countryside, people were also in the [sic] similar situation as their work and benefits were tied to the agricultural, fishing, or handicraft cooperatives). (Le Bach Duong 1998, 31, quoted in Hardy 2001, 192)

Because the *hộ khẩu* was tied to residence, rights and access to goods and services were only granted where one resided. Aiming to prohibit spontaneous migration, the government implemented rules governing the *hộ khẩu* that created bureaucratic impediments to visiting or moving to other locales. It was easy for city residents to move to rural areas and for rural residents to move to remote upland regions, but it was very difficult for rural or upland people to move to the cities. This is because the government considered urban growth "detrimental to economic progress" (Hardy 2001, 192).

Bureaucratic impediments to leaving the place where one resided, even temporarily, while possible to overcome, made seeing and spending time with loved ones who worked elsewhere difficult and infrequent. The *hộ khẩu* and "other regulations prevented people from traveling beyond their own subdistricts without permission. Consequently, communication, networking, or coordination among people in different parts of the country—even different parts of the same district or province—was exceedingly difficult without official involvement" (Kerkvliet 2005, 27). Restrictions on moving to urban areas meant that rural single women mostly had to stay put even if they had the means to relocate. Hội, born 1952, for example, said, "I have yet to leave Sóc Sơn. I have always been here—I farm the land." While restricted mobility would not have been a problem prior to the war, high male mortality and the mobilization of men for the war effort and later for nation-building projects diminished many women's chances of meeting a potential spouse.

Gendered Mobility in the Early Years of Đổi Mới

Prior to the 1980s, the *hộ khẩu*, employment, and nonstate economic activity channeled and controlled most population movement. With the socialist planned economic system showing serious signs of failure by the early 1980s, the state began to relax portions of the *hộ khẩu* system.[15] Gradually the cooperatives, which were already being undermined by informal market sector activities, were dismantled, and with them the "economic benefits and residence status enshrined in the *hộ khẩu*" (Hardy 2003, 269). As a result, in the early 1990s (the early years of Đổi Mới) "people increasingly turned to social mechanisms other than the state, including family, friends, and the open market, to find jobs, housing, and opportunities" (Lê and Khuất 2008, 39). The development of private enterprises prompted people to move about the country as they wished, as opposed to being directed by state concerns (Doan, Henaff, and Trinh 1998).

In the early years of Đổi Mới, economic privatization did not render rural women as mobile as men (Tran and Le 1997). While the state had successfully mobilized women for the war effort and postwar socialist enterprises, "at the end of the American war in 1975, women's participation in the public domain dropped precipitously," partly due to men returning from the war and to "the socialist-state's partial ideological concession to the male-centered kinship and family domains" (Luong 2003, 205, 207). Many of the gains that women had made during the war demonstrating their value outside the home did not carry over after the war (J. Werner 2002; N.A. Trần 2002).

Prerevolutionary practices based on the notion that women's primary responsibilities lay at home restricted women's mobility in the absence of war. Lacking the independence of single men, many women remained at home to help family members with agricultural production, maintain the household, or care for elderly relatives and other family members, constricting their marriage prospects. When both of Ty's parents died, as the oldest of five siblings, she became responsible for her sisters and brothers, forcing her to forgo marriage. Quỳnh, whose parents died when she was seventeen, sacrificed her own chances of marrying by staying at home, raising and caring for her younger brothers and sisters, and making sure they all married. In part, Quỳnh was caught between the older matchmaking customs, when parents arranged one's marriage, and the newer socialist ways, where meeting a potential spouse was left to chance or one's friends. Quỳnh's friends tried for years to introduce her to young men, but she was too embarrassed to đi chơi (go out to have fun) with them. As a result, she remained single, devoting her time to the Women's Union. Chi, whose brother went off to war and whose sister left home to work as a civil servant, stayed home to care for her father: "If I had taken a husband, then my father would have had to be alone by himself. I thought that if I love my father then I should not take a husband."

Rural men, on the other hand, prompted by overcrowding in the Red River Delta, moved temporarily or permanently to towns or cities to find employment. Because male migration exceeded female migration, "whole villages [were] being depopulated by men in search of work" (Werner and Bélanger

2002b, 26).[16] The movie *Thương nhớ đồng quê* (Nostalgia for the countryside) by Đặng Nhật Minh, released in Hà Nội in 1996, eloquently portrays the dilemmas of village life at the time: young men were mostly absent, leaving the villages to young women, children, and the elderly. In 1996, Thi Xuân, a young woman I interviewed who was coming of marriageable age, quipped, "There are hardly any young single men in Sóc Sơn to marry; see all of us young single women here! I want to go to China to get a husband. I know of about five girls from this village who went up there. They write that they are happy." This anxiety was also reflected in stories circulating about country boys who became "intoxicated" by city life and abandoned their girlfriends back in the countryside in the hope of marrying a city girl. But, as Tiên, my young Vietnamese teacher, pointed out, few city girls would marry a country boy; you can take the boy out of the countryside, but you can't take the country out of the boy. "He would have been too *nhà quê*," she said, using a slur I often heard Hanoians use to describe people from the countryside whom they considered simple, like a "country bumpkin."

The same gendered maxims that kept women from migrating also inhibited geographic mobility in their everyday lives and how they spent their free time. Rural single men were free to visit other villages, to *đi chơi* (go out, go for a walk, visit), but for the most part single women, such as Hội (born 1952) from Sóc Sơn and Sinh (born 1959) from Phú Lương, stayed within their own villages. Nor did they have the time, money, or means to *đi chơi* in their own villages, let alone far beyond their villages. As a result, their ability to meet young men was circumscribed: they could meet them in school, through relatives, visiting other villages, or since Đổi Mới, at festivals. Principally, rural women met men who came to them rather than the other way around. Young urban women, on the other hand, had a much easier time meeting men. The cities offered different kinds of employment, a variety of continuing education opportunities such as the increasingly popular English classes for those who could afford them, and public places such as parks and cafes where young men and women could meet.

AGE AND MARRIAGEABILITY

> I was old already. I was twenty-five. At that age we should have
> been wives, had children already. Married women of twenty-
> five or twenty-six had two or three children. My friends and I,
> we knew our chances of marrying had been thwarted. My male

friends who did return from the south took wives five to seven years younger than them. If women my age wanted to marry, we would have to marry a man around forty years old. And at that time, a man forty years old would have a wife and a child already. Therefore, most of us decided to remain single.

HÀ, born in 1957

In addition to high wartime male mortality, gendered employment practices, limited migration, and population displacement, women's chances of marrying were further complicated by a host of other considerations, such as where they stood in the sibling order, their family's social and economic situation, parental permission, and personal attributes such as beauty, level of education, type of employment, personal demeanor, skills, talents, and general character. While all of these factors were in play, the most direct and obvious effect of Cold War and revolutionary politics was simply that women, having devoted their marriageable years to the nation, were too old to marry when the war ended (for women who came of marital age during the war) or after the war (when gender imbalances limited women's ability to meet men when they were of marriageable age).

Analysts who have examined changes in marital trends in Vietnam during the latter part of the twentieth century divide trends in terms of three marriage cohorts: the war cohort, who married between 1963 and 1971 when Vietnam was at war; the reunification cohort, who married between 1977 and 1981, after north and south Vietnam were reunited; and the renovation cohort, who married between 1992 and 2000, after the implementation of economic reforms (Đổi Mới), when its effects were well underway. The mean age at marriage between these three cohorts did not differ substantially (war cohort: 21.56, reunification cohort: 22.23, renovation cohort: 21.56; Jayakody and Vu 2009, 217). The women I interviewed who asked for a child belonged to either the war cohort or the reunification cohort: born between 1945 and 1969 (the majority in the 1950s), they came of marital age in the late 1960s to the mid-1990s (the majority in the mid-1970s). In the years after the war cohort, the probability of parents and relatives introducing their children to a future spouse steadily declined, especially in urban areas (Jayakody and Vu 2009, 225).

Three aspects of age contributed to how women conceptualized their marriageability: chronological age, gendered relational age, and physiological age. In chronological terms, age reflects your place in society and in the family. Age designates your relationship to other people; it determines what pronouns (terms of address) you use to refer to yourself and to others; and it determines if someone is a suitable spouse.[17] <u>Chronologically, women were considered, and often considered themselves, to be unmarriageable after a certain age.</u> This idea was reinforced by Vietnamese colloquialisms, which ranged from phrases that revealed the presocialist (or "feudal," as it was often called) conceptualization of marriage, such as *ế rồi* or *bị ế* or *ế chồng* (on the shelf already) to more benign phrases such as *quá lứa* (overripe, past the best age) or *lỡ thì* (missed the marriageable age). *Ế*, not a polite reference, literally translates as "do not sell" or "to be in little demand"—a reference to goods and commodities that are rotten and therefore no longer hold value.

While the concept of *ế rồi has* remained constant, the age at which a woman becomes *quá lứa* has changed over time due to government edicts and family planning campaigns promoting a later minimum age at first marriage. In the north, prior to 1959, girls tended to marry by age fifteen or sixteen. At age twenty they were considered *ế chồng*. The state then raised the minimum legal age at marriage to eighteen for women and twenty for men. In 1988, to reduce population growth, the government enacted Decision #162, which raised the minimum legal age of marriage to twenty-two for women and twenty-six for men (Nguyễn Hữu Minh 2009).

As the age at marriage rose, so too did the age at which women were considered *quá lứa*, but not as much. *Quá lứa* also varied according to location and source of income, with women living in rural areas, such as Phú Lương and Sóc Sơn, hoping to be married by age twenty-five, and certainly by age thirty in Hà Nội. Attitudes about age and marriageability were reinforced by proverbs such as "A man in his thirties is still in his youth, a woman in her thirties is verging on old age" (*Trai ba mươi tuổi đang xoan, Gái ba mươi tuổi đã toan về già*).

<u>The second consideration, gendered relational age, refers to the notion that husbands should be older than wives.</u> This belief is rooted in Confucian precepts, in particular the Three Submissions, which obligate a woman to obey her father when she is a child, her husband when she is married, and her eldest son if widowed. As *trụ cột* (pillars) of the family, men were responsible for educating themselves about public affairs, creating advantageous social connections, and providing economically. Women, "generals of the interior," were responsible for domestic affairs. The attitude that men were more worldly and more knowledgeable than women was reflected in the pronouns husbands and wives used to refer to one another on a daily basis. Wives used the personal pronoun *anh* (older brother) to refer to their husbands and referred to

themselves as *em* (younger sibling/sister). Husbands likewise referred to wives as *em* and themselves as *anh*. This reciprocal pronoun relationship also designated distance and respect. This hierarchy was reinforced by people's preference (in both urban and rural areas and across generations) that there be a four- to five-year age difference between spouses (Bélanger and Khuất 1996). Laws legislating a lower minimum age for women than men reinforced the notion that men ought to marry younger women.

The third factor, physiological age, refers to the contingent relationship between a woman's beauty, how her body ages, and her reproductive potential. The Vietnamese aphorism "A talented man and a pretty woman will make a perfect couple" (*Trai tài, gái sắc*) does not just refer to criteria for choosing a spouse; it also alludes to the idea that women should remain attractive to their husbands in order to ensure a happy marriage. According to many women, bearing and raising children take a toll on a woman's body, causing her to age faster than her husband. For this reason, they asserted, a woman should not marry a younger man. Thắm, for example, would not marry her boyfriend. "We truly love each other," she said. "But we cannot marry each other. He is seven years younger than I am. We don't have any problems now, but in five or ten years, then our extreme age difference will make life difficult to bear. When I get older, he will no longer be able to find me attractive. . . . At first, I thought we could have a progressive marriage, but then I decided that our problem could not be overcome. . . . I don't want to get into that kind of situation, so I won't marry him. He will eventually find a younger woman and marry her."[18] Sinh, who is sixteen years younger, reiterated Thắm's opinion: "A boy wants a girl younger than himself because once a woman bears and raises children she will get ugly and old, so younger women are better."[19]

Women also thought of their body's age in terms of its reproductive capabilities. They referred to their fertility not in linear terms, but in contingent terms—the ways in which their bodies aged as a result of participating in the war effort (cf. Bledsoe 2002). When the first wave of women went off to work for the war effort, they were young teenage volunteers. When they returned home in 1975, "they were perceived as less desirable, as damaged by disease, malnutrition and other hardships they had endured in the jungle."[19] Parents of young men refused to let their sons marry girls whose bodies appeared too weak to bear children. Such was the case for a woman from the city of Ninh Bình, sixty miles north of Hà Nội. "Oh, how the jungle aged me," she said.[20] Malaria and malnourishment left her feeling weak; she also did not think she would be strong enough to bear children.[21]

Between 1993 and 1996 I attended a few weddings in which the bride, considered *quá lứa*, had suddenly announced she was getting married after a very brief courtship. Men at similar ages, in contrast, were still considered "young and promising" (Tran and Le 1997). There were limits, however; few women wanted to marry a man who was much older. Hiền, for example, could have married an older man who had a good retirement pension and was willing to buy land in her village so they could live near her family. But Hiền felt he was too old; he was fifty, almost twenty years older; some women suggested that by age forty single men were *ế rồi*.

The difficulties that attitudes regarding marital age presented to unmarried women were often publicized in the newspapers. Some articles recognized the reality (and thus plight) of women who were unable or reluctant to marry because they were older than their boyfriends, while others provided examples of happy couples where the man was younger than the woman.[22] The moralizing tone in a number of these articles suggests that the journalists sought to change public opinion and were motivated by broader political interests. In a 1990 *Báo Phụ nữ Việt Nam* article titled "Hạnh phúc ấy quá mong manh" (That fragile happiness), a reporter writes about the shock upon realizing that the bride in a wedding procession looked significantly older than the groom.[23] The journalist noted that the crowd gossiped and commented on this age difference, referring to the woman as *cóc đế* (very old, stricken in years). In another article, recognizing the difficulties older women faced finding men to marry, the author suggests that it is possible for older women to find happiness in marriage and provides an example of an older woman who was able to marry because she found a man from a lower socioeconomic status. Her husband was poorer and had a lower educational level than she did, but they were happy nonetheless. While some women were willing to "marry down," women I met who asked for a child were not, a clear indication of their agency.

For unmarried women nearing the age at which they were considered *quá lứa*, life often proved quite trying. The pressure to find a husband could be intense and could result in a woman retreating from society rather than embracing social life to meet a man. The three questions "How old are you?" "Are you married yet?" and "Do you have a child yet?" are among several *hỏi thăm cho vui* (questions asked out of habit and for fun). Other, less obvious *hỏi thăm cho vui* some of my older unmarried friends were asked were *Có gì mới không?* (Anything new?) and *Bao giờ cho ăn kẹo?* (When are you going to let me eat sweets?), a reference to the hard candies served at weddings.

However innocent, the cumulative effect of these questions could easily trouble or annoy those to whom they were directed, depending on their age, marital status, and childbearing status. For Thủy, a twenty-five-year-old woman from Hà Nội, what once seemed lighthearted questions—jokes tossed back and forth among friends—became a source of anxiety when she neared the age when she was considered *quá lứa*. Thủy suffered greatly from these questions. Dreading contact with people outside her family, she became "hesitant to talk" (*ngại nói*) to people. Day by day, she withdrew further from society, limiting her contact with outsiders to avoid *hỏi thăm cho vui*. As a result, she rarely met new people and had less and less contact with friends, which made it even more difficult to find someone to marry.

Other women, such as Mai and Hương, dismissed the questions but felt angered and irritated by them. Tuân was skeptical that marriage at her age would bring happiness. Nam asserted that "if you are not able to marry someone good" because you are *quá lứa*, "then marriage would be more difficult than living alone." Thích simply said marriage would have been "too difficult" for a woman her age. Age, it turns out, was not simply a reason women could not marry; it was also a reason some women decided against it.

I myself was not immune to these questions. In 1993, the female proprietor at the corner magazine store slipped me an issue of *Gia đình ngày nay* (Families today), which contained a feature article on how to find a husband. I routinely found my marital and reproductive status the subject of conversation among other customers at the morning *phở* (noodle soup) stall. When I left Vietnam in 1994, the Vietnamese family with whom I was living gave me a white linen tablecloth colorfully embroidered with a scene depicting a traditional wedding ceremony featuring a cat and a mouse. When the eldest son handed it to me, he kindly said, "Mai Hương, get married before you return to Vietnam." When I returned to Vietnam in 1995, my friends were delighted to hear I had married but surprised that I had married a younger man.

LOVE AND THE NEW SOCIALIST WOMAN

War, male mortality, skewed sex ratios, and age were significant structural factors limiting women's ability to meet men they might marry. Yet women were not simply victims of circumstance; they were agents who ascribed their single status to ideological factors. Beyond the issue of age, all of the women who asked for a child, regardless of circumstance, attributed their single status to love or lack thereof. Women's appeal to love as a reason they did not marry derives from changing notions (circulating from the revolutionary era on) regarding whom one should marry, who decides, and for what reasons. The women's narratives thus illustrate "the interrelatedness of structural change and ideological transformation" (Hirsch 2003, 12) and how "structural and cultural changes mutually reinforce one another" (12).

Women who asked for a child belong to the Kinh ethnic majority, which has a rich literary and folk tradition on love that informs everyday practice. This syncretic tradition, informed by Confucian, Buddhist, and indigenous Southeast Asian folk beliefs and customs, traditionally revolved around an individual's relationship and obligations to their family and extended kinship network—in particular one's husband's family. Because people primarily conceptualize themselves in terms of their relations to others, the Kinh concept of the individual is self-consciously relational rather than atomistic or singular. When considering marriage, it has been necessary for people to consider the effects of their decision on the larger extended family. As a result, there may be a disjuncture between whom one falls in love with and whom one decides to marry.

The disjuncture between whom one loves and whom one marries has roots in prerevolutionary Vietnamese society (pre-1945), when parents arranged their children's marriages, polygyny was a common practice among high-status families, and women were socialized to be self-sacrificing and subservient to men. Most marriages were not built on love. When people spoke about conjugal relationships, they rarely mentioned love but frequently referred to *tình nghĩa vợ chồng* or *tình nghĩa phu thê* (emotion or responsibility). *Tình nghĩa* was considered to be a deeper, wider, and more sustainable emotion than romantic love, which could be strong but would shortly die. The implication was that love is too romantic for daily practice; *tình nghĩa* is more important because it grows from the mutual support, respect, attachment, and so on of daily interaction. Conjugal love was thus a sentiment that developed over time as couples lived, worked, aged, and became intimate with one another. Bearing and raising children provided the necessary *sợi dây* (string) to bind a couple, enabling them to live together until "their hair was gray and teeth were loose" (đầu bạc răng long).[24]

Vietnamese I met recognize the importance of *tình nghĩa* and having children for marital stability and happiness but foreground the necessity of individual choice, love, and respect when entering into marriage. This generational shift has a history that comprises Vietnamese intellectuals' call for individual romantic love in the 1930s, revolutionaries' call to devote one's affection above all to the homeland from the 1940s on, and socialist efforts to reform marriage and love to create a new socialist society from the mid-1950s on.[25] While each of these ideological efforts influenced how single women who asked for a child thought about love, the most impactful was the state's decision to carefully govern marriage as part of its effort to create a "new socialist person" (*con người xã hội chủ nghĩa*).

In 1959, the DRV promulgated a new Law on Marriage and the Family (implemented in the north in 1960 and throughout the country in 1975). The law derived from the 1959 Constitution, which promised, among a number of freedoms, gender equality "in all spheres of political, economic, cultural, and social and domestic life" (Sidel 2009, 51, 50). The 1959 law aimed to eradicate the feudal marital system by promoting one that was free and progressive. To accomplish this goal the government raised the legal age at marriage and forbade child marriage, coerced or involuntary marriage, bride price, and polygamy.[26] Love became a *legal* basis for marriage for the first time in Vietnamese history. Article 13 of the Luật Hôn Nhân và Gia Đình (Law on Marriage and the Family) stated, "The husband and wife shall be obligated to love, respect, care for and help each other; to bring up the children, participate in productive labor, and to build a harmonious and happy family."

On the one hand, the law simply codified what many people had long wished for and what some were already practicing (Nguyễn Hữu Minh 2009). On the other hand, it was politically motivated and was aimed at promoting the interests of the state. Hồ Chí Minh viewed the Law on Marriage and the Family as "an integral part of the socialist revolution." At the Central Party Congress in 1959 he proclaimed, "This law aims at the emancipation of women, of half of society. . . . It is necessary to liberate women, but it is equally necessary to destroy feudal and bourgeois ideologies in men. . . . For their part, women should not sit and wait for Government and Party decrees. They must struggle. . . . The Party must take the lead from the elaboration to the promulgation and application of this law, because this is a revolution" (quoted in Mai and Lê 1978, 220). For Hồ Chí Minh, like Friedrich Engels ([1884] 1995), the institution of marriage and the patriarchal family reproduced many of society's inequalities because they were based on and served to maintain a system of private property.[27] The key to emancipation therefore lay in the state liberating the individual, in particular women, from the traditional family. The law gave the state, not the family, the authority to create families—and to define what a family would be.[28] In doing so, the law aimed to shift the basis of authority and the structure of obligations: the individual would no longer be principally subservient to the extended family, and the conjugal couple would become obligated both to one another and to the state.

The 1959 Law on Marriage and the Family was a pivot point for social change and personal empowerment. The law formally institutionalized a concept of love that brought together elements of romantic and revolutionary love. Advocates for romantic love stressed the importance of the individual, of deciding one's future, and recognized the tensions inherent between personal individual desire and one's obligations to one's family. Proponents of revolutionary love provided a political vision for how women could emancipate themselves from their families: by devoting themselves to the nation. Socialist love, symbolized by the 1959 Law on Marriage and the Family, linked individual romantic love to marriage and women's emancipation to revolutionary praxis.[29] Having promoted a concept of the modern socialist family based on marital love and women's emancipation, in contradistinction to the prerevolutionary feudal traditions, the state had to support women's decision not to marry should love be absent.

Decades later, when I asked single women why they did not marry, I was struck by their reference and appeals to love. The similarity of their responses signified a particular historical narrative of explanatory currency that they drew on to explain and justify their decisions not to marry and to have a child outside marriage. They were drawing on emancipatory notions of individual romantic and socialist love. In 1996, Thắm (born in 1959) said, "I would never marry for the sake of getting married. That would be a feudal act." All of the single women I spoke with held to this belief; they refused to marry men they did not love. "Actually," explained Đào, who came of marital age in the mid- to late 1980s, "it is not at all that all men are bad. There are some good men, but I have yet to throb with emotion [rung động]. It wasn't that I didn't want to marry, but . . . no one satisfied my hopes, aspirations, and desires, so I did not marry." Hiền, who was twenty-seven, not yet married, and without a child, said, "I have not been able to choose a man that I fully sympathize with." Hiền's mother and sister urged her to marry, but she could not bear the thought of it. "I don't want just any husband. The model that I like is when two people get to know each other and spend time with one another." Nam had lost her love to the war. Phương told me that Nam loved her boyfriend so much she was unable to consider anyone his equal: "She would not and will not marry anyone else. She is a beautiful woman and has had many suitors, but she would rather live alone than live with someone she does not love. I am also the same. I have loved someone so I would not want to love again."

Ngọc, Đào, and Hiền appealed to love to explain their decision to remain single. Thắm and Nam chose to remain faithful to their loves. Hà, Tuân, Sinh, and Thích claimed they were too old, too ugly, or unsuitable for a man to marry and in so doing situated themselves outside marital desire, marriage-ability, and conjugal love. This was not a rejection of the institution of marriage itself, but a rejection of a loveless marriage. As Hương (born 1954) said in 1996, "Marriage is good. I don't oppose it, but it is not absolutely necessary." The notion that women did not need to marry was a significant departure from the previous generation's beliefs about marriage. Unobtainable conjugal love, however, did not foreclose women's decision to seek what many said was a far more valuable and enduring love: the love of a child.

CONCLUSION

> The stories of Việt Nam. . . . I should start with the one that sticks in the heart of any Vietnamese: the birth of the nation, which is told according to the legend of our totem the great mother Âu Cơ, who married the dragon father Lạc Long Quân. They gave birth to one hundred eggs, which later turned out to be one hundred sons. They were happy for a while, but cultural differences led to an inevitable separation. Fifty children stayed in the mountainous area with their fairy mother, and the other fifty went to the Red River delta and the coastal area with their father. . . .
>
> In one way the story of the nation's birth tells us that we are united as one country, that we came from one family. But in my childhood, I always wondered why a family had to separate. Why did our ancestors choose that legend to tell us about the foundation of our nation? Was it a fatal legend?
>
> PHAN THANH HẢO 2021, 9

In this excerpt from a personal memoir, the journalist and translator Phan Thanh Hảo tells the story of a family living through the turmoil of the revolutionary era. It is a tale of love and lost love, of faithfulness and pain, and of sacrifice, familial dispersion, and personal hope. Looking back at her life and to the tale of Âu Cơ, Phan Thanh Hảo wonders about her ancestors' motivation for telling the story and about the choice to disperse in order to ultimately be reunited. By questioning the origin and continual retelling of the tale, Phan Thanh Hảo calls attention to the ways in which tales of the past and of the nation's origin were invoked to explain the present and make it familiar. Phan Thanh Hảo's rendering of Âu Cơ mirrors the stories I was told—in many different manifestations—by women from Sóc Sơn, Phú Lương, and Thanh Liệt. Both Phan Thanh Hảo and Mai, described in the vignette, call attention to the ways in which Cold War politics and socialist efforts to build the nation altered the social, familial, and moral landscape, which intimately affected the trajectory of their lives.

Mai Thi Tu and Lê Thị Nhâm Tuyết began their 1970s socialist revolutionary history of the nation, *Women in Viet Nam*, with the same legend, but did not question Âu Cơ's historiography. Indeed, for them the tale served as a foundational nationalist history of population migration and family dispersion. Such moral framing aimed to justify the DRV's call for its citizens to set aside personal concerns for the benefit of the nation. Reinscribing a Vietnamese national female essence, Mai Thị Tú and Lê Thị Nhâm Tuyết portray dispersion in romantic and sacrificial terms by quoting a song women reportedly sang frequently:

> Darling, we are still near each other
> Though separated by a hundred mountains and a thousand rivers.
> Our family affairs, as well as those of the village
> Whatever they may be, I will attend to them in your place.
> (Mai and Lê 1978, 260)

These two renderings of Âu Cơ, starkly opposed, belie the complicated nature of sacrifice. While the stories of lived experience and the anguish of familial dispersal disrupt the official narratives of willing sacrifice and loss, such sacrifice illuminates the effects of war and postwar socialist policies. They also hint at the way in which the government sought to redirect people's affections from one another to the nation.

Women whose lives had been circumscribed by their parents' familial concerns participated in radically new spatial and social arrangements. These arrangements, principally organized and managed by state interests, introduced women to an alternative public world and, at the same time, provided them with the opportunity to redefine themselves in unconventional ways. For women like Mai and Hà, leaving home and traveling to other parts of the country meant being introduced to—and possibly falling in love with—people they would otherwise have never met. Women who joined the party and became involved in revolutionary activities developed new skills and new trades, providing them with a glimmer of what it could mean to be economically and socially independent of their families. Having been asked by the state to postpone marriage to devote their time and energy to the country, these young women were indirectly given the message that there might be more important things to think about than marriage. Married women, forced to endure separation from their spouses for long periods of time, were confronted with the possibility of developing other intimate relationships. Gendered notions of work led to high concentrations of women working in certain industries, some of which were located in remote areas, rendering many single women geographically unable to meet men, let alone get married. And for those women who remained at home, population management via *phân công* and the *hộ khẩu* system could mean that there were no or few men remaining in the village or no men to meet at state forestry farms.

It is clear that larger structural factors, which many women glossed as "fate" (*số phận*), either eliminated women's chances for marriage or severely curtailed their options.[30] Yet women also referred to their marital fate in terms of love.[31] Women who cited age, beauty, health, and unsuitability as reasons they had not married also made it clear that it was for these reasons they had not fallen in love or had been loved. Women who had loved but remained unmarried said their love had been "thwarted" (*lỡ làng tình duyên*): thwarted as a result of a boyfriend going off to war and never returning, or perhaps returning but marrying someone younger; thwarted by parents who did not consider it a suitable match; or thwarted by the need to remain home to take care of younger siblings or an aging parent. Some women simply never had the chance to fall in love, whereas others had managed to disentangle themselves from a loveless marriage and for this reason were single. Given the frequency with which women cited love as a reason for not being married, I began to realize that, for them, affect played as important a role in why they were single as had war, socialist demographic policies, and marital law. Love, war, and politics were intimately entwined. Sinh's statement, "I have not married because of fate," took on new meaning.

PART 2

REPRODUCTIVE AGENCY AND VIETNAMESE GOVERNMENTALITY

CÀ MAU

It was 1986 and we were one of the first official delegations from the north to visit the Cape of Cà Mau since reunification. We went to the hamlet of Xóm Mũi.[1] As leader of the delegation, I was invited to stay at the local party leader's house. Because there was no local guesthouse, the other men were sent out into the village to find places to sleep. The next morning I waited and waited for the men to come back. Seven a.m., eight a.m. passed. I wondered what was keeping them. Around nine a.m. the men came back, tired and accompanied by a fairly large group of women.

The women insisted we postpone our return trip, and they requested I take a message back to Hà Nội. The women wanted men. They wanted the government to send down military men to protect the area. "There are no men," the women complained. "So many were killed during the war, the only men we do see travel up and down the river on patrol boats. . . . It is the government's duty to protect our rights, and the first right of a woman is to have a man. After that a child," they told me lest we construe their behavior the previous evening as illegal. As far as they were concerned, it was natural, a free custom, and their right. The women then bought some sea shrimp, cooked up a great meal, and provided the men with snake wine to restore their health, as the women had tired the men out the previous night.[2]

THIS IS THE STORY A WELL-KNOWN HISTORIAN AND FOLKLORIST RECOUNTED to me over tea in his house one morning in the spring of 1996. I had come to talk to him about *xin con*. Like so many other Vietnamese scholars I spoke with, he began our discussion with a personal story or a Vietnamese legend. The professor had taken this trip to Cà Mau in the mid-1980s. When he finished the story, he sat back and mused with admiration, "The women demanded their rights. They were not ashamed and spoke with no shame. . . . It is unusual. Vietnamese women usually speak of sexual relations with shame." He went on, "Since the war, Vietnamese women are becoming more and more dynamic and aggressive and provocative."

CHAPTER 3

Xin Con, "Asking for a Child"

A Novel Path to Motherhood

BY THE 1980S, WAR, MALE MORTALITY, POPULATION DISPLACEMENT, GENDERED divisions of labor practices in state enterprises, and government efforts to create a modern socialist society had dramatically shifted the familial, marital, and reproductive landscape for single women. These external structural factors both opened up and foreclosed women's options for participating in social life. They contributed to women's ability to enter social worlds outside the family (to join the revolution, to fight, to work, and to study), but they also severely constricted chances and choices for marriage. One might suppose that the inability to find suitable men to marry, a fundamental effect of these larger sociopolitical processes combined with cultural and ideological constraints on expected behavior, would have dashed single women's reproductive desire and ability to give birth to their own children. It did for many single women but not all.[1] Ironically, these larger forces also provoked single women's decision to actively find other ways to become biological mothers.

This chapter examines *xin con* as a form of agency, a deft maneuver that traverses maternal desire, marital custom, family law, and gendered notions of sexuality and reproduction. I explore how single women navigated conventional yet malleable moral parameters surrounding reproduction and, in the process, produced and articulated codes of conduct that would help render *xin con* a socially intelligible reproductive practice. Consistent with the principle that agency is "never a thing in itself but is always part of a process" that constructs and reconstructs "larger social and cultural formations" (Ortner

2006a, 134), asking for a child instigated social change that broadened the permissible horizons of family formation in modern Vietnam.

PARAMETERS OF *XIN CON*

> I intentionally had a child; it was not accidental.
>
> CHUNG, born 1948

Three characteristics together defined the parameters of *xin con*: maternal desire, age, and intent. First, and most obviously, maternal desire was the driving force for *xin con*. A woman who asked for a child wanted a child to love so she would not be lonely and to have someone to take care of her as she aged. On the one hand, there was nothing unique about single women's maternal desire; normative discourses at the time asserted that all Vietnamese women desired children. Conventional maternal desire envisioned a particular kind of maternal subject, one constituted through and subsumed within the patriarchal family. On the other hand, *xin con* represented a new kind of maternal desire, in which single women envisioned and performed a novel maternal subjectivity outside the old bounds of the patriarchal family.

After desire, the second salient feature of *xin con* was the way age demarcated marriageability. Asserting that they were *lớn tuổi rồi* (old) and therefore past marriageable age, women embraced an ostensibly constraining subjectivity and reinterpreted it through the perspective of their own desires: they no longer considered marriage a desirable or necessary route to bearing a child.[2]

Intent, the third defining feature of *xin con*, was the fundamental distinction between single women who planned to get pregnant and those who accidentally did so. If a single woman was past marriageable age when she became pregnant, it was highly likely that she would say she had intended to get pregnant and had done so by asking for a child, whereas if a single woman was still of marriageable age when she became pregnant, it was highly likely that she had *not* intended to do so.[3] Older women designated their reproductive intent by using one of two phrases, *kiếm con* (finding a child) or *xin con* (asking for a child). The younger single mothers still of marriageable age with whom I spoke did not refer to their pregnancies in terms of "asking for" or "finding"; rather they said they had not intended (*không có ý định*) to get pregnant.

Intent is a clear indication of agency. But what kind of agency? What the professor of history and folklore (born in 1934) found remarkable about the women he visited in Cà Mau in 1986 was not that they desired sex or a child but that they demanded the right to have a man, to have sex, to bear a child—and they were not ashamed of their actions. Since the women framed their desire as a right to be protected by the state, perhaps there was no need to be ashamed.[4] In the history professor's eyes, the women's candor and requests or demands of the men marked a significant break from how Vietnamese women were "supposed" to comport themselves. In 2017, a female social scientist recently retired from the Vietnamese Academy of Social Sciences (VASS) explained, "One reason a single woman would not have had a child in the past is that she would never have been able to *ask* a man to have sex and get her pregnant. . . . They would not have broken social conventions. The need for sex was not discussed—it was a taboo topic. Women were supposed to be passive with regard to initiating sex."[5]

The social conventions regarding sexuality to which the social scientist referred derive from the Confucian moral precepts called the Four Virtues (*Tứ đức*) and the Three Submissions (*Tam tòng*). The Four Virtues stipulate that "every young woman must fully practice and scrupulously conform to four virtues: be skillful in her work, modest in her behavior, soft-spoken in her language, faultless in her principles" (Trinh 1992, 83).[6] The Three Submissions called upon a woman to obey the men in her family depending on her marital status: her father, her husband, or her son. Under Confucianism, a woman's childbearing serves the patrilineal family; she must therefore remain a virgin before marriage and maintain sexual fidelity to her husband. Unmarried women gained respect by being chaste filial daughters. Unmarried daughters risked inciting familial opprobrium and bringing shame upon their families by getting pregnant out of wedlock, but also by ignoring female mores that denied women's sexual agency. But if single women wanted to birth a child, they had to ask men to have sex to get them pregnant; there were no other options.[7] Asking for a child broke with conventional sexual and reproductive morals and practices. For this reason it was remarkable and, given the predominant social values at the time, also quite brave. *Xin con* represents both sexual and reproductive agency.

It is telling that women "asked" for a child. While *xin con* clearly diverged from social convention, it retained the appropriate female discursive comportment. Literal translations of *xin* include "to ask," "to beg," "to pray," or "to offer." *Xin* is used at the beginning of a humble request, an invitation, or an offering; it indicates modesty and politeness. It is used when you hope someone will give you something or agree to let you do something. (*Con* simply means "child.") Linguistically, "asking for a child" enabled women to walk a fine line of femininity: the new socialist woman asserting her right to a child, but doing so in a feminine mode of appealing for assistance, one that aligns with how women are "supposed" to comport themselves, unlike the women in Cà Mau whose "aggressive" demands so surprised the professor. This is one reason that *xin con* has become a recognized discursive category.

Intent is a necessary condition of *xin con*. It indicates forethought, negotiation, and planning. It includes "all the ways in which action is cognitively and emotionally pointed *toward* some purpose" (Ortner 2006a, 134). However, one should be wary of imputing intent to people in general and cautious about asserting a definitive relationship between intent and agency, "because what are presented discursively by actors as intentions are often after-the-fact rationalizations" (Ortner 2006a, 135). Some theorists, such as the sociologist Anthony Giddens, worry that theories of intentionality that presuppose "'definite goals consciously held in the mind'" do not leave room for the role of the unconscious (Giddens 1979, quoted in Ortner 2006a, 135). Social theorists such as the anthropologists John and Jean Comaroff argue that "too much focus on explicit intentions obscures the fact that most social outcomes are in fact *un*intended consequences of action" (Ortner 2006a, 135). The anthropologist Sherry Ortner agrees with these points but contends that "if one is too soft on intentionality, one loses a distinction . . . between routine practices on the one hand, and 'agency' seen precisely as more intentionalized action on the other" (Ortner 2006a, 135). Ortner conceptualizes the notion of agency as having "two fields of meaning": "In one field of meaning 'agency' is about intentionality and the pursuit of (culturally defined) projects. In the other field of meaning agency is about power, about acting within relations of social inequality, asymmetry, and force. In fact 'agency' is never merely one or the other. Its two 'faces'—as (the pursuit of) 'projects' or as (the exercises of or against) 'power'—either blend or bleed into another or else retain their distinctiveness but intertwine with one another in a Moebius-type relationship" (139). *Xin con* could be considered a kind of "cultural project." At the same time, since the two fields of meaning are not really "two different 'things'" (Ortner 2006a, 143), *xin con* is also about power because asking "brings into play relations between individuals" (Foucault 2000, 337). By necessity, single women were in a subordinate position to the men from whom they asked for a child; they needed men's help. As a reproductive strategy, *xin con* also functioned in relation to kinship norms that situated and marked single women as outside conventional patriarchal reproductive practices. And given the appeal of the women in Cà Mau to the government official, it is clear that their reproductive objectives are somehow also intimately entwined with the state. Single women's "desires or intentions . . . emerge[d] from structurally defined differences of social categories and differentials of power" (Ortner 2006a, 145).

Keeping in mind theoretical and methodological concerns regarding agency, I frame the women's decision to ask for a child in terms of intent because women were explicit about the process through which they came to ask for a child: they deliberated about their decision, they took full responsibility, and their child was an intended consequence of their actions. Indeed, birthing a child was an accomplishment.

At the same time, I heed cautions about "treating agency as synonymous for free will" (Ahearn 2001, 113) and instead tease out "the ways in which agency is constituted by the norms, practices, institutions through which it is made available" (Lalu 2000, quoted in Ahearn 2001, 115). Asking for a child necessitated that single women navigate their local moral worlds without threatening normative values of marriage and reproduction; embrace pragmatic practices employed by previous generations of married women unable to conceive with their own husbands; secure cooperation and compliance from men; and be willing to risk and manage the familial, social, and economic consequences of getting pregnant out of wedlock, drawing on support where it could be found. Each of these facets of intent distinguish *xin con* as a unique form of agency that "is not an entity that exists apart from cultural construction" because "every culture, every subculture, every historical moment, constructs its own forms of agency, its own modes of enacting the process of reflecting on the self and the world and of acting simultaneously within and upon what one finds there" (Ortner 1995, 186).

ASKING FOR A CHILD

The cases presented below, organized in terms of intent, illustrate how women's decision to ask for a child is an example of agency. The care, patience, and consideration women put into asking for a child demonstrate that their actions were not solely dictated by their circumstances, age, or the lack of men. Women were choosy; they chose whom to ask to get them pregnant and did so according to their own criteria, even if the choices were limited. They intentionally developed relationships with the men and negotiated terms of agreement regarding the child before getting pregnant. The women were brave; they kept their heads down to quietly overcome patriarchal ideology and familial and social obstacles that prohibited single women from bearing and raising their own children. *Xin con* was not accidental or circumstantial, but a deliberate choice. *Xin con* was also a discursive strategy that signaled reproductive intent and that some older women appealed to in order to justify holding on to a pregnancy.

While desire, age, and intent were consistent features of *xin con*, the women's paths to motherhood otherwise varied according to disparate personal factors such as romantic history, residential location, occupation, attitudes toward familial or public opinion, and resolve. Probably the most significant factor differentiating the women's strategies was the year when they asked for a child. This is because in 1986, the government passed a new Law on Marriage and the Family, which was widely interpreted as recognizing all women's right to bear a child regardless of marital status. The law provided legal support for single mothers and their children; it was a first step toward changing social opinion about households headed by single women. About half of the older single women I spoke with regarding *xin con* chose to do so before the law. The other half did so knowing the law provided legal and social support. As implied above, agency and governmentality respond to one another.

Prior Intent, Asking Old Acquaintances: Bích and Hội

Bích (born in 1958) and Hội (born in 1952) both developed the intent to *xin con* prior to having an intimate relationship with the men they would eventually ask. When Bích wanted to get pregnant, she looked for a man "who was wise, lively, strong, and healthy—and an ethical and moral person." In other words, Bích was unwilling to get pregnant with just any man; she was selective. Hesitant to describe her own personal situation in much detail, Bích instead spoke about the other older single women with whom she worked at her cement factory south of Phú Lương. Ten out of forty single women at the factory had asked for a child. When I asked her how difficult it was for the single women at the factory to find men with whom to get pregnant, she said:

> It is very difficult for them to find a man who would help. Women look
> for a man who is decent [*tử tế*], serious minded [*đúng đắn*], a man who has
> a wife. These men are friends, men they have known for a long time, not
> someone they just met for the first time. The man must fully grasp the
> woman's situation and be sympathetic. As for the men, they look at the
> ability of the woman to raise a child and make sure she is not just playing
> with them and taking advantage of them. The women make an agreement
> with the men that the women will raise and take care of the child; it will

not be the man's responsibility. Some men give the woman a little money for food when the child is born—the amount depends on the man.[8]

Some of the factory workers' children knew their father's identity; others did not. According to Bích, if a man agreed to help a woman get pregnant in the hope that she would give birth to a boy and she did have a boy, then he would maintain contact with the mother and the child. Otherwise, he would not. Ultimately Bích decided to ask for a child from an old friend who lived far away; she did not tell her family or her child the father's name. Bích gave her child her own family name (*họ*).

Bích and the other women who worked at the cement factory were fortunate to give birth in a sympathetic environment (cf. Nguyễn Thị Khoa 1993; Lê Nhâm 1994). During the 1980s and 1990s, women in Phú Lương tended to be married by age twenty-two; thirty was considered to be *lớn tuổi* (old). According to Bích, for over fifteen years the personnel office at the cement factory had accommodated their single female employees' decision to bear children out of wedlock as long as they were *lớn tuổi*. If a woman did not have a family to return to for her maternity leave, the office appointed another worker to help her during the initial postpartum period. But, said Bích, "they help each other out not because it is their duty or responsibility, but because of *tình cảm* [sympathy]." A shared understanding between single mothers meant they were willing to care for another's child when the need arose. "Nowadays, everyone knows the law, so that when they are *lớn tuổi* they have a child." However, they were only supposed to bear one child. Bích noted, "None of the women want two children; they only want one in order to be happy and to have someone to lean on when they are sick. There isn't enough money to raise two children, and the office will discipline them if they have more than one child."

Hội, from Sóc Sơn, asked for a child from a man she had known as a teenager. He was one of her brother's friends and younger than Hội by two years. In 1982, he came through her village doing carpentry work. He was married and had five or six children. Hội asked him for a child and gave birth when she was thirty years old. The father's wife did not know he helped Hội have a child; Hội did not want her to know. She gave her child her own *họ*. Hội's parents died shortly after the child was born. She told them and others she was pregnant. Courageous in the face of social opinion, Hội said it did not matter to her what people thought: "It would be my child, I will be the one giving birth, and I will raise it." Hội lived near a number of her relatives, but they were also poor and busy taking care of their own children; she said she did not rely on them for help. Although she knew of other single women in Sóc Sơn who had also asked for a child, she did not *đi chơi* (go out or spend time) with them mostly because it had not occurred to her to do so, but also—as many mothers pointed out to me—because single mothers don't *have* leisure time.

Prior Intent, Finding a Man to Ask: Quỳnh and Nga

Quỳnh (born in 1952) and Nga (born in 1948) undertook strategies similar to Bích's: they first decided they wanted a child and then found a man. But in Quỳnh's and Nga's cases, they were not formerly acquainted with the men from whom they asked for a child. Quỳnh, who lived most of her life in Thanh Liệt, was a dedicated worker for the Women's Union. She was thirty-one when she began to think "very seriously about having a child." When she was forty, her friends introduced her to a man her age from Hà Nội whose wife had been living and working in Germany for some time. He and Quỳnh developed a close relationship, and she eventually got pregnant. "My friends advised me to *xin con* and when they found out I was pregnant they congratulated me for having a *chỗ nương tựa*, a child to lean on (literally, "a place to lean on"). "Principally because there was a law, I decided to have a child. If there had been no law then I would not have dared go ahead and have a child on my own." Quỳnh gave the child the father's *họ*. He used to visit regularly and give Quỳnh money for the boy, but when his wife returned from Germany he only visited about once a week.

When Nga turned thirty, she had already been thinking about asking for a child for some time prior to forming a relationship with a man stationed at the nearby army base in Sóc Sơn. Nga asked her family (with whom she lived) and her friends what they thought about her getting pregnant. All agreed she should have a child, so she went ahead and did so. When Nga was thirty-three, she gave birth to a baby girl and later to a boy. She wanted a boy to carry on her business and to rely on when she was older. Nga gave the children their father's *họ*. Nga and the father had an agreement that he would provide some money for the children's clothing and food, but he was poor and could only help periodically. After fifteen years of being in the army, ten of which were spent at Sóc Sơn, the man returned to his wife, who lived in another province.

Prior Intent, Asking a Current Boyfriend: Thắm and Lý

Thắm (born in 1959) and Lý (born in 1956) developed their intent to ask for a child after being in a relationship for a while. Thắm, from Hà Nội, was thirty-five when she began to think about getting pregnant with a boyfriend she had met through work. She did not want to marry him because he was so much younger. "I made the decision to get pregnant two years before giving birth." She said she spent those years thinking about her desire and about the implications of getting pregnant and giving birth without being married. "There were times when I was alone and of two minds as to whether it was a right decision or not. Many times I vacillated." At the end of 1994, when Thắm asked her boyfriend to get her pregnant, she drew up a formal written agreement (thỏa thuận) for herself and her boyfriend that established the parameters of his relationship with the child. To prevent claims arising in the future, the contract detailed the rights of the child, Thắm's rights, the rights of the father, and the rights of his relatives. Thắm insisted that her boyfriend relinquish any and all claims to the child. He would not be responsible for raising or providing money for the child, nor would his family have rights to the child. Thắm said he could visit the child—"It is not a problem"—but she would not accept any money from him. Thắm gave birth to a girl, to whom she gave her own họ because she wanted her daughter to have her own family name.

Thắm, having grown up in a well-established Hà Nội family, said, "In order to overcome feudal [phong kiến] thinking and the reactions of my family and society or my close friends, I must fight against tư tưởng [ideology]." Referring to her parents, who were in their late sixties and early seventies, Thắm said, "They don't agree with me. They think that my actions are contrary to the custom, habits, and traditions of our country."[9] Nonetheless, Thắm boldly got pregnant. She considered the younger generations more accepting: "Society today considers women who have a child on their own to be normal, like other women. It does not have the heavy [nặng nề] opinions of the past." Moreover, like Bích, Thắm had the support of the personnel office at the state agency where she worked. She had obtained its support prior to getting pregnant so she would not lose her job or her government housing.

Lý, from Thanh Liệt, explained that she had been unable to marry due to a physical disability that left one of her arms paralyzed. Lý said she met her boyfriend one day when he came to work on her house. "We got to know each other voluntarily [tự nguyện]. We had the same voluntary love." He was forty-two at the time, with a wife and three boys. He did not want more children, but he did want to help Lý have a child because "of his love for me." She spent one year thinking about whether to get pregnant and then waited to find a good time to do so. When her mother traveled to the south to visit relatives, Lý's boyfriend visited frequently. She had deliberated, patiently waited, and now acted on her intent. By the time her mother came home, Lý was pregnant. At first, her mother chastised her. "She was angry and nervous because she was fearful of neighborhood gossip." But when her mother began to care for Lý and the child, Lý realized that "actually she was secretly very happy for me." After Lý gave birth to a boy, the father tried to visit, but the villagers beat him so he did not dare return. Lý explained that her relatives and the villagers were afraid he would take the child. Even so, Lý gave the boy his father's *họ* rather than her own. Lý said that the 1986 Law on Marriage and the Family "created the conditions for me to register the birth of my child and after that for my child to have a favorable situation for learning. Therefore, mainly because of it, I was able to decide to have a child. . . . Had there been no law, then it would not have been right."[10]

"Traditional" Intent, Becoming a Concubine or Second Wife: Yến and Ngọc

A couple of the women I interviewed agreed to become a concubine (*làm lẽ*) or a "second wife" (*vợ hai*) [11] in order to ask for a child.[12] In doing so they were drawing on Vietnamese practices of polygyny and concubinage, culturally recognized principles of Vietnamese kinship that "have remained essentially intact at least in the twentieth century, if not for half a millennium" (Luong 1989, 744). Despite a legal prohibition on polygamy, married men continue to engage in "unofficial arrangements that constitute second wife relationships" (Pashigian 2009a, 50). Whereas seventeenth- and nineteenth-century legal codes and cultural practices clearly differentiated a woman's relationship to her husband and her rank from those of other women with whom her husband bore children, today "the informality and illegality of these relationships make it difficult to categorize whether someone is a second wife, lover or surrogate mother" (Pashigian 2009b, 179).[13] Most pertinent for single women choosing to be a second wife is that "the child born of a second wife is ultimately considered, socially, to belong to her, not to the first wife because she is the one who birthed the child" (Pashigian 2009a, 50).

Yến (born in 1956) was living with her mother when I met her. She said no one would marry her, so she reconciled herself to "becoming a concubine" (*làm lẽ*) in order to "find a child" (*kiếm đứa con*). She wanted a biological child but she did not want to adopt, so she "sneakily married" (*cưới trộm*) a man from a village somewhat far away: "sneakily" because she did not want anyone to know she had "married." She did not register the marriage. He was a thirty-eight-year-old married man with three children. At age twenty-seven, Yến gave birth to a girl. A few years later she got pregnant again in the hope of having a boy but had another girl. Both girls have their father's *họ*. When I asked Yến if the man's wife knew about her two children, Yến said that his wife, whom she referred to as the "first rank wife" (vợ cả), initially did not know but later found out. The wife did not say anything. She did not act jealous. She simply did not recognize Yến as a second wife. In contrast to women who did not call themselves concubines or second wives, Yến openly maintained contact with the biological father. Though he lives elsewhere, she has visited him twice, and he has visited the children a couple of times; they know who he is. Yet, when I met with Yến in 1996, she was raising the children on her own; the father had financial difficulties and no longer focused on the children. Yến had not seen him in a while. Some of the villagers were sympathetic to her decision to get pregnant a second time to try to have a boy, but others were not. Yến said she struggled to care for her two girls on her own, but she does receive help from her father and mother as well as her uncles.

Ngọc, who was born in 1952 and is from Thanh Liệt, initially decided to become a second wife (vợ hai) in order to have a child. One day when she and her sister were out and about, she met a man from another village, and they fell in love. It turned out that his wife, who had given birth to four girls, had sent him out to "ask for a boy." Ngọc and the man developed a relationship, and after a year he asked her to become his second wife. But when word got out in his village, he succumbed to social pressure and withdrew his marriage proposal. According to Ngọc, some villagers didn't think he should marry a middle-aged woman with poor eyesight. But, said Ngọc, he did agree to get her pregnant. When he and his wife learned that Ngọc had given birth to a boy, he apologized and again asked her to be his second wife. He and his wife invited Ngọc and her son to come live with them. Ngọc rejected the offer. In doing so, she incurred her mother's wrath. She was thrown out of her house and treated with scorn by her relatives. "But," said Ngọc, "I was fortunate because I had the help of two different women." Ngọc said, "Everyone in the village knows of the situation—it is public." Clearly it was not easy to keep such dealings secret.

Yến and Ngọc turned to "feudal" practices, which had accommodated older single women's desire to become a mother in the past but no longer functioned the same way. Their strategies remind us that old and new patterns of social action often coexist.

Ambiguous Reproductive Intent: Sinh and Nhân

Sinh (born in 1959) and Nhân (born in 1958) were not forthright or definitive about their intent to have a child. Sinh, who is from Phú Lương, was unwilling to state whether she had planned or intended to have a child prior to getting pregnant; she gave mixed messages. At the beginning of our conversation she said that she had thought about it because she was *tuổi cao* (advanced in age) and wanted to have a child to lean on, to take care of her when she was sick. Yet later in the conversation she said she did not intend to have a child, but when she got pregnant she decided to keep it. In either case, she said, referring to the 1986 Law on Marriage and the Family, "the law influenced me to have a child out of wedlock." She was twenty-seven when she gave birth to a boy whom she gave her family's *họ.* Sinh did not want her son to know who his father was. The father, who lives in Hải Phòng, tried to visit but was afraid to do so because Sinh's family knew he already had a wife and child. Though Sinh's parents did not agree with her decision, her mother and her sister eventually helped her take care of the child.

Nhân, who is also from Phú Lương, began a courtship with a man when she was nineteen years old. They courted for eight or nine years. She said because she was *nhẹ dạ cả tin* (weak-minded and gullible), she trusted everyone; she trusted him and got pregnant. "I had become pregnant with my boyfriend; we loved each other, but the two families did not agree to the match." When she was pregnant, Nhân realized that she was *tuổi cao* and needed a child "to lean on" (*cho dựa*), so she went ahead and gave birth. "At first I thought I had a bad reputation, but when I considered the age I had the child, I was twenty-eight. Even though my family and my relatives understood that I had become too old to marry, they still did not accept the idea of my raising a child on my own. Now they have a law that gives women the right to be a mother. When I had the child, I still had to heed the rules of the Women's Union and the Youth Association, which in this case meant not engaging in nonmarital sex. My friends thought little of me. After the law, many people were consoled." The 1986 Law on Marriage and the Family, by providing single mothers legal recognition and social legitimacy, relieved single mothers, and by extension their families, of moral stigma. Nhân visited the father when her son was three years old. After that first visit he married and had two children, so Nhân no longer visited. "When he was born, I gave the child his father's *họ,* but when he goes to school he will use my *họ.* Even though the father lives nearby, he takes no responsibility for the boy. The child knows that and never goes near the father's house because he knows who cares for him."

For Sinh and Nhân, age was the key defining element in their decision to give birth. Their reproductive intent was fuzzy. Though Sinh said she had asked for a child, her discussion was inconsistent. Nhân did not use the phrase *xin con* or *kiếm con.* But the Women's Union officials who took me to meet them did so because they knew I wanted to meet women who had asked for a child. For these officials, the phrase *xin con* adequately encompassed Sinh and Nhân's reproductive circumstances. By 1993, when I was conducting predissertation research, the term *xin con* had already become part of the nomenclature, and by 1996 Women's Union officials and older single women used the phrase because it signaled a particular reproductive configuration and provided social legitimacy. By discursively encompassing otherwise fuzzy circumstances in terms of *xin con*, the Women's Union regularized it and in doing so produced a new maternal subjectivity it would strive to govern.

NAVIGATING LOCAL MORAL WORLDS

Single women's ability to untether marriage's hold on reproduction depended on their ability to successfully navigate their local moral worlds without threatening normative values of marriage and reproduction. They did so by (1) appealing to socially sanctioned narratives regarding the importance of bearing one's own biological child, (2) drawing upon strategies used by married women whose husbands were infertile, (3) not seeking to challenge the institution of marriage, and indeed by trying to safeguard marital stability for the men who got them pregnant, and (4) by being open to the possibility that familial and social support might not be forthcoming, thus braving the unknown. *Xin con*, albeit a clear demonstration of sexual and reproductive agency, was bounded by culturally informed mores, practices, and conditions. As Ortner (2006a, 130) points out, "Social agents . . . are always involved in, and can never act outside of, the multiplicity of social relations in which they are enmeshed."

Pragmatic Women, Practical Strategies

In 1995, when I was looking for people to talk to about *xin con*, I was introduced to a gynecologist who worked at the Ministry of Health in Hà Nội. During the course of our conversation she told me that it was not uncommon for married women whose husbands were infertile to go to the hospital to get inseminated. I was puzzled because there were no sperm banks in Vietnam. The doctor laughed. "You in the West," she said, "with all your technology. You make everything so complicated." She then explained that a woman goes into a hospital room, lies down on a bed, and covers herself completely with a sheet—for privacy and to hide her face. Then an "unremarkable" (*bình thường*), average-looking man enters the room to inseminate her: "unremarkable" so his child's biological paternity would not be easily identifiable. The sperm donor and the woman remain anonymous to one another.

I was, admittedly, a bit skeptical of her account. Was she playing with me? I began to recognize that my incredulity disclosed more about me and my limited knowledge of practical kinship than anything else.[14] As I inquired further, I learned about other such strategies. The history professor who told me the Cà Mau story also told me that it was not unheard of for an infertile man of an older generation (born around 1920) to tell his wife to leave home and return when she was pregnant, which was referred to as *thả cỏ*, which means to "graze in other fields or greener pastures" (Pashigian 2009a, 55). A Vietnamese doctor (in his mid-thirties) who practiced traditional Vietnamese medicine said that "in the old days" an infertile man might bring a stranger into his home to impregnate his wife. Acquaintances in Hà Nội told me that men who had become infertile or were fearful of giving birth to a severely deformed child as a result of being exposed to Agent Orange (a tactical herbicide used by the United States military in Vietnam from 1959 to 1962 to defoliate the landcape and destroy food crops) during the war would take his wife to the hospital to be impregnated.[15] In each of these cases, the identity of the man (the sperm donor) remained unknown or hidden, and no one revealed that the child was not biologically related to the father. I also heard the obverse—a more recent story about a husband who threatened to divorce his wife when she suggested she become impregnated by another man—and a story about a man who did divorce his wife upon finding out that his wife had done so.[16]

Narrative accounts of alternative reproductive strategies challenge notions that there was once "a traditional Vietnamese family" that had been disrupted by war and revolution. They also reveal that Vietnamese have engaged in practical flexible kinship practices that did not rely on paternal blood to ensure patrilineage (*dòng họ*). Instead, the stories reveal a highly pragmatic solution for achieving a couple's desire to create a family ostensibly linked by blood. They also indicate that the strategy of asking a man to intentionally impregnate a woman other than his own wife, a woman with whom he would not maintain an ongoing relationship, was not a new reproductive practice in Vietnam.

What was innovative about *xin con* was that women (with the exception of concubines and second wives) did not ask men to get them pregnant to continue a man's patrilineage, but rather for themselves. By creating her own "uterine family" (Wolf 1972), a woman displaced "the absent presence" of the "patriarchal man" as the originating center of kinship: while he served as a "biological agent," he was not a "social agent" of reproduction (Dorow and

A single mother and her son. Sóc Sơn district, ca. 1990. Photograph shared with the author in 2013. Used by permission.

Swiffen 2009, 565), if only for a generation.[17] Single women who asked for a child created a new kind of family, an alternative to the patriarchal, patrilineal, and patrilocal kinship system.

Pregnant Negotiations, Pregnant Secrets

It is an obvious point but one worth highlighting that for single women to succeed in their goal of bearing children, they needed to obtain the cooperation of men. Bích, Quỳnh, Thắm, and the others in their various ways secured the support of men who already were or would become close friends, acquaintances, or boyfriends. Because the women would need to have sexual relations with the men and because the men were usually married, they needed to negotiate terms of agreement and the parameters of their relationship. The terms of agreement were aimed at protecting the happiness of the man's family, ensuring that their sexual relations would not threaten the emotional or financial foundations of his marriage. The parameters shed light on the ways in which Vietnamese social norms, practices, and institutions shaped *xin con* as a form of agency.

In most cases, men's willingness to impregnate an older single woman who had asked for a child derived from mutual agreement that the man would relinquish all responsibility for the child. All of the women agreed to take full responsibility for their child: there was no question about that. They were not of like mind, however, regarding the men's involvement in their child's life. Quỳnh was happy to have the father of her child continue to visit even after his wife returned from Germany. More typically, Bích, Nga, and Lý did not want nor expect long-term ongoing involvement from the biological father, though they were happy to receive a tiny bit of money or an article of clothing for the newborn. Aware that the men lacked resources, the women were resolute that they did not want any money. Nor did they want him lingering around. While Thắm's decision to draw up a contract with her child's biological father was unusual, none of the women wanted the man to have rights to their child. After all, they had each asked for a child for themselves, not for anyone else.[18]

In contrast to what women told me regarding their disinterest in men's involvement, Hanh, one of the editors at *Báo Phụ nữ Thủ đô* (Women's capital city newspaper), said in 1996 that in her opinion, "though a woman initially intends to 'ask for a child' not wanting anything from the man, once the child is born, the woman secretly hopes that the presence of the child will bind him [the man] to her. . . . This is because people view children as the string that binds (married) couples together." "Also," she said, citing a Vietnamese idiom, "people always want more than they have" (*được đằng chân, lân đằng đầu*). Regardless of how women felt, however, it was imperative for them to assert that they would take all responsibility for the child. According to Hanh, this agreement of responsibility was the single most important reason men agreed to help women get pregnant.[19]

From Hanh's perspective, because agreeing to take full responsibility for the child was imperative, a precondition to getting pregnant, the women were subordinate to men's stipulations; it was not necessarily a balanced agreement of mutual benefit. Hanh also dismissed the idea that a woman could have a child with a man without wanting either his emotional or financial involvement; single women were not getting what they "really wanted." I was troubled by Hanh's assertions. As a well-educated and well-intentioned woman, an employee of a government newspaper, she had the power to represent and speak for single women who had asked for a child. Her expert opinion, which imputed intent, silenced the women's own voices (Das 1995).

How was I to make sense of the disjuncture between Hanh's assertions and the women with whom I spoke? Single women said they wanted full responsibility for the child in part because they did not want the man to have any claims on their child. On this matter Thắm had been adamant. How Hanh and Thắm interpreted the negotiations and agreements was shaped by their quite different marital and social positions in Vietnamese society, which in turn shaped their perceptions about whether a woman would actually want to raise a child on her own or could be happy without a man present in her life. The ubiquity of marriage in Vietnam, the importance of the institution of marriage, the fact that few married women were willing to divorce their husbands regardless of how problematic or unhappy their marriage might be (Phinney 2010), and concomitant social patriarchal norms that construct men as the pillars of the family made it difficult for Hanh and many other married women with whom I spoke to perceive single women as anything but victims of circumstance, to be pitied because they had not been able to marry (Lê Thi 2005).

Notably, one of the more common Vietnamese phrases used to refer to single (*độc thân*) women at the time was *cô đơn* (lonely woman). From Hanh's perspective, *xin con* was more of a compulsion in which women made a virtue of necessity. For Hanh, *xin con* was not a form of agency, because older single women basically had no choice; they needed a child to survive and to take care of them in their old age. This is a very different way of thinking about *xin con* as a form of agency than how I interpret the women's stories. The women in Phú Lương wanted assurance that I "would *not* pity them." Older single women, while discursively subjected to a Confucian patriarchal ideological frame, nonetheless challenged norms that proscribed a social space for single mothers outside the patriarchal family. From my perspective, single women who asked for a child, while subjected to power relations, were simultaneously active agents, women on the margins who, while they may not have sought to resist the social order, did transform it—and themselves. Hanh perhaps was unable or unwilling to view single mothers through a different lens.

Women who asked for a child were not all that different from women in other countries who went to sperm banks, chose sperm based on a list of men's personal characteristics, got pregnant, and took full responsibility for the child. As Bích explained above, the women tried to pick carefully given the limited selection. The importance of being picky was illustrated one afternoon in 2004, when I returned to Sóc Sơn to visit the women I had interviewed in 1996 (see also Lê Nhâm 1994). Hà, Trước, Hội, Dần, and I were sitting around Hà's living room admiring her new armoire, her TV, and the view over the rice paddies from her recently constructed second-story bedroom when they began to tease her about her sickly boy. Having complained that he was always getting colds, Trước teased, "You should have been more picky—you chose a weak man." The other women hooted with laughter.[20]

But this pickiness only went so far. Unlike sperm banks in the West where women choose among a cast of "characters" and access sperm through a mediated, commodified transaction, asking a man for sperm took place in a relation of power. Men controlled the sperm women wanted access to and thus the bargaining chips. Even if the men were willing to gift their sperm, the women's negotiations "emerge[d] from structurally defined differences of social categories and differentials of power." It was "not free agency" (Ortner 2006a, 145).

Men's willingness to impregnate a single woman who asked them for a child also derived from the women's promise to keep the men's identity a secret.[21] This is one reason many women did not ask for a child from men who lived in their village or who would be readily identifiable. Keeping the man's identity a secret served a number of purposes. Remaining anonymous would keep him from being recognized as the father of the child and potentially becoming susceptible to admonitions to contribute to the child's well-being in the form of money, school fees, or inheritance. Anonymity also ensured that his wife and children would not learn that he had sexual relations with another woman who had given birth to a child. After the 1959 Law on Marriage and the Family promoted love-based marriage and decreed polygamy illegal, it was important that a woman who asked for a child not be accused of trying to break up a marriage. Hà (born 1957) said, "There was a man who came to me. He had a wife already and wanted me to be his second wife [vợ hai]. I did not like him. I only wanted to have a child, to live pleasantly and independently, and then after that not affect his wife and child anymore." Again and again women told me in no uncertain terms that they did not want to ruin the man's family happiness; they only wanted a child.

Anonymity guarded against social condemnation (Nguyễn Thị Khoa 1993). A woman reduced the risk of being considered an immoral person by not telling anyone the man's name or where he was from, as well as by declaring no interest in seeing him in the future or making any effort to do so. According to Phương, the Women's Union official from Sóc Sơn, in the family's or villagers' eyes, once an older woman who asked for a child had given birth to her child, there was no reason for her to continue the relationship. Keeping the man's identity a secret and taking full responsibility enabled the woman to maintain proper moral boundaries. To do otherwise would indicate she was not an honorable person.

The need to take full responsibility, to keep the men at bay and disavow interest in them, to hide the men's identity, and to keep one's head down suggests that the parameters of women's choices and thus their agency were narrow. Perhaps such demeanor is more in keeping with the Four Virtues and Three Submissions than one might think. What was a private matter between two people was also a matter of social compliance. Adherence and submission to a few patriarchal norms, not all, constituted an important mode of their agency (also see Mahmood 2005).

Given that word travels quickly and it is difficult to keep secrets in communities where everyone knows one another, I could not help but wonder how successful women were in protecting the men's identity or how important it was to keep the secret. In some cases, children knew who their father was, but their mother did not maintain contact with him. In some cases neighbors knew and prevented the biological father from returning to visit, either fearing he would take the child or because they knew he had a wife and children. Clearly some wives knew their husbands had helped a single woman get pregnant, as revealed in their letters or their husband's letters to the editor at *Báo Phụ nữ Thủ đô* and *Báo Phụ nữ Việt Nam* seeking advice. Hanh, the editor at *Báo Phụ nữ Thủ đô*, told me that any wife would know if her husband had been having a relationship with another woman, especially in a small village or in Hà Nội. Moreover, she said, "single women are easily exposed because their goal has been achieved and they are exceedingly happy to be a mother. For that reason they leak the secret."

During subsequent visits to Sóc Sơn in the mid-2010s, I learned that some women who previously asked for a child had, in fact, been in contact periodically with the biological father. Improved transportation and economic conditions beginning in the late 1990s and especially after the early 2000s as a result of Đổi Mới facilitated men's mobility, enabling them to check in on the child they had fathered many years earlier. For some men, it was no longer necessary to maintain the secret. In 2017 Phương from the Sóc Sơn Women's Union said, "In 1995 and 1996 no one knew who the fathers were. In the past, it was essential they keep the father's identity hidden. But now, yes, certainly everyone knows." Now that the women's own children had grown, and they had a little money and a motorbike, it had become okay to reconnect.

In some ways, this secret of the father's identity resembles the "public secret" I witnessed in 2004 when conducting research on men's extramarital relations in Hà Nội (Phinney 2010). In that context, and in many other locales, "'the secret' is one that men keep from their wives (and sometimes wives from their husbands), but it is also a secret that wives and husbands share together as they keep it from their neighbors" (Hirsch et al. 2010, 3). Michael Taussig's notion of the "public secret"—"That which is generally known but cannot be spoken" (1999, 50)—parallels the collective effort to hide the identity of men who fathered a child out of wedlock so they could maintain the fiction of having monogamous marriages.[22] *Xin con* was not a rejection of the institution of marriage but a paradoxically tacit recognition of its value for married people.[23]

MATERNITY CARE

In Vietnam, it has been and remains customary for married women to return to their natal home to give birth or after giving birth in a commune health station or hospital. When feasible, women were strongly encouraged and sometimes forced to rest (no walking around), stay in a room for at least a month, keep doors and windows closed to avoid chilly drafts, refrain from washing their hair so they didn't get wet, and have someone prepare or provide food that would bring the mother's yin and yang back into balance. What about single women who asked for a child? The kind of support they expected or received depended on a variety of factors, including whether they had discussed with family members or friends their decision to ask for a child ahead of time, whether they worked for the state, and if they chose to keep their intent and their pregnancy a secret.

By and large, the single women who discussed their plans in advance could count on postpartum support from those who were sympathetic to their desire to have a child or had encouraged them to ask for a child. Bích (born in 1958) from Phú Lương, who worked at the cement factory but lived in her parents' home, decided to ask for a child when she was twenty-seven because her brother advised her to do so. "It was his idea. He said that if I could not get married then I should have a child to rely on. He was worried I wouldn't have anyone to care for me when I get old."[24] Her brother's wife did her best to care for and help Bích after the birth. Quỳnh from Thanh Liệt, whose work friends had encouraged her to ask for a child, received their support.

Women who worked for governmental organizations received support from the the state. For the most part, women who worked for state enterprises were able to maintain their state housing and were eventually given paid maternity leave regardless of their marital status. Because of the preponderance of women living in some of these enterprises, women benefited from the support of other women like themselves; together they looked after one another and each other's children.[25] Such was also the case at the cement factory where Bích worked in Phú Lương. In 1990, her personnel office, responding to women's requests, built small houses around the factory so the single mothers and their children could have their own residences. According to Bích, single mothers were treated the same as other women; they were not discriminated against, nor were they given special provisions.

Thắm, who worked for a state agency in Hà Nội, made sure she could keep her job and maintain her state employee housing when it became clear that her parents did not and would not support her decision to ask for a child. After giving birth in the hospital, she returned to her flat to rest during her paid maternity leave, during which time she was looked after by supportive friends and fellow employees. Women who kept their intent to ask for a child or their pregnancy a secret as long as possible strategized when and where to get pregnant in order to minimize social condemnation.

In 2017 I learned about two single Hà Nội women, now in their late fifties, who each had left home to give birth to a child. When they returned home, they each claimed the child was adopted so they would not be criticized. Lý did not tell anyone she planned to ask for a child because she felt it was safer to keep it to herself. She arranged to get pregnant when her mother was away and did not know how her mother would react when she returned home. At first Lý's mother chastised her, but eventually she came around and took care of Lý and her child. One woman I met got pregnant by a man she loved who lived in another city and then left the country to study because she didn't want to deal with negative reactions from family and friends. When she finished her studies, she returned home with a little boy whom family members and friends readily accepted: it was a fait accompli.

There were limits, however, to familial, social, and governmental support for single women who asked for a child, regardless of the women's efforts to maintain a low profile. Two conditions stand out. First, the state's position was contradictory; single Women's Union officials and schoolteachers were expected to model appropriate feminine behavior. This made it difficult when they too wanted a child. When a Women's Union cadre leader from Quảng Bình Province asked her superiors for permission to bear a child out of wedlock, they told her to go elsewhere to ask for a child so as not to shatter a local family's happiness.[26] Single schoolteachers were advised to take a leave of absence or move elsewhere.[27] As role models for students and as individuals to emulate, teachers who asked for a child would send an inappropriate message to their students that it was acceptable to have extramarital sexual relations, which the state did not advocate. Two teachers I interviewed in 1996 had decided not to ask for a child because, as teachers, they would suffer social condemnation for not being good role models. One teacher, Bốn from Phú Lương, adopted a brother's youngest daughter so she would have a child to keep her company.

Second, it was generally understood that single women should only ask for one child, no more. Bích's personnel office at the cement factory made this stipulation quite clear. Most women with whom I talked asserted that they only wanted one child. However, a few women justified getting pregnant a second time in order to have a boy. Such was the case of Nga, who wanted a boy who could inherit her business, Yến, who considered herself a concubine, wanted a boy because girls leave home when they marry. The same applies to second wives who are trying to bear a son for the man who needs a son to pass down his patriline. Only the latter reason held sway among people with whom I spoke.

Most people explained the one-child limit in terms of economics; simply, it was just too difficult for a single woman, on her own, to raise two children. It was hard enough to raise one child. There was an element of moral censure for single women who had more than one child. I clearly remember Phương shaking her head disapprovingly when she told me about a single woman who had two children; she considered it a "selfish" act.

In each of these cases, women's calculations regarding what kind of social response and support they could receive and from whom shaped their plans for getting pregnant. Family circumstances, fear of ridicule, unwillingness to confront unsupportive family and friends, and how they made their living circumscribed women's reproductive agency. Single women chose to ask for a child for themselves; it was thus an individual desire. Their reproductive decision-making must nonetheless be viewed within larger Vietnamese "discourses of reproductive responsibility" (Gammeltoft 2014, 63), informed by gendered kinship and state ideologies. Having more than one child was viewed not only as economically untenable but as morally irresponsible—for the child, the society, and the nation.

CONCLUSION: THE GENERATIVE POWER OF HUMAN CREATIVITY

Anthropologist Heonik Kwon (2008, 85), referring to historian Jay Winter's accounts of commemoration after World War I, writes, "I believe that Winter opens a powerful new perspective to the social history of modern war, in which the phenomenon of war appears not merely in terms of its destructive power to tear apart the fabric of social life but also in relation to the generative power of human creativity to confront its mechanism of destruction and embrace its ruins."[28] I would argue that *xin con*, albeit a far cry from the spirits Kwon speaks of in his book *Ghosts of War in Vietnam*, represents just such a form of human creativity. Like the ghosts who had sacrificed for the nation, whose presence illustrated the contradictions of war, and who prompted new forms of kinship, *xin con* emerged out of the debris of the American War and out of revolution. But not all was debris; governmental responses to the war created and expanded social, economic, political, and educational opportunities, as well as skills for women.[29] New political and social forms and ideologies created the opportunity for older single women to carve out a new reproductive space. Taking advantage of and exceeding the bounds of the socialist revolutionary agenda for female emancipation, older single women demonstrated not only that a husband is not necessary for creating a family but that women can reproduce for themselves. Yet their narratives did not reflect a complete break with patrilineal reproductive ideology even if their actions did. Instead, women drew on and navigated existing cultural values and practices regarding marriage, sexuality, and women's place in society that themselves were in flux.[30]

Xin con signifies a new kind of sexual and reproductive agency. But what kind of sexual and reproductive agency? Clearly asking for a child entailed a transgressive act; women not only broke Confucian edicts bidding women to be subservient to men, but they also rejected the notion that women should be sexually passive. As such, *xin con* demonstrated political agency, a form of "everyday politics" in which women adjusted norms and rules regulating sexuality and reproduction to accomplish their goals even if their aims were not organized or political (cf. Kerkvliet 2005, 22).

I would not argue that *xin con*, however, as manifested at the end of the twentieth century, was a form of resistance against the patrilineal and patrilocal family or a rejection of the institution of marriage, as has been suggested (cf. Turner 1998). It would be a mistake to "misattribut[e] to them forms of consciousness or politics that are not part of their experience—something like feminist consciousness or feminist politics" (Abu-Lughod 1990, 47). In 2013 and 2017, women from Sóc Sơn with whom I have kept in touch over the past twenty years have been delighted to tell me about their children's marriages. Their children's ability to marry demonstrated their success as mothers and their belief that marriage, as long as it was based on love, was good. And the childrens' proper and conventional marriages reflected morally and socially on the women themselves. Single women's acceptance of and participation in a modern ritual of matrimony demonstrates that the women not only support but are reproducing dominant ideologies about marriage and reproduction, not subverting them.

For most women, *xin con* represented a form of individual autonomy that was unusual given the social expectation that an individual consult one's elders or other family members when making important life-transforming decisions that would reflect socially on the larger extended family (Gammeltoft 2014). Such women stated that they asked for a child on their own without the support of family and friends. For other women, such as Bích, Quỳnh, and Nga, who were encouraged by family or friends, their decisions suggest a more relational form of reproductive agency.

Regardless of the conditions of their intent, I would not want to "devalue their practices as prepolitical, primitive or even misguided" (Abu-Lughod 1990, 47), as if they were not aware of the social import of their actions. Even if the women said they were not rejecting the institution of marriage, their actions did resist fundamental ideological tenets regarding the relationship between marriage and childbearing—and their readiness to deflect their iconoclasm affirms their awareness of it. We could attribute women's keeping a low profile to a desire to adhere at some level to Confucian moral precepts, to shame, to deference toward the Happy Family (the heterosexual monogamous family), or as recognition that their actions did untether marriage's hold on reproduction. It was a site of struggle, an example of how "women both resist and support existing systems of power" (Abu-Lughod 1990, 47).

But it takes more than just women to bear and raise a child. Why did men cooperate? In the end, men's willingness to provide sperm, as well as the decisions of family, friends, and employers to assist women who had asked for a child, all tacitly recognized the cultural and personal significance of motherhood, the cultural significance attached to the womb, and acknowledgment that children bring joy. Women who asked for a child were seeking a conventional subjectivity, one that readily prioritized a maternal identity. While women had stepped outside the patriarchal box, they did so knowing that becoming a mother was the most socially valued identity and role a woman could undertake. Indeed, single women's trailblazing ask signaled an effort to belong to the traditional world of women.

To achieve this objective, women needed to reject notions of monogamy promoted by the socialist state and instead draw on alternative customary strategies for bearing children. At the same time, the economy of kinship and the discourse of maternal desire that prompted many single women to ask for a child are themselves forms of power. Therefore, *xin con*, as a form of agency, is perhaps best viewed as a maneuver that refers to, and works with and through, different strategies and relations of power. The same gesture that flouts some norms roots one all the more deeply in parallel ones.

Gender performance, however, never completely reiterates what it seeks to perform; instead it reveals its own instability (Butler 1990). A natural extension of revolution by the people ought to affirm the revolutionary practice of those same people, ineluctably making those same practices orthodox. As Hạnh, who came of marital age in the mid-1950s and remained unmarried and childless, said, "I did not once consider having a child out of wedlock. In the past, they shaved women's necks [napes]. . . . I remember situations where they humiliated and shamed the women. I would have been afraid of public opinion. . . . But that was a different day. In general, now this village considers it normal."

CHAPTER 4

Governing *Xin Con*

The State's Embrace

WHEN I FIRST MET LÊ THI (DƯƠNG THỊ THOA), DIRECTOR OF THE CENTER FOR Scientific Research on the Family and Women (CSRW), in her office on a drizzly Hà Nội day in 1995 to talk about single women who had asked for a child, she told me a story.[1] Long ago, she said, a rural farm girl working in the fields around Đồ Sơn "was raped by a lord traveling by" (*bị ông vua đi qua đó hãm hiếp*). When her parents and the villagers saw she was pregnant, they tied a stone around her neck and threw her into the sea; she had disgraced her family and her village. But her body rose and floated on top of the waves. The villagers were alarmed. Word of this mystery eventually reached Lord Trinh (Chúa Trịnh), who returned to claim responsibility. His admission in conjunction with the girl's floating body convinced the villagers that the girl was a genie, a spirit. To redress the wrongs they had committed against her, they built a temple on top of a mountain in Đồ Sơn that overlooks the ocean and named it Bà Đế in her honor.[2]

I was not sure, at first, why Lê Thi prefaced her discussion about *xin con* by recounting this tale. Clearly the story of Bà Đế was also about sexual transgression, sacrifice, and rectification, albeit of a different order than *xin con*. Eventually it became clear that CSRW's ongoing research and advocacy efforts paralleled the narrative arc of the legend; because of the king's response, Bà Đế had a temple built in her honor where people could go to pray, whereas women who asked for a child became objects of scientific inquiry and state efforts to incorporate the women into its larger project of governing the population.

Why did *xin con*, a private interaction between two people intent on keep-ing it a secret, become a focal point of government interest from the mid-1980s to the early 2000s? Having drawn the state's gaze, how did government actors respond? Answering the first question requires understanding the goals of the new Đổi Mới state. Answering the second necessitates examining the way government agents discursively framed the women's actions within the intel-ligibility of family and state. State actors became interested in and responded to the phenomenon of *xin con* through legal, social scientific, pedagogical, and economic tactics, each of which facilitated inclusion of the women into the modern state's agenda as well as social and legal acceptance of their reproduc-tive agency.

The Vietnamese government's response to single women's reproductive agency is an instance of governmentality, a particular form of modern power. At the same time, it illustrates how governmentality is an interactive process that shapes and is shaped by the agency of the governed. Attention to the tech-niques, tactics, arts, and methods utilized by the Vietnamese government reveals the discursive and nondiscursive effects of this form of power and illuminates how social and cultural change takes place.

Governmentality, a term pioneered by the French philosopher Michel Foucault, is an exercise of political power whose purpose is the manage-ment, welfare, and improvement of the population. The overarching aim of governmentality is to preserve the strength of the state itself. This is not a hierarchical form of domination but a complex intention that circulates through individuals, institutions, and agencies. It exists "wherever individuals and groups seek to shape their own conduct or the conduct of others" (Walters 2012, 11). Foucault viewed this "conduct of conducts" as a "space . . . where tech-nologies of government and technologies of the self intersect" (Walters 2012, 15) such that people unconsciously come to structure their own decisions and actions as objectives of the state. To achieve this alignment, "government operates by educating desires and configuring habits, aspirations, and beliefs. It sets conditions, 'artificially so arranging things so that people, following only their own self-interest, *will do as they ought*'" (Li 2007, 5). Power, then, is not a thing that is possessed but a strategy that is expressed.

Governmentality unfolds and operates differently in various historical moments and cultural contexts. The politics of *xin con* illustrate a specific field of governmentality in which management of the population (the various tac-tics and techniques deployed) was informed and driven by Vietnam's Confu-cian heritage and the Communist Party's 1986 decision to implement Đổi Mới policies. Attention to the ideological conditions in the postreform era (post-1986) provides ethnographic insight into a culturally specific and gendered form of governmentality (cf. Kipnis 2008; Harms 2012).

Historically, the public and private spheres of Vietnamese society have been "closely entangled with one another" due to the country's Confucian heritage, which does not differentiate between "state and political relations, on the one hand, and social and family relations, on the other" (Rydström and Drummond 2004, 7). Conveniently consistent with techniques of governmentality, Confucian philosophy and the socialist state both regard self-cultivation and self-discipline as necessary for the state's success, the family as the core of society, and reproduction as a duty, rendering *xin con* a natural object for governmentality.[3] The Đổi Mới state's emphasis on women's reproduction "connects a continuous process of reconstitution of the Vietnamese nation state with the construction of women/girls in terms of motherhood" (Rydström and Drummond 2004, 9).

The government's response also illustrates how governmentality is an interactive process that shapes and is shaped by the agency of the governed. The actors concerned with and invested in improving the lives of single mothers—legal scholars, social scientists, journal editors, and Women's Union representatives—did not begin with an a priori policy. Instead they worked to establish what practices were being lived and what concerns or problems people encountered, including the practice of *xin con* by older single women desiring children. Then they developed their policies and plans for guiding behavior. The strategies and tactics they deployed to render single women's decision to ask for a child socially intelligible are notable for the way in which people in positions of authority first sought input from their fellow citizens. As a result, their efforts resonated, influencing how people responded to single mothers and how single mothers thought of themselves. It is in such instances, when people recognize themselves in the policies applied to them, that governmentality emerges clearly. This led to the appearance of *xin con* as a socially recognized discursive category and, as a result, the emergence of a specific "structure of feeling" (R. Williams 1977): a new way of thinking about and responding to single motherhood.

ĐỔI MỚI AND THE HAPPY FAMILY

Đổi Mới is a series of economic reforms the state initiated in 1986 to transition to a socialist-oriented market economy. The sociologist Thomas Lemke (2001) provides a useful way of thinking about Đổi Mới and the Vietnamese state's logic of governmentality (Phinney 2010). Lemke writes about the manner in which neoliberal governments transfer responsibility for social risks to collectivities such as families or associations, and ultimately to individuals. According to Lemke, a neoliberal government endeavors to achieve "congruence . . . between a responsible and moral individual and an economic-rational actor" (Lemke 2001, 201). This describes Vietnam's shift in policies quite well. Instead of viewing Đổi Mới in terms of the state's "withdrawal" from family life, we should view it instead as a "reorganization or restructuring of government techniques, shifting the regulatory competence of the state onto 'responsible' and 'rational' individuals" (202). By rendering economic the social domain, the Vietnamese state, like neoliberal governments, was able to "link a reduction in (welfare) state services and security systems to the increasing call for 'personal responsibility' and 'self-care'" (203). In Vietnam, this entailed a process whereby the state transferred economic, social, and moral responsibility from itself to the family and the household.

Concurrent with implementing new economic policies, the DRV began to intensify its deployment of what Foucault referred to as "biopower" (a form of governmentality): "Power exercise[d] over persons specifically in so far as they are thought of as living beings: a politics concerned with subjects as members of a *population*, in which issues of individual sexual and reproductive conduct interconnect with issues of national policy and power" (Gordon 1991, 5). While the DRV had launched family planning policies in the early 1960s in the north, it was not until the mid- to late 1980s that they were able to systematically collect demographic data and employ cadres to implement a comprehensive family planning program. In 1982, consistent with modern forms of governmentality in which expert knowledge is utilized to inform policies for governing the population, the Ministerial Council (Hội Đồng Bộ Trưởng; responsible for managing and implementing activities of the state) ordered a scientific inquiry into the state of marriage and the family in thirteen provinces and the centrally controlled municipalities. Research concluded that there had been an increase in extramarital affairs, requests for divorce, premarital sex and pregnancies, and underage marriage and polygamy.[4] It was also clear that there were a large number of widows and other women without husbands raising children on their own.

Having identified and subsequently characterized specific familial relationships as social problems (single mothers struggling, children living without fathers, unhappy marriages) and thus points for intervention, the

This "Happy Family" campaign poster declares "Stable Population, Prosperous Society, Happy Family" (Dân Số Ổn Định, Xã Hội Phồn Vinh, Gia Dình Hạnh Phúc). Hà Nội, 2017. Photograph by the author.

government, in its "will to improve" (Li 2007), formulated a plan to educate and manage the population. In the late 1980s, the National Committee for Population and Family Planning launched a new campaign, the Happy Family Campaign. The Happy Family is orderly, with an adequate income, stable conjugal relations, and two children whose parents educate them properly. Family planning billboards depicted the Happy Family as a well-dressed mother, father, boy, and girl. One slogan read, "Stable population, prosperous society, happy family" (*Dân số ổn định, xã hội phồn vinh, gia đình hạnh phúc*). Family planning messages linked family size, family finances, family happiness, and national wealth. As Werner and Bélanger (2002b, 40) note, by "linking small families to happiness and prosperity," the state "harnessed the promise and lure of modernity to the developmental project of the state." The family planning posters replaced revolutionary posters, which had called upon women to participate in the war effort, with calls for women to focus on their domestic lives. It was under the guise of helping people create and maintain happy families that the state sought to maintain its authority through the biotechnologies of the family planning program.

Trying to educate desires and configure habits was not a new tactic for the DRV; during and after the war era, the state configured itself as the primary object of affection for a martially mobilized and ordered citizenry (Phinney 2008). With Đổi Mới, educating desire was geared to a different goal, that of revalorizing the private family sphere by relocating the individual back within the family. As was the case in China, "population [became] the means to express the persistent problem of how to produce a modern citizenry . . . , a problem that acquire[d] new urgency with the dissolution of collective agriculture and with the new freedoms accorded to the household economy" (Anagnost 1997, 123).

THE 1986 LAW ON MARRIAGE AND THE FAMILY

In 1986, in conjunction with the Happy Family Campaign, the state updated the 1959 Law on Marriage and the Family. The 1986 law was designed to address the myriad social changes that had taken place over the past thirty years and to facilitate the shift toward a market-based economy. To help households successfully take responsibility for their own economic welfare, the state legislated with far more specificity, extending family members' obligations and responsibilities to one another.[5] The 1986 law addressed many more issues than had the 1959 law: it specified minimum age at marriage, legislated cohabitation and paternity, and provided for divorce proceedings. And the law reminded citizens that the state would play an important role in family affairs. In essence, the more detailed legal provisions in the 1986 law, while affording "better guidance for courts and citizens" (Walsh 2011, 102), provided more rationales and sites for the state to use the family *as an instrument* through which to govern—a hallmark of governmentality.

How did single mothers, particularly those who had asked for a child, fit into the state's strategy for governing in the Đổi Mới era? In many ways, they represented a fissure in the state's vision of the modern socialist family. Their reproductive agency and embodiment of a new kind of family had not been part of the socialist state's imagined future. In its efforts to create a modern family, the state had eradicated previous legal subject positions, such as a concubine or a second wife, that had enabled many women to create a uterine family. At the same time, the state did not alter notions of marriageability that informed and constrained women's marital choices. As marginal members of society who struggled to be accepted by families and neighbors, and who did not participate in Women's Union activities designed to educate wives about population policies (e.g., the importance of having no more than two children), single mothers and their children fell outside the state's plan. This was a social problem that needed rectification, and not just because it was a humanitarian thing to do. Bringing single mothers and their children within the purview of the state would make it possible for the state to more fully recruit them to the state's economic and social agendas.

The state's first step toward bringing single women who asked for a child specifically into the state's purview was embodied in the new Law on Marriage and the Family. Family laws, like other laws, are tactics of government, "tools to educate desires" and "reform practices" (Li 2007, 196). The 1986 Law on Marriage and the Family was the first to formally acknowledge the importance childbearing had for all women regardless of marital status. In doing so, the state met people's desires by constructing itself as needing to administer to newly visible subjects: single women who asked for a child.

Mai, Ngọc, Năm, and many other people I spoke to about the 1986 Law on Marriage and the Family referred to it in general terms, stating that it provided legal justification for single women's decision to ask for a child. I was surprised, therefore, to discover that there are no articles in the law explicitly condoning this practice. Rather, there are a series of articles that together are interpreted as providing this right. The vagueness of the law led to different interpretations over whether the state awarded rights directly to women or directly to their children, or to both.

Many Women's Union officials, legal scholars, and social scientists pointed to Article 3 in Chapter I, "General Provisions," to assert that women's reproductive rights were given directly to women. Others pointed to Articles 30, 31, and 32 in Chapter V, "Determining Parentage," to assert that the law awards rights to the child, from whom women derive their reproductive rights.

Article 3 in the 1986 Law on Marriage and the Family reads, "The state and society shall protect the mothers as well as their children, and shall assist the mothers in fulfilling their noble tasks of motherhood" (Thế Giới 1993, 297; Nhà Xuất Bản Phụ nữ 2001). Hiên, a senior lawyer at the Ministry of Justice (Bộ Tư pháp) whom I met in Hà Nội in 1996, explained that regardless of the fact that single mothers were not mentioned in the law, Article 3 recognized the right of all women to have a child. The news agent Thế Lan, reporting on the National Assembly session where the 1986 law was ratified, wrote that Article 3 was included to "ensure impartiality between mothers (among whom are single mothers)."[6] The editors of *Báo Nhân Dân* corroborated Thế Lan's and Hiên's interpretations.[7] However, Nguyễn Thị Định, president of Vietnam's

Women's Union (Hội Liên hiệp Phụ nữ Việt Nam; 1982–92), qualified the state's inclusivity: "The state does not encourage relationships between men and women that are not legal, but it does show concern for single mothers."[8] This was the first time unmarried women would gain legal status from bearing children.

The logic behind Article 3 derived from the common belief, discussed in chapter 1, that maternal desire is "instinctual" (*thiên bẩm*), a "thirst or a craving" (*khao khát*).[9] Because maternal desire is an instinct, it must therefore be a natural right. Justifying the link between maternal instinct and maternal rights, Nguyễn Thanh Tâm (1991, 113–14), sociologist at the Center for Family Studies, asserted,

> With the function bestowed by the creator, it is needless to debate the problem of the woman's right to enjoy the happiness of the mother in the family. . . . It is clear that when a woman does not get married for whatever reason, then the act of having a child is a practical requirement of her personal need for individual happiness. This need is more powerful than old customs and habits and is victorious because it is the embodiment [*hiện thân*] of deep longing [*khát vọng*] for personal happiness. If they are not able to have husbands, it is imperative [*nhất thiết*] that they have a child, even though their lives are poor and difficult.

Nguyễn Thị Khoa (1993, 58), a senior psychology researcher also at the Center for Women's Studies in Hà Nội, argued, "Humanity recognizes a legitimate instinct in a woman to have a child. The new spirit of the Law on Marriage and the Family does not reflect the need to remedy a social defect; it is rather a response to the right of women." In other words, according to Nguyễn Thị Khoa, single women's reproductive rights originated not from social circumstances such as the postwar gender imbalance that made it difficult to find suitable men to marry, but from the essential nature of being female.

Article 3, according to these scholars, was a just and legal recognition and a practical response to older single women's reproductive agency, to the fact that women had *already* chosen to ask for a child, and more were likely to do so. Lê Thị Nhâm Tuyết (1993, 65), professor of anthropology and director of the Research Center for Gender, Family, and Environment in Development (RCGFED), highlighted women's agency when she wrote that older single women were "prompted by maternal instinct" to "demand a child" out of wedlock, and they, along with women elsewhere in Vietnam, "consider it their innate, obvious and sacred right to be a mother" (108). Women I interviewed in 1995 and 1996 echoed these sentiments. Article 3 acknowledged women's "natural" right under the law, and in doing so recognized and legitimized their reproductive agency.

If the intent of the writers was to assert that biological motherhood was a natural right, it would have been helpful for them to say so explicitly. I suggest four possible reasons for the lack of clarity. First, it may well have been that, in 1986, the state authorities were not comfortable directly proclaiming that all women, including single women, had a right to biological motherhood. Perhaps they worried about potential negative effects or did not think society was ready for such a law.[10] Second, ambiguity enabled the state to deny requests for special economic assistance for families headed by single women, which in turn would have signaled greater confirmation of the women's choices. Third, the law was not, in actuality, meant to inhere equally to all women and all circumstances. The lawyers, social scientists, and Women's Union officials with whom I spoke emphatically stated that the law was not meant to justify young, marriageable women's decision to have children out of wedlock. Nor was it meant to encourage single mothers to have more than one child, given the difficulty of raising two children alone.[11] Fourth, the state viewed women's reproduction in terms of their contribution to the nation (not solely for the women's own benefit), which would then justify state regulation of that right. At play was the "ideological work of the government" (Nguyễn-Võ 2008, 255), which, in the end, sought to sustain the patriarchal family: marriageable young women must be available to reproduce for a man's family; it is too late for older single women.[12]

This latter reasoning pertaining to governance is embedded in alternative readings of Article 3. Nguyễn Thị Định interpreted Article 3 as follows: "Aside from the general duty of men and women as citizens, women still have a private function: giving birth to and raising children. This function preserves the existence of the race and is truly glorious, but is also a truly heavy responsibility especially given our country's situation when we still have many economic difficulties. In order to fulfill this function, women must receive the protection of the state and society, help via practical and concrete policy."[13] The law recognizes reproduction as a private function, but also as a service to the nation. Nguyễn Thế Giai (1993, 31–32), an editor for the National Political Publishing House, also made this link explicit in her reading of Article 3: "The issue of reproducing oneself and [humankind] through the means of bearing children gives women an elevated position as mother in the family and society. Bearing children in order to reproduce for the family simultaneously reproduces the existence of the race, the nation, and develops society and the population. This matter requires that we must protect mothers and create excellent conditions so that each mother is able to fully realize the function of bearing children and of raising their children." These interpretations of Article 3 view women as reproducers for the family, society, and the nation. For Nguyễn Thị Định and Nguyễn Thế Giai, the law protected women's reproductive rights because women are responsible for the future of the nation: they reproduce and raise the children.

Beyond these readings of Article 3, throughout the 1990s some journalists, social scientists, and state officials referred to Articles 30, 31, and 32 in Chapter V, "Determining Parentage," as the legal basis for women's reproductive rights.[14] Articles 30, 31, and 32 referred to children born out of wedlock and were considered supplemental to Article 3.[15] Article 30 stated, "Recognition of a child born out of wedlock shall be attested and recorded in the Birth Register by the People's Committee of the commune, city ward or town where the child resides." Article 31 stated, "A child born out of wedlock may ask to be recognized as somebody's child, even when such parent has already died. The mother, father, or foster-parents may request the determination of parentage of a child born out of wedlock, if the child is still under age."[16] Article 32 stated, "A child born out of wedlock who has been recognized by his father or mother or by the People's Court shall have the same rights and duties of a child born in lawful wedlock" (Thế Giới 1993). These clauses functioned to grant all children equal rights under the law: women's "natural right" to become mothers was effectively an adjunct to the equal rights held by children. The goal, according to Nguyễn Thế Giai (1993), was to eradicate social prejudices toward children born out of wedlock, to protect their interests equally, and to avoid situations where the father—or mother, but particularly the father—evaded responsibility to the child by refusing to accept parentage. "Morally and ethically the socialist doctrine requires that all people who have given birth to a child must accept the responsibility of mother, father toward the child that they have borne into the world" (100).[17]

At the same time that the state asserted more control over the parent-child relationship, it opened up a new legal space for reproducing.[18] This is because "the recognition that an illegitimate child is not an unwanted child allows for a reconstruction of unmarried motherhood" (Silva 1996, 4). For this reason many scholars pointed to Articles 30, 31, and 32 as the legal basis for women's reproductive rights. One of the most explicit references to Articles 30, 31, and

32 came from Phạm Thanh Bình, a member of the Supreme People's Tribunal (Tòa Án Nhân Dân Tối Cao).[19] She argued against the state taking disciplinary action against an older single woman who had given birth, because, she contended, the women's "craving" (*khao khát*) for bearing children out of wedlock was a legitimate but *unique* circumstance resulting from the war. From this perspective, single women's desire for a child was not a natural right embedded in women but a right derived from social circumstances—in contrast to the position of Nguyễn Thị Khoa and Lê Thị Nhâm Tuyết. Rather than point to Article 3, Phạm Thanh Bình pointed to Articles 30, 31, and 32 as "indirectly recognizing [women's right] to give birth out of wedlock." Having linked the rights of older unmarried women to the rights of children born out of wedlock, she argued, "Bearing a child out of wedlock does not violate the law." Phạm Thanh Bình's assertion that women derive their rights from the child suggests that the state's interest was located in the child; the mother's private reproductive desires were secondary.

The advantage of principally deriving women's rights from the child was that it justified the state's intervention in and regulation of women's maternal behavior more effectively than by focusing solely on the essential personal right of the woman to bear a child. If women's reproductive rights were based on women's natural instinct alone, then the state would have no role. If women's reproductive rights were designated solely a private right, then *xin con* would represent a disjuncture in the socialist Happy Family project. Recentering the focus on the child was consistent with party philosophy and the goal of creating a new socialist society through the successive improvement of each generation. This line of analysis is in keeping with the reading of Article 3 by Nguyễn Thị Định and Nguyễn Thế Giai, both of whom frame women's reproduction in terms of the family, society, and the nation and call for policies to protect women and children.

Legal scholar M. M. Slaughter (1995, 75) points out that the "law is a discourse produced by social power that both constitutes and legitimates . . . social arrangements. It is part of a normalizing system that regulates and constructs subjects." In this case the law set in motion efforts that would lead to the construction of a new subject position, that of "single mothers." The irony of the 1986 law is that while it granted all women the right to reproduce, by doing so they became subject to new state efforts to govern families. The law created the legal foundation for regulating and constructing subjects far more than had the 1959 Law on Marriage and the Family; the 1986 law indicates the beginning of a trend in which the state, with increasing specificity, delineates different kinds of people, laying out their duties, obligations, and the nature of their relationships with one another. The 1959 law had provided legal justification for the state inserting itself into family affairs, first by seeking to replace parental authority over marriage with that of the state, and second, by its implicit message that bearing and raising children should not perpetuate the feudal confines of the Confucian-influenced patriarchal family, but should serve the nation. The 1959 law thus provided an opening for a different conceptualization of reproduction, an alternative meaning of why women reproduce; the 1986 law expanded upon this precedent. And it made the right to reproduce a defining characteristic of women who were fulfilling their own desire to bear children. In doing so, the law contributed to the formation of a new kind of Vietnamese feminine subjectivity.

BIOPOWER AT WORK: VIETNAMESE SOCIALIST RESEARCH, DISCOURSE, AND ADVOCACY

To achieve the goal of bringing women's reproduction into line with state policies, the government tasked trade unions, the Women's Union, and the Communist Youth Organization with the responsibility for educating citizens about the 1986 law, implementing it, demonstrating the ethics and morals of the socialist society, and preserving the interests of mothers and children.[20] This pedagogical effort was the second aspect of governmentality; it sought to render *xin con* socially intelligible to the populace.

The 1986 Law on Family and Marriage, having broadened the state's authority for governing through the population, created a space for CSRW and other research organizations to gain a more in-depth knowledge of family dynamics.[21] CSRW's mission, as a state organization, was to help the Committee for Social Sciences of Vietnam and other connected government bodies "to draw up a programme of social research on women's problems, which would then serve as a basis for the outline of options, policies and regulations of the State [sic] relation to women" (Việt Nam Women's Union and Center for Women's Studies 1989, 95; cf. Evans 1985). This was "a new relationship among socioeconomic dynamics, knowledge, and social policy" in Vietnam (Nguyễn-Võ 2008, 158).

From 1987 through the early 1990s social scientists (the majority of whom were women) from CSRW, the Institute for Reproductive and Family Health (IRFH), and the Research Center for Gender, Family, and Environment in Development (RCGFED) began to conduct research on single mothers in the north at state agricultural cooperatives and state forestry enterprises. Their research revealed that many kinds of single mothers (divorced, widowed, separated, and never married) had been ostracized, scorned, or treated with suspicion, and their children were teased by other children for not having a father (Lê Thi 2002).[22] Single women who asked for a child, in particular, became objects of the state's gaze and "will to know" (Foucault 1978, 73).

CSRW and the Women's Union developed three strategies to improve the living conditions of single mothers and their children: framing the discourse on *xin con* in the media, normalizing single motherhood, and advocating for policies as well as concrete help for single mothers.

Efforts to support women who had asked for a child were at once personal, humanitarian, and governmental.[23] In 1996, one Women's Union cadre in Hà Nội quietly suggested to me that perhaps one reason some Women's Union officials in Hà Nội and elsewhere sought social and legal legitimacy for *xin con* was because they too had asked for a child.[24] In 1995, when a foreign NGO (nongovernmental organization) representative asked a local Women's Union team in Đà Nẵng to organize a theatrical skit on what they saw as the most pressing needs of women in the area, the women performed a skit in which single women tried to find men to get them pregnant. It turned out that the local leaders were dramatizing their own desires as much as those of others. The humanitarian concerns of CSRW and the Women's Union were based on knowledge of the sacrifices older single women had made during the war and of the difficult lives they were living. The Women's Union cadres' efforts are indicative of a "politics of agency" in which individuals, invested in their own cultural projects, work to instigate social change based on their own desires (Ortner 2006a, 152). And yet these personal maneuvers engage a larger, governmental apparatus, which carries on past the circumstances of individuals who set it in motion.

Framing the Public Discourse

CSRW sought to demonstrate how *xin con* was a practical response based on conventional gendered ideologies and was not a threat to the Happy Family. To do so, social scientists published articles in newspapers and academic journals that addressed the public's misunderstandings, prejudices, and concerns. During the late 1980s and into the 1990s, social scientists took advantage of the new role the Đổi Mới state permitted the Vietnamese press; shifting away from their pre-reform role as "tools of state propaganda," newspapers began to "investigate social reality." The press began "to take a more genuinely meditative role—at once conveying official policy to readers and presenting a version of 'the people's' interest to the authorities" (Pettus 2003, 115). However, "the purpose remains, in the Confucian and socialist tradition, pedagogic. The journalist may report on social ills, as long as he or she poses a problem as moral predicaments, either between evil actors and innocent victims or between 'external' influences and 'internal' values" (117). Single mothers who asked for a child were construed as innocent victims of war who unwittingly faced a moral predicament of bearing a child out of wedlock.

Women's Union officials, interested in educating people about social issues, often used the "letter to the editor" format to provide advice or to generate a *diễn đàn* (discussion forum) on a particular topic. Chị Thanh Tâm is the pseudonym for a group of women who read and responded to personal letters individuals around the country mailed to *Báo Phụ nữ Việt Nam* seeking advice. The letters enabled the newspaper's editors to gain a sense of what people were concerned about; at the same time they provided a pedagogical opportunity. The editors chose a topic to address based on the frequency or timeliness of a particular subject matter.[25] Chị Thanh Tâm then publicly offered her "personal" advice on the matter at hand. *Báo Phụ nữ Việt Nam*, the official newspaper of the National Women's Union, provided advice more or less consonant with the party line. The letters, stories, and advice therefore serve both normative and productive functions.[26] To advance their agenda of encouraging people to be sympathetic to and understanding of single mothers who had asked for a child, CSRW and journalists framed their discussions in the newspapers around two main issues: loneliness and sexuality.

Loneliness

Women who asked for a child said one reason they wanted a child was so they would not be lonely. Social scientists and journalists published a number of articles in newspapers such as *Báo Phụ nữ Việt Nam*, *Báo Phụ nữ Thủ đô*, *Báo Pháp luật*, and *Báo Tuổi trẻ* that raised the specter of women's loneliness to generate understanding and sympathy and to justify women's decision to ask for a child. Võ Thị Hảo depicted this loneliness in her short story "Người sót lại của rừng cười" (Left behind in the smiling forest; 1990), which is about women who, having their beauty and youth snatched away by the war, did not want to return home.[27] They remained in the remote mountainous area where they had been working. But unable to bear their loneliness, their health deteriorated, and they died. Ngọc Văn argued, "Children not only satisfy the need for *tình cảm*, but have a material and spiritual value: they provide happiness for women."[28] Bùi Đình Nguyên thought older single women should be able to have a child "so they can hold a babe in their arms with all of a mother's sentiment, to hear the voice of a young child babble, to make a happy house, and to have someone to comfort and console, to lean on, to take care of them when they are old."[29] Such arguments made cultural sense and garnered sympathy.[30]

Sex, Gender, and the Happy Family

The most pressing public concern *xin con* prompted was what to do about the fact that single women were asking married men to get them pregnant. How should government officials respond to actions (extramarital relations) that during the war and postwar era had been cause for dismissal from the Communist Party and subsequent loss of employment—especially for women (Khuất 1998; Phinney 2010)?[31] This concern and the government's response are nicely illustrated in a letter published in a May 1989 issue of *Báo Phụ nữ Việt Nam* asking for guidance from the newspaper's personal advice columnist, Chị Thanh Tâm.[32] The letter, from a government office at a state forestry farm (*lâm trường*) in Bắc Thái Province, relayed the situation of a Communist Party member and "model cadre," a married man with two children who had secretly helped a thirty-five-year-old single woman get pregnant. When the woman was five months pregnant, rumors began to circulate. Fearful his wife and family would find out, the man asked to "receive all discipline and rules of conduct" in the hope that his office would not spread the news to his family. His superiors were divided as to how to proceed. One cadre said that since "the law recognizes children out of wedlock, we should not and cannot consider disciplining a comrade that has met the hopes of another woman." A different cadre said, "This situation lacks faithfulness, it lacks morality and it lacks ethics because Nguyen H. already has a wife and children, especially since he is a comrade." Office "Y" wrote Chị Thanh Tâm for advice on how to proceed.

Receiving permission to print the letter from the Bắc Thái office, Chị Thanh Tâm opened up a *diễn đàn* (discussion forum) so *Báo Phụ nữ Việt Nam* readers "far and near [would] be able to submit their opinions." The stated goal was threefold: to help the office come to a resolution, to allow other state leaders in similar situations to provide advice based on their own experiences, and to encourage greater understanding of and sympathy for older single women and children born out of wedlock. After receiving varied responses and opinions from individuals and party cadres in various provinces, the editors of *Báo*

Phụ nữ Việt Nam summarized the most popular opinions and ended the *diễn đàn* by advising readers to read the adjacent article, "Discussion on the Matter of Children Born out of Wedlock," printed on the same page of the newspaper.[33] The author of that article was Ngọc Văn from the Institute of Sociology, who had conducted scientific research on single mothers at state enterprises where there were significantly higher proportions of women than men.

In her article, Ngọc Văn did not advise a single correct course of action. Nor did she consider it pertinent how single women got pregnant or with whom. In fact, she and her research colleagues deliberately had avoided asking women such questions, because they were more concerned with letting the women, all of whom had passed what was considered a marriageable age, be at peace with their children. Acknowledging that sometimes the "happiness of one family is the unhappiness of another," Ngọc Văn reminded *Báo Phụ nữ Việt Nam* readers that the 1986 Law on Marriage and the Family gives children born out of wedlock the same rights as other children. She then reiterated the significance of the law, remarking that it constitutes "very important social progress." Thus, while not definitively stating a correct course of action, Ngọc Văn did nonetheless steer the readers toward recognizing the legitimacy of older single women's decision to ask for a child.

The Bắc Thái official's letter to the advice columnist Chị Thanh Tâm at *Báo Phụ nữ Việt Nam* suggests that he wrote to seek advice on how to respond to this extramarital relation. I found it a bit curious that a government official from a state forestry farm, under the purview of the Ministry of Forestry, would reach out to Chị Thanh Tâm for advice on how to proceed. Couldn't officials have decided among themselves? In point of fact, sociologist Rita Liljeström's report on the Bãi Bằng Forestry Project indicates that brigade members and leaders had already decided to support older single women's decision to get pregnant. According to one brigade nurse, "'It is her right to choose between giving birth or having an abortion. It [the abortion] can be done at the enterprise clinic. But we do not tell her to do so. . . . The right to be a mother has recently been written into our constitution. The way she takes care of this right is not our concern'" (Liljeström 1987, 28). The letter to Chị Thanh Tâm from the Bắc Thái forestry official, then—regardless of whether it was a real letter or a contrivance—provided the Women's Union and CSRW with an opportunity to air public concerns and to provide advice.

The press described numerous other scenarios in which older single women sought extramarital relations in order to have a child. These letters provided Chị Thanh Tâm with an opportunity to steer the newspaper's readers to think about *xin con* in particular ways. By and large the letters evoke anxiety about the implications for extramarital sex, family happiness, and stability. How should a daughter respond to the knowledge that her father agreed to impregnate her teacher, a single woman? Should a man who fears that villagers already know the little boy living with a single mother is his biological child inform his wife? How should a wife react to a husband who helped another woman get pregnant?[34] Responding to these questions, Chị Thanh Tâm reminded readers that all women have maternal instinctual desires, and the law gives single women the right to fulfill these desires and have a child to take care of them in their old age. But they do not have the right to ruin a family's happiness. Chị Thanh Tâm encouraged people not to turn their backs on older single mothers who only desire happiness. She advised men to terminate relations with the single women, and wives to have sympathy for women who have less than they do.[35]

While acknowledging wives' extremely difficult position, as well as their frustration, jealousy, and anger, neither Chị Thanh Tâm nor the respondents in the Bắc Thái debate seemed to worry about the enduring strength of the marital relationship. This is due, I suggest, to culturally gendered beliefs about sexuality at the time. In the mid-1990s, when I inquired about the differences between men's and women's sexuality, a male social scientist simply quoted the proverb "A man has several hearts [livers], one stays with his wife, others wander to other women" (*Đàn ông năm bảy lá gan, lá ở cùng vợ lá toan cùng người*). Covering her smile with her hand, my Vietnamese teacher relayed another: portraying men as sticks and women as sand, the proverb states, "Men go from place to place poking holes in the sand, leaving a trace behind but forgetting where they have been" (*Đàn ông đi hết nơi này đến nơi khác chọc lỗ trên cát, để lại dấu vết nhưng quên mất chúng ở đâu*). No one cited proverbs about women's sexual desire. Typically, people depicted women as passive victims of male desire (Khuất 1998; Phinney 2010). Women were said to engage in sexual intercourse principally to have a child and demonstrate love for their husband.

Nguyễn Cư, one of the participants in the Bắc Thái debate, differentiated between two kinds of children born out of wedlock by distinguishing between two kinds of sex: sex engaged in to satisfy the sentimental need for a child and maintain the mental health of a woman who cannot have a husband, and sex engaged in as an act of love.[36] Nguyễn Cư argued that the former is acceptable because the man's family can remain intact, but the latter is impermissible because it leads directly to family ruin. Because a man is capable of engaging in sexual intercourse without loving a woman, his decision to get an older single woman pregnant was permissible. Such sexual relations do not risk his relationship with his wife, which is supposed to be based on love.[37]

The Bắc Thái debate was part of a larger discussion being aired in newspapers "from 1988–1990s in which the public heatedly debated premarital sex and adultery . . . regarding both as examples of decaying ethics" (Khuất 1998, 38). But while decaying ethics could also be attributed to the effects of war, extramarital sex in the context of *xin con* was framed differently. In this context, journalists indexed sex as an act both of necessity and of sympathetic understanding: for the older single woman sexual intercourse was a necessity, whereas for the man it signified sympathy and understanding. This reframing illustrates a tactic of governmentality, one that arguably reinscribes child-bearing as the moral legitimation for women's sexual desire.

It is notable that *Báo Phụ nữ Việt Nam*—whose content was generated and controlled by state officials—aired governmental concerns as an open public forum. While the *diễn đàn* enables the state to profess its concern for the happiness of its citizens and its willingness to intervene in their most intimate affairs on their behalf, it does so in order to assert its ongoing role in their lives. Indeed, rather than disciplining single women who asked for a child or the men who impregnated them, the *diễn đàn* "designates the way in which the conduct of individuals or of groups might be governed. . . . To govern in this sense, is to structure the possible field of action of others" (Foucault 2000, 341). By not coming to a resolution in the *diễn đàn* and pointing to the law recognizing all women's right to bear a child, Ngọc Văn evokes individual freedom to choose how to act, a necessary precondition for the exercise of power.[38]

At the same time the reframing of sex as an act of necessity and sympathy rather than degeneracy may shape the kinds of choices people make. It is a "management of possibilities" and an education of desires (Foucault 2000, 341) that, in Vietnam, shows how government policy is being constructed publicly and dialogically. This interaction opens the possibility that governmentality in Communist countries works differently than it does in neoliberal democracies. For example, United States government discourse during this same time period, driven largely by moral absolutist premises rather than single women's desires or needs, portrayed single mothers of all ages as promiscuous and inadequate mothers, blamed them for their poverty, and depicted their families as pathological (Briggs 2017; Geronimus 2003; Luker 1996; Mullings 1995, 129; Nathanson 1991). Such portrayals perpetuated and contributed to the stigmatization and marginalization of single mothers and their children.[39] This is in marked contrast to Vietnamese governmental authorities who listened to single mothers and then worked to help them feel a sense of social belonging. This Vietnamese form of biopower, which was responsive and inclusive, illustrates the "affective aspects of state policies" in which the Vietnamese state was "motivated by a sense of responsibility" to the reproductive concerns of its citizens (Gammeltoft 2014, 57).[40]

In 1993, Nguyễn Thị Khoa wrote, in reference to Articles 30, 31, and 32 of the 1986 law:

> These legal provisions have gradually changed the views of the family and society regarding single mothers and extra-marital children. Single mothers who are functionaries or employees are treated in the same way as married mothers: annual vacations, full salary during childbirth period, social security allowances during absences to take care of sick children, and allowances for childbirth. Far from being an object of contempt and isolated, single mothers have now begun to receive better treatment from the family and society, which take care of her and her child. (48)

I would add that CSRW, sympathetic journalists, and Women's Union officials also contributed to the general shift in attitude. Their efforts illustrate what the history professor who visited Cà Mau (described in the vignette) meant when I visited him to talk about *xin con*. Making a soft gliding motion up and down with his hand in the air, he said, "On the surface things seem very hard and rough, but underneath they are softer," adding that "Vietnamese people are generous and sentimental; they can understand the plight of these single women." Precarity called not for condemnation but for understanding, leniency, and support.[41]

By 1996, it was clear that the 1986 Law on Marriage and the Family, CSRW's dissemination of its research in the public media and the academic press, discussions about *xin con* in the newspapers, and calls for the state to help single mothers had begun to shift social attitudes regarding older single mothers and their children. Everyone I spoke with in Hà Nội knew about *xin con*, acknowledged older single women's loneliness, and agreed that it was their right to have a child. Lan, a single woman who worked at the Women's Union in 1996 and had recently given birth to a girl, said she was motivated and no longer afraid to have a child on her own when she saw that two older single women who held senior positions at the Women's Union had both asked for a child.[42] The creation of a legal space for older single women to reproduce signaled a change not just in society but in women themselves. For Nguyễn Thị Khoa (1996, 131),

Their initiative to find happiness for themselves is one step toward changing the traditional psychology of women's inferiority complex, their passivity, and their tendency to hide secret feelings and aspirations to a point of taking the initiative to affirm their right to happiness. . . . From a place of accepting, being shy, timid, and bashful, of maintaining one's virginity and faithfulness . . . to a place where they display boldness to dare to destroy inferior feelings, to dare to preserve individual happiness. As one forestry worker said, "I must be bold with society in order to have a child."

But there were limits to this inclusion; not all kinds of single women who had a child out of wedlock were treated with leniency. Women's Union officials, journalists, and social scientists, such as Lê Thi, did not support younger women's decision to bear a child out of wedlock. Newspaper advice columnists such as Chị Tâm Giao and Chị Thanh Tâm encouraged young marriageable women to get an abortion and forget the boyfriend who got them pregnant.[43] The specification is important for understanding the meaning of *xin con* as a form of social action and as a discursive category. First, as it pertains to *xin con*, the 1986 Law on Marriage and the Family was widely interpreted, within a special moment in history, to support the reproductive desires of older single women who had sacrificed their youth to the nation and who could not find a suitable man to marry. *Xin con* was understood as a response to the demographic imbalance caused by war (Lê Thi made this quite clear at the International Workshop on Vietnamese Families in the Context of Industrialization, Modernization and Integration in Comparative Perspective held in Hà Nội in 2013). Second, at the time, the phrase *xin con* evoked a unique reproductive strategy with defining characteristics: women intentionally got pregnant out of wedlock, attributed their decision to their advanced age, and agreed to keep the man's identity secret; they did not expect economic support. They wanted a child of their own to raise and carefully framed their narratives in terms of maternal desire, loneliness, and the need for old-age support.

The combined effect of single women's use of *xin con*, the policing of younger women's reproductive behavior (they were too young to either ask for a child or attribute their pregnancy to having intentionally gotten pregnant), and the public discourse about women who asked for a child led to the stabilizing of *xin con* as a discursive category—such that when I returned to Hà Nội and Sóc Sơn in 2010, 2013, and again in 2017, people knew exactly what I was referring to when I spoke of *xin con*.[44]

Normalizing Single Motherhood

CSRW's second strategy was to normalize *xin con*. Lê Thi and her colleagues folded women who asked for a child into a broader group of older single mothers who had also suffered from the wartime and postwar economic policies that had dispersed families. Lê Thi told me repeatedly that while she understood I was interested in women who asked for a child, I needed to recognize that they were just one kind of female-headed household among many others. I came to realize how important this situating was: women who asked for a child drew attention. *Xin con* was easily sensationalized, as most people were intrigued by it. But in order to help women it seems it was necessary to desensationalize *xin con*, to show that it made perfect sense and was not a threat to the Happy Family. To do so, CSRW subsumed and incorporated women who asked for a child within a larger group of mothers (widowed, divorced, or separated) who were also raising children without support—or with minimal support—from the biological father.

It is instructive to trace the trajectory over time of how Lê Thi and other social scientists characterized and labeled older single mothers and their children in their publications. In 1991, CSRW published *Người phụ nữ và gia đình Việt Nam hiện nay* (Women and family in Vietnam today), which includes two chapters on older single mothers who chose to get pregnant out of wedlock or who had absent husbands.[45] Nguyễn Thị Khoa (1991, 37) characterized these families as "incomplete families" (*gia đình không đầy đủ*) in contrast to "complete families" (*gia đình đầy đủ*), a nuclear family in which wife, husband, and children live together in one home. Nguyễn Thanh Tâm's (1991) chapter "Về những gia đình phụ nữ cô đơn, thiếu chồng" (Lonely women, families without husbands) discusses the various factors that led to the appearance of a new kind of family, one that only includes mothers and their children living together.[46] As the title of her chapter indicates, Nguyễn Thanh Tâm decided to call this "new family model" (*gương mặt gia đình mới*) "families without husbands."[47] Notably she also portrays the women as lonely—because women without husbands were typically characterized as unhappy and lonely. By pointing to "absence," the label reasserted the norm of a married heterosexual couple with children: "When speaking of the cozy family, people easily imagine a snug home, brimming with the laughter of children, sunshine, gentleness, and kindness, the grave manner of the father, the soft sweet honest mother" (117, 111–13).

Subsequently, in 1996, Lê Thi edited a volume devoted solely to single mothers. Following Nguyễn Thanh Tâm, she titled the book *Gia đình phụ nữ thiếu vắng chồng* (Women families without husbands).[48] The chapters describe the poor living conditions of a diverse group of single mothers struggling to raise their children in the absence of men: widows, divorced and separated mothers, older single women who had children, mothers whose husbands worked far away, women whose husbands had abandoned them, and women who did not have husbands but did have children.[49] Despite the disparity in reasons for raising children without the support of a husband and the varied circumstances in which they lived, Lê Thi folded them all into a single category, a single type of family. At the time, whether or not single mothers wanted a husband present, their families were considered incomplete because they were without husbands.

A decade later, in 2002, Lê Thi wrote a book on single women titled *Cuộc sống của Phụ nữ đơn thân ở Việt Nam* (Life of single women in Vietnam).[50] The book is a sociological analysis of single women in northern Vietnam based on the research CSRW had conducted from 1987 to 1999. Lê Thi traces the emergence of single female–headed households among women born in the 1950s and the 1960s. She describes their social history, their "real life experiences," and the kinds of support they have received from family, the community, and the state. The title she chose for the book formally designates a new subject position, that of single women. They are no longer defined in relation to complete families, nor in relation to an absent husband, nor as an appendage to their natal families. They are not in some way lacking by virtue of being single, unmarried. Instead Lê Thi portrays them as single women struggling to raise children as best they can.[51]

The change in Lê Thi's accounts over time illustrates both the efficacy and iterative nature of this instance of biopower. Social science is a "form of power" that "categorizes the individual, marks him by his own identity, imposes a law of truth on him that he must recognize and others have to recognize in him. It is a form of power that makes individuals subjects" (Foucault 2000, 331).[52] In the space of a decade, Lê Thi and her colleagues changed how they referred to single women who asked for a child. In turn, the research they had conducted on single women who asked for a child, which led to the stabilization of *xin con* as a legitimate category of social action, was a key factor enabling Lê Thi to construct a positive (neither pejorative nor defined by lack) subjectivity (single mothers) that lay outside the confines of the patriarchal family. In 2011, friends who had grown up in and around Hà Nội, reflecting on the change in terminology, commented that people no longer used the pejorative phrase *không chồng mà chửa* (no husband but pregnant) to refer to single mothers, as they had in the 1970s. They thought it wasn't until recently, perhaps in the mid- to late 1990s, that people began to refer to them as *mẹ độc thân* (single mothers). The 1986 Law on Marriage and the Family had created an opening for the construction of a new subject, that of single mothers. CSRW helped normalize and solidify it.

"Sympathy Is Not Enough": Advocating for Policies and Concrete Help

Having drawn up a program of social research on women's problems in alignment with its mission, educated the populace about single mothers in the newspapers, published their research findings in academic journals, and designated female-headed households a social problem, CSRW called upon the state to take action (Nguyễn Thanh Tâm 1992, 79; 1994). A social problem, after all, offered a mechanism for the state to become involved. CSRW and the Women's Union asked the state to provide female-headed households with education for children living in remote areas, maternity and childcare benefits, cultural entertainment, access to newspapers and magazines, improved housing, construction of private housing, conditions for an improved social life for women living on remote forestry farms, and welfare subsidies.[53]

While it is unclear to what extent changes in policy were the direct result of efforts by CSRW and the Women's Union, the government has acted on behalf of single mothers. In May 1989, the Women's Trade Union Association passed a circular that stated, "Women civil servants who have not yet had the means to take a husband but have a child can receive a salary and regulation subsidies like women who have borne their first child with a husband" (Nguyễn Thanh Tâm 1994, 21). This legal provision was limited to state employees but nonetheless represented a shift in state perceptions of single mothers. The same year, the state enacted a legal provision stating that single mothers could no longer be expelled from mass governmental organizations, subjected to various sanctions such as self-criticism, be transferred to another workplace, have their salary reduced and rewards canceled, or be criticized for bad conduct (Nguyễn Thị Khoa 1993, 50).

The state was not willing, however, to provide welfare subsidies for poor single female-headed households, a request the Women's Union first made in 1995 (Lê Thi 1996). According to a lawyer associated with the Ministry of Justice, the government declined because the state did not want to provide preferential treatment for one kind of poor family over another. This decision was consistent with the Đổi Mới government's effort to transfer economic responsibility from the state to the household.

Undaunted, Women's Union officials pressed on. Shortly thereafter, the Women's Union began to work with foreign NGOs to deliver microcredit programs for single female–headed households in rural areas. The programs were designed to provide single mothers with access to capital and training in small business enterprises so they could adequately support themselves and their children—and become economically independent.[54] The microcredit programs illustrate a tactic of governmentality. The state, responding to its citizens' behavior and their needs, makes itself relevant to the people in a manner that enables the state to achieve its own objectives.

In 1996, I conducted research under the auspices of two such NGOs, one in Sóc Sơn District, Hà Nội Province, run by DEVAID (a Finnish NGO), and the other in Phú Lương District, Bắc Thái Province, run by CIDSE (Coopération Internationale pour le Développement et la Solidarité).[55] CIDSE's program had been up and running for a short time, whereas DEVAID had just begun: I attended its second meeting with single mothers.

Hoping to reconnect with the single mothers I had first met through DEVAID in 1996, I first returned to Sóc Sơn in 2004. I visited with ten single mothers, nine of whom I had met in 1996. In 1996 they had *agreed* to talk to me; this time they clearly *wanted* to talk to me. Yes, they did remember me; some still had the photos I had sent after my visit. This time, they spoke at length about their children, and they proudly showed me their gardens and fruit trees, their newly painted or newly built houses, and their new appliances. As for the microcredit program, Nam said, "It is a lot of fun because we help one another when we have no one nearby to help. We check in on each other if someone is sick and help each other if someone is unable to work or attend the monthly meeting. In the rainy season we help each other work for a few hours." For these reasons, San said, "I am happier, not so glum, and less sad." Đào spoke of social changes and of her own personal transformation:

> Before the program I did not feel confident; I had pain in my heart because when I met other people, I knew they did not perceive me as I see myself. But when I participated in the project, I experienced what it felt like to have other people show an interest in me and to pay attention to me. Then I made friends, so now when I am alone by myself out in society I feel much more at ease [*thoải mái hơn*]. I no longer feel ashamed or self-conscious or

that I am scorned and hated. And as for the economic changes in my life, I have eradicated my poverty. I know how to work to improve my production. I know how to take care of my child. I know how to plan to achieve results so I can improve my life.

By the mid-1990s the distinctiveness of *xin con* had been firmly established and become broadly recognizable. But for Lê Thi, Nguyễn Thanh Tâm, and other advocates working to improve the lives of single mothers and their children, the uniqueness of *xin con* would be downplayed. The platform from which CSRW, DEVAID, and the Women's Union could most effectively act was based on subsuming *xin con*'s specificity into a larger category of "single mothers."

The microcredit program created opportunities for single women who asked for a child to meet other single mothers, to make friends, and to develop a support network. It changed how they felt about themselves and how they viewed themselves. In the process of being lumped in a larger category of single mothers and subsequently becoming objects of state intervention, how they got pregnant no longer mattered. Women who had asked for a child became merely "single mothers." In 1996, they had not labeled themselves one way or another, unless they described themselves as concubines or second wives; instead they spoke of their desire, their intent, and whether or not they received support for their child. They did not talk about their identity. It was when they became objects of the state's gaze that they referred to themselves as "single mothers." Li (2005, 386) notes, "The stability of a discursive formation is demonstrated when elements that are pragmatically 'lashed up' become systematized, their discrepancies submerged. . . . Most significantly, it is stabilized when it comes to inform individual behavior and to act as a grid for perception and evaluation." In 2004, the Women's Union decided, after a bit of debate, that single female–headed households could also earn the official designation of "Model Vietnamese Family."[56] Notably, "operations of classification, interpretation, and connection do simplify, but they also generate something new: new ways of seeing oneself and others, new problems to be addressed, new modes of calculation and evaluation, new knowledge, and new powers" (389).

CONCLUSION

One February morning in 1996, I rose early and bicycled to Lý Thường Kiệt street in Hà Nội's Hoàn Kiếm district to visit the recently opened Vietnamese Women's Museum (Bảo tàng Phụ nữ Việt Nam). As I walked up the staircase into the lobby, rising boldly in front of me stood *Mẹ Việt Nam* (Mother Vietnam).[57] In my fieldnotes, I wrote,

> *Mẹ Việt Nam* is a golden statue, majestic and heroic, elegant. She has
> notably large breasts and she carries a boy child on her left shoulder.
> He too, majestic, raises his arms wide welcoming life, welcoming the
> future. *Mẹ Việt Nam's* right arm extends downward, her palm toward
> the ground as if to squash life's difficulties. *Mẹ Việt Nam* stands under
> the center of a rising four-story breast-shaped cupola and directly under
> a silver chandelier. The chandelier's main down light is oval shaped. Five
> arms, with large milky white light bulbs at each end, radiate out and
> downward from the middle rod (the font) creating a lighted dome over
> her and her boy. According to the director of the museum, the oval is
> meant to represent a woman's breast, the long metal arms milk ducts,
> and the bulbs drops of breast milk. Indeed, the sky is raining milk and
> behind *Mẹ Việt Nam* is a mural—a blue-tinged river of milk streams by
> as do clouds filled with milk.

There were four floors to the Women's Museum, each of which focused on
a different theme depicting Vietnamese women's relationship to the nation
over time. Outside the museum in an adjacent building, the Women's Union
provided classes in aerobics, cooking, sewing, and how to apply cosmetics—a
marked departure from the state's war era efforts to eradicate signs of femininity and a clear signal that women should learn to make themselves desirable.[58] As I was leaving the museum compound, two buses pulled up to the
gates. More than sixty women in rubber sandals and wide-legged black
cotton-polyester pants and blouses, many carrying their conical hats (*nón lá*),
poured out of the buses and into the compound. They had arrived from the
countryside, brought by their local Women's Union to be educated about a
shared history curated by the state.

Nguyễn Thị Định, president of the Vietnam Women's Union, had con-
ceived of the museum in 1985; she felt Vietnam should have a museum devoted
solely to women. The museum's director, Đặng Thị To Ngân, "hope[d] that the
museum [would] provide local women with insights and guidance on what it
means to be a model Vietnamese woman" and also "a place where women
[could] beautify themselves."[59]

Mẹ Việt Nam and the classes in self-improvement at the museum demonstrate two distinctive yet intersecting exercises of state power, one ideological

Statue of Mother Vietnam in the foyer of the Hà Nội Women's Museum, 2013. Photograph by the author.

and the other a form of governmentality. *Mẹ Việt Nam*, a contemporary manifestation of a long history of governmental efforts to frame motherhood in nationalist terms, "hails"[60] women to reproduce for the nation.[61] The self-improvement classes, on the other hand, operated principally on technologies of self-management, sought to shape women's conduct, "to educat[e] their desires, configur[e] their habits, aspirations and beliefs" (Li 2007, 275). Both worked together in conjunction with the Happy Family Campaign to promote the patrilineal family: Mẹ Việt Nam has a boy rather than a girl sitting on her shoulder.

In 1996 single women who asked for a child were not excluded from the museum's representation of women, but they also were not fully present. They had sacrificed for the nation and were mothers but had done so outside the bounds of normative patrilineal kinship practices. In contrast to the maternal sacrifices made by Heroic Mothers, the sacrifices women who asked for a child had made (their youth and optimal marriageable years) were not recognized. Nor were single mothers targets of the self-improvement classes designed to make women attractive to husbands or would-be suitors. By 2011, however, the museum had been renovated. Mẹ Việt Nam still welcomed visitors to the museum, but she was no longer surrounded by rivers of milk, and the chandelier was gone. Behind her were stands of flowers and swirling above were conical hats painted colorfully with geometrical designs in white, red, orange, and yellow.

On the second floor, a new space constructed to house rotating exhibitions displayed an exhibit titled "Chuyện những bà mẹ đơn thân" (Single mothers' voices). The exhibit was a collaborative effort between the Vietnamese Women's Museum, the Embassy of Finland in Hà Nội, and the Tân Minh Women's Union. According to Professor Nguyễn Văn Huy, an adviser to the exhibit whom I met in June 2011, the exhibit's curators had two goals: the first was to generate a public conversation about single mothers' lives, to get people to understand the circumstances that led them to become single mothers, the difficulties they had experienced, how they had benefited from the microcredit program, and how they made a living. The second goal was to give the women a voice in how they represented themselves. In the introduction to the book that accompanied the exhibit, Nguyễn Thị Bích Vân (2011, 5), director of the Vietnamese Women's Museum, wrote,

> Twenty single mothers from Tân Minh Commune in Sóc Sơn District, Hà
> Nội, received training and cameras to photograph themselves, their lives,

and subjects of importance to them. The 100 images introduced in this exhibit have been chosen from the 1,000 photographs the women took. The exhibit also displays portraits of 18 single mothers. Here are true stories, words shared from lives of women with "one shoulder but two yokes," for these women must serve as both mother and father yet must also overcome fixed gender prejudices and low self-image to achieve happiness. This exhibit also shows the change in the community's perceptions and actions regarding the issue of single women. It invites each of us to join hands to eradicate every hindrance and prejudice and to participate in realizing the goal of equality.[62]

Many of the women I know from Sóc Sơn were featured in the exhibit. It was remarkable to see their faces on large posters displayed on the wall, to know they had chosen the photographs and decided what they wanted people to know about their lives. I couldn't help but reflect on my first meetings with some of them fifteen years earlier, when they had spoken quietly and demurely.[63] The exhibit provides a testament to the microcredit program that helped women change their lives economically and socially. It is also an example of a Vietnamese form of neoliberal governmentality that enacted policies and programs designed to help single female–headed households strive to become (and want to become) economically independent.

The exhibit parallels the shifting place of Mẹ Việt Nam. While motherhood remains the driving force behind women's lives, her reproductive importance has been muted: women are no longer symbolized in general terms by their reproduction or sacrifice to the nation, but rather as complex individuals with their own stories, their own voices, and in particular with an ability as single mothers to become economically self-sufficient—indicative of the Vietnamese household economy. Motherhood is no longer the defining element of their identity: they are friends, members of loan fund management boards, skilled at animal husbandry, sewing, and roof repair. Their identities are more nuanced, more multifaceted. For single mothers who had asked for a child, their agency is also present; it was their reproductive choices that led the state to respond to their needs.

When I asked Professor Nguyễn Văn Huy what specific message the exhibit curators wanted to convey, he said they had no clear purpose. They did not want to have a set message, but wanted to let viewers take away their own thoughts. The exhibit was meant to be reflective. The curators themselves provided no conclusion, no evaluations, but instead presented multiple voices—a stark contrast to the 1996 exhibits. In 2011, representations of women who had asked for a child were fully present; their voices, choices, struggles, and accomplishments were integral to shaping the gendered discourse on single mothers.

The transformation of single mothers on display at the Women's Museum reflects the arc taken by the state's response to single mothers as a whole. *Xin con* was both a normative and a transgressive reproductive strategy. The state had a choice in how to respond. Rather than focus on the transgressions (having extramarital sex and bearing children out of wedlock), the state took the opportunity to elevate the normative aspects of women's decision to ask for a child (women are inherently maternal and reproduce for the nation). In doing so, the state, following the women's lead, broadened the normative horizon of reproduction. Rather than take an antagonistic stance by restricting *xin con* or by insisting on a singular family model, the Vietnamese government accommodated both single women and the state.

This outcome was not inevitable but, much like the women's choices themselves, was shaped by historically specific cultural, economic, and political forces. The Đổi Mới state confronted the challenges posed by women who asked for a child at a time when it sought to shift the responsibility for social and economic risks from the state to the household. By conferring legitimacy on their choice to bear children, the state (via the 1986 law, the social scientists, and the press) reinforced single women's efforts to take responsibility for their own future. This dynamic relationship illustrates a distinctive Vietnamese form of governmentality, the effects of which would prompt state actors to once again respond to the reproductive agency exerted by single women. This time it would be to "conduct the conducts" of the next generation.

PART 3

XIN CON AT THE TURN OF THE CENTURY

OANH

I FIRST MET OANH IN 2013 DURING A TRIP TO SÓC SƠN. SHE WAS BORN THERE in 1967 and came of marital age in the early 1990s. She was raised by her mother, a war martyr's widow. Oanh had a busy life, raising her seven-year-old son, tending to her garden, feeding her cow, helping her mother, and participating in activities for the microcredit program, which provided her with ash for fertilizer, seeds to plant her garden, and money for her son's school fees. But she took time to sit with Tuyến and me for a couple of hours to tell us about her decision to ask for a child. Her mother and her son joined us. With their permission, I recorded our lively conversation. Here are snippets and paraphrases of that conversation. I began by asking Oanh whether the skewed sex ratio had limited her marital choices.

OANH: No, it did not.

HARRIET: Why didn't you marry?

OANH: I don't like men. . . . I have not experienced love. . . . Each person has their own fate. . . . I didn't think about a husband or children . . . and my mother never told me to marry so I didn't. If she had pressured me, I probably would have.

OANH'S MOTHER: I saw no reason my child should marry. I have managed without a husband. I saw the young men her age drinking, gambling, and fighting in the village. The idea of a marriage with this kind of man scared me. So I did not force her to marry.

OANH: When I was about thirty-six or thirty-seven, Mother advised me to *kiếm con* [find a man to ask for a child]. I needed a child so I would have someone to lean on.

OANH'S MOTHER: You were getting old, but you were still healthy enough to birth a baby.

OANH: I thought for some time about birthing a child, but I didn't think I could do it. Many people told me I needed to make a decision; I was getting older. When I finally decided to get pregnant, my sister-in-law said she would find a person to help. But I made it clear that I was not interested in getting married and that if I have a child, I will care for it myself. I certainly would not expect someone to take responsibility for me or it at all.

TUYẾN: How did you choose the person to ask?

OANH: I did not want to *kiếm con* from a man who lived nearby. I was afraid his wife and children would find out and feel humiliated and hurt. I thought I needed one person who lived a little bit far so that no one would be hurt. I didn't want trouble [*gặp rắc rối*].

Initially Oanh's sister-in-law was going to find a man for Oanh, but in the end a friend of her brother's found a man living in another province who was willing to help. He was married and had a grown son. A year later, in 2004, Oanh and the man started to get to know each other. Before they tried to get pregnant, Oanh introduced him to her family.

OANH: We had a ceremony with three trays of rice to smooth relations between him and my family. . . . This was not a second marriage. This was so I could have a child.

Getting pregnant was not easy going. Because Oanh's menstrual periods were irregular, she needed to pay a doctor to regulate them. After she took traditional medicine for four to five months, her periods became regular. Then the man came again, and Oanh got pregnant. She had planned to give birth in Sóc Sơn, but her sister-in-law was worried about the high rate of maternal mortality at the local hospital, so her family took Oanh to Hà Nội, where she was well cared for. She gave birth to a baby boy. The boy's biological father visited them in the hospital so Oanh could put his family name on the birth certificate and the *hộ khẩu* (household registry).

OANH: That was a foolish decision. I wish I had given the child my family name.

TUYEN: Did you keep how you got pregnant a secret?

OANH: Yes, we did not make it public. He told his son and his wife, but she was not really capable of understanding due to an illness. In the beginning he visited when possible and sent money for school fees. But then he had an accident, and now his health is declining so he no longer can help. . . . He encouraged my son to study well so that when he is older, he will not have a difficult life. . . . His son visits my child periodically—they are on good terms.

HARRIET: After the birth did the neighbors visit?

OANH: They certainly did. Younger and older women in the neighborhood came to *đi chơi* [go out, have fun]. Some gave money; some gave presents.

Before we left, Oanh said, "I am happy I have a child. I have someone to take care of me when I am old. I have single friends who did not have a child, and they regret it. Now when I look into the future, I have a son. People always tell me I have gold [*vàng*]."

CHAPTER 5

"This Was My Choice.
It Is My Life."

ON NOVEMBER 19, 2013, THE HIP NEW MANZI ART SPACE IN HÀ NỘI HOSTED the November edition of the talk show *Đúng hay sai?* (*Right or Wrong?*) on a discussion titled "Tình yêu thời thổ tả" (Love in the time of cholera).[1] A focal point for discussion was what the moderator called "the single mum phenomenon," in which single women were intentionally choosing to get pregnant and raise children on their own. I was particularly interested in this conversation because one of the major questions prompted by women's decision to ask for a child in the 1980s and 1990s was whether *xin con* was a blip, a postwar aberration, or whether it presaged a fundamental change in women's reproductive strategies. Once the sex ratio of marriageable women and men balanced out, would single women still ask for a child?

The promotion of the discussion at the Manzi Art Space about single mums seemed to answer this question. However, one of my original informants, whom I first met in 1993—a sociologist from the Institute for Gender and Family Studies in Hà Nội—wondered why, in 2013, I was still asking about single women's intent to become mothers. According to her, women who asked for a child were no longer of any real interest because, she said, "it is no longer a social problem." She, along with most other Vietnamese social scientists who had researched and written about *xin con* in the 1980s and 1990s, had since identified and moved on to other social concerns, such as domestic violence, ethnic child marriage, and trafficking of women.

I was admittedly a bit confused by the disparity between the excitement at the Manzi Art Space and the social scientist's dismissal of my question. Why would intentional single motherhood be of obvious interest in the media, but *xin con* of little concern to social scientists? In 1996 the discussion in the media had mirrored the concerns of social scientists; indeed, the social scientists had been the ones who framed that discourse. In 2013 the discursive disparity between the authorities and the public surrounding *xin con* called for investigation.

In many ways, this disparity is explained by the evolving dynamic between women's agency and governmentality explored in the previous chapters. Contemporary single women who choose single motherhood act on ground that has already been reshaped by women who asked for a child in the late 1980s and 1990s. The absence of social scientific interest in their actions denotes a shift in governmentality, while the continued public interest indicates a change in the meaning of the women's agency. These shifts in governmental focus and meaning in turn reflect socioeconomic and policy changes that provide the newer generation of women with more economic and social mobility. Women who asked for a child before 1986 did so before or during the nascent stages of Đổi Mới, whereas contemporary single women have done so when the effects of Đổi Mới policies have demonstrably changed the tenor of life in Vietnam.

In the 2000s and 2010s, single women continued to engage in the actions that constitute *xin con* but explained and framed their decision to bear and raise a child out of wedlock differently than their predecessors. They did not attribute the same significance or meaning to *xin con* as had women in the 1980s and 1990s. The younger cohort of single women was cultivating new "modes of being" (subjectivities) by undertaking a different kind of cultural project than the previous generation (Biehl, Good, and Kleinman 2007, 6). The diverging descriptions of women's continued exercise of their reproductive agency alerted me to the shifting cultural ground of this relatively recent innovative practice. While *xin con* had emerged into a recognized category of social action by the early 2000s, "a discursive formation is never complete or finished. In fact, neither is it really singular: It is always subject to contestation and reformulation by a range of pressures and forces it cannot contain" (Li 2005, 386).

This chapter explores what subjectivity tells us about the shifting meaning of *xin con* and vice versa. In chapter 4 I spoke of subjectivity in Foucauldian terms: the way in which governmental actors discursively constructed the subject position *mẹ độc than* (single mothers). I now turn to a different notion of subjectivity, the "complex structures of thought, feeling, and reflection, that make social beings always more than the occupants of particular positions and the holders of particular identities" (Ortner 2006b, 115). Doing so shows how governmentality, agency, and subjectivity bump up against and shape one another.

Single women's reproductive agency in the mid-1980s and 1990s was rooted in their sense of themselves as gendered social beings who, reflecting on their circumstances and their desire to achieve a culturally valued gendered identity, chose to ask for a child. "The idea of agency itself," Ortner points out, "presupposes a complex subjectivity behind it, in which a subject partially internalizes and partially reflects upon . . . a set of circumstances in which she finds herself" (Ortner 2006b, 127). And because distinct subjectivities emerge from particular social, political, and economic formations that "shape and provoke subjectivity" (Ortner 2006b, 111), the next generation of single women embodied different gendered subjectivities. Attention to the gendered effects of Đổi Mới economic reforms, and to contemporary women's experiences, perceptions, and concerns resulting in part from those reforms, provides insight into the shifting meaning of *xin con*.

THE CHANGING LANDSCAPE OF *XIN CON*

Contemporary single mothers' attitudes toward marriage, their decision to get pregnant and raise children outside of marriage, and the public's responses must be considered in relation to the gendered effects of the Đổi Mới policies on the family and the state's evolving efforts to govern the population.

Love, Sex, and Marriage in the Market Economy
When I interviewed single mothers in the mid-1990s, they rode bicycles rather than motorbikes, they did not have phones, there was no internet, and their access to foreign media (magazines and TV) was expensive and limited to urban areas. Their mobility was circumscribed due to lack of money and time. They had had limited opportunities to meet marriageable men before becoming too old to find a suitable spouse. Some had fallen in love; others never had the chance.

By 2004, the circumstances within which women and men formed relationships were markedly different. The gender imbalance among men and women of marriageable age was no longer an impediment to finding a husband. The age at marriage had risen, giving women more time to find a suitable husband before being considered too old to marry. Đổi Mới led to a widening of employment and educational opportunities, increased mobility, and access to an abundance of consumer items, enabling people to develop new skills and forge "modern" identities advantageous for successfully participating in the expanding market economy (Drummond 2012; Phinney 2010).

The availability and accessibility of motorbikes, cell phones, and the internet radically changed how often and in what ways young people met, communicated, and gathered. Young people were now able to work, live away from parents, become economically independent and mobile, develop a private life, and meet a potential spouse from another province (D. L. Trinh 2007; Kwiatkowski 2008). Single women were more engaged in social life outside the family compared to the previous cohort of single women (Nguyễn Thị Thu Vân 2015). Moreover, access to foreign media provided alternative images of marriage, love, romance, sexual intimacy, and sexual relations. Single women were able to read about women in other parts of the world living different kinds of lives, making different kinds of choices. A dramatic increase in divorce, premarital and extramarital sexual relationships, and experimentation with different kinds of family models, such as cohabitation, demonstrated a loosening of Confucian-oriented sexual mores.[2]

By 2010 and 2013, the sense that Đổi Mới had overwhelmingly transformed parts of Vietnamese society was inescapable. As Nhung, who was living in Hà Nội, said, "More exposure to information from the outside world has changed society's perceptions about marriage and the family. This has made Vietnamese know more and accept other family models and ways to become a mother."[3] Indeed, gay love and gay relationships have become more visible (Newton 2012).[4]

Though marriage was based on love, it remained predominantly structured by gendered divisions of domestic labor that since the advent of Đổi Mới provided married men with opportunities for extramarital relations in more ways than it did their wives. Married women, still primarily responsible for domestic chores, cared for children and family members, whereas their husbands were free to spend more time outside the home with male friends and colleagues. For some men, the need to successfully compete in the market economy rendered economic fidelity more important than sexual fidelity, prompting men to engage in extramarital relations as a means to demonstrate a "modern" form of masculinity and to secure access to social and economic status and resources (Phinney 2010; Nguyễn-Võ 2008).[5] They did so with single and married women.

Ongoing Population Management

During the 2000s, in order to address ongoing rapid social change, the Vietnamese government updated the laws on marriage and the family more frequently and with far more specificity than previous administrations. The 2000 Law on Marriage and the Family stressed the rights of individuals, rather than the family as a whole or as a collective. As a result, Vietnamese sociologists consider its individualistic spirit to be a significant departure from the 1986 law (Vũ et al. 2002). The 2014 law addressed issues pertaining to cohabitating or separated married couples, increases in divorce among younger people, and premarital and extramarital sexual relations. One year later, the 2015 law removed the legal prohibition against same-sex marriage.[6] In effect, each new law incrementally legislated increased personal responsibility and independence, a departure from the ideological tenets of the Confucian-based patrilineal kinship system.

Along with these legislative changes, the Vietnamese government also launched the Population Quality Campaign in 2001, a new population strategy that remains in effect. One of the primary goals of the campaign is "to improve population quality and develop a human resource of high quality in order to meet the requirements of industrialization and modernization, making a contribution to the rapid and sustainable development of the country."[7] "Population quality" refers to the "physical, mental, and spiritual" (*thể chất, trí tuệ, tinh thần*) aspects of an individual, the family, and the nation.[8] The Population Quality Campaign is a form of biopower; it is a moral project similar to previous forms of Vietnamese governance through which the state calls upon families to act responsibly both for their own benefit and for the good of the nation.[9] Specifically, the campaign calls upon women to bear and raise quality children who will be productive members of society. The campaign shifts governmental focus from how people form families to how they raise children, a focus echoed in the public discourse on single mothers in the 2010s.

Consistent with the Population Quality Campaign, in February 2003, the Vietnamese government explicitly recognized single women's legal right to become biological mothers. The government passed Decree 12/2003/NĐ-CP, "On Childbirth by Scientific Methods," which regulates the use of in vitro fertilization (IVF) and artificial insemination (AI) for infertile couples and single women.[10] Promulgation of Decree #12, an amendment to the 2000 Law on

Marriage and the Family, clarified the ambiguity of single women's maternal rights inherent in the law, first promulgated in 1986. In doing so, the decree legally solidified the subject position of single mothers first described and labeled by Lê Thi and her colleagues at CSRW (now named the Institute for Family and Gender Studies).

These government responses to changing social dynamics both enabled the state to recognize the emergence of new identities and family formations and to advance its legislative ability to manage the population. We can view these recent tactics as attempts to govern in a socioeconomic arena in which the state had more or less lost its monopoly on pedagogical and discursive authority over the family—a result of its decision to enter the global market economy. The dynamic relationship between agency and governmentality illustrates that the state itself changes, in turn giving rise to new subjectivities.

DISMISSING MARRIAGE

The fact that women continue to ask for a child in the present day typically begs the question of why they did not marry. Three main considerations contributed to women's decision to remain single: personal experiences with love, the women's reflections on their own character and suitability for marriage, and a desire for a certain kind of marital relationship. Although some of these considerations echo the experiences of the earlier generation of *xin con* women, they also reflect the changed circumstances of the Đổi Mới era and the women's construction of a new subjectivity.

A Broken Heart

Tuyết, Châu, Linh, and Nhung had grown up imagining they would marry and raise children, and each had fallen in love. However, like many women of the previous generation, their lives did not follow the trajectory they had envisioned for themselves when they were young girls. For example, Tuyết, who was born and lives in Hà Nội, fell in love at age twenty-one and married her boyfriend years later, in 2007. Four years into the marriage her husband asked for a divorce because he had met someone else. Tuyết was stunned and devastated. She found herself at age thirty-three divorced and childless; they had waited two years to try to have a child, until they were financially secure, and after that he was often away for work. After the divorce Tuyết's parents encouraged her to get to know someone else. Tuyết was not interested. "I did not think that way. . . . I believe that love is predestined from heaven. I just wanted to have a child." Tuyết's appeal to love as a reason for not remarrying mirrored women from the previous generation whose loves had been thwarted due to war and circumstance.

Character and Marital Suitability

Some younger women, like their predecessors, also pointed to their own shortcomings (calling themselves old, ugly, physically unattractive, or weak) as reasons they had not fallen in love and therefore would not marry. Thị Mai, who was born and continued to live in Hà Nội, was skeptical that any man would want to marry her because of her weak legs, so she never paid much attention to the men who showed interest in her. In any case, she had been too busy running her hairdressing business to worry about love or marriage, and she needed to take care of her parents.

However, when other single mothers spoke of themselves, they did not attribute their single status to circumstance (situations out of their control), but rather to their own character. Rather than saying they were unlovable or unmarriageable (factors outside their control), they reflected on what kind of person they were and came to the conclusion that they were not temperamentally suited for marriage. Linh (born in Thanh Hóa Province and living in Hà Nội), for instance, had fallen in love at age seventeen with a man seven years older. "We were in love. He was always affectionate, honest, intelligent, and dignified. . . . He was the only man I ever loved, but I could not marry him." Their relationship had gone through "so many difficulties, and ups and downs in love [đau khổ, sóng gió trong tình yêu]" that she decided not to marry. "Previously I thought I would be a good wife and a dutiful daughter-in-law. I considered myself a traditional woman who if she got married would fulfill her duties. Eventually, I decided I didn't want to marry; I just wanted a quiet and peaceful life [cuộc sống bình lặng]." Similarly, Oanh (described in the vignette) considered herself to be self-sufficient; she never felt the need or desire to have a husband.[11]

Companionate Marital Aspirations

In contrast to the earlier cohort of xin con women, many women, having reflected on their own and others' experiences with love and marriage, determined that the men they had fallen in love with would not make suitable husbands and that they wanted a different kind of marriage.

Châu eventually decided that the man she had fallen in love with was not a suitable person for her to marry. Suitability could refer to a range of characteristics: character, profession, family background, place of origin (urban or rural), or compatible zodiacs. While Châu chose not to specify why her boy-friend was unsuitable, I surmised based on her other comments that he was already married. When I said there didn't appear to be a shortage of men, Châu pointed out that availability does not necessarily translate into suitability. "Many people believe that a beautiful woman who has a good job can easily find a husband, but that is not so."

Linh and Nhung were interested in marrying only if they could develop a specific kind of conjugal relationship with their husbands. For example, Nhung, who was born and still lived in Hà Nội, had been in a relationship with a man she loved for seven years. When she first met him, he had told her he was divorced, but actually he was only separated from his wife. Eventually Nhung decided he would not be a suitable husband: "He is not the kind of man I would marry because he is conservative, but I think he is a good person." Nhung's idea of marriage was one in which two people share thoughts, similar views, and a commitment to building a family but still can maintain independence.[12] "I would not be interested in a marriage where only one person does all the work and/or they are supposed to change who they are to be suitable for the other person."

In the end, at age twenty-seven, Nhung decided marriage was not for her.

Marriage would be difficult for me. I am an independent strong woman, not the docile [dễ bảo] type. . . . Moreover, I see so many women in Vietnam (including my mother and a lot of my friends) when they married they had to serve and care for all of their husband's family and they are responsible for worshiping the ancestors. I know I can't do that, and I don't want to do that. If marriage makes a woman dependent on a man, I would never marry. So I think it is a good option for me to have a child and then have different kinds of relationships. . . . Actually I love my parents very much, and I do not want to share my love to serve other people.

Nhung's rejection of marriage was based on her sense of self and filial duty, but also on her unwillingness to enter into a marital situation that would structurally place her in unequal power relationships with her husband and her in-laws. While her desire to take care of her parents echoed the previous generation of women, her concern with gender inequality illustrated a different kind of subjectivity.

Nhung, Linh, and Thị Mai all knew of young women in urban areas who were choosing not to marry. Nhung said, "I know four to five women like me.

They are economically independent, well educated, have more contact with Western culture, and as a result their thinking is more open. They look for husbands who would understand and respect them, give them space to think freely and make their own decisions. They don't need to get married or rely on a man or they don't want to be legally bound to him." Lan, a young urban married woman, remarked, "There are benefits to not marrying. If a woman does not marry, she would have more freedom. She would not have to deal with a mother-in-law and live in her house, nor would she have to suffer her mother-in-law's interference in raising her child."[13] Suitability now encompassed a range of criteria that indicated women were looking for "companionate marriages" in which love, companionship, and equality, rather than economic security or even love alone, were the principal marital goals.[14]

These women's perceptions of and experiences with men made it unlikely they would find a suitable man to marry.[15] One young woman age thirty who had married a foreigner explained Vietnamese women's reluctance to marry as follows:

> Vietnamese men are romantic and kind to their girlfriends, but once they marry they are not so nice; they are bossy and they expect their wives to do everything around the house. The men hang out on the street drinking tea, and they comment on women walking by. The men are loud—they comment on women's body parts so they can hear. These are younger and older Vietnamese men. Even guys my brother's age act this way; once they marry they think they are superior to their wives.

I heard a similar story from a recently divorced shopkeeper: "Vietnamese men—it is in their blood. After they marry, they believe they are in charge of their wives." Nhung said, "There are plenty of reasons women don't marry. For the majority, they have either lost confidence in men, or they don't want to be tied down, or they want to reserve their time for studying or their career. . . . But I have noticed that they still have a happy life." In contrast to the previous generation of women, who chose to remain single on the basis of love and age, Nhung and her friends rejected marriage because of men's attitudes and behavior toward women, and because they envisioned a different kind of marriage than that of their friends and mothers.[16]

Linh and Nhung compared their generation to previous generations of women (born 1948–68). Linh said that for her mother's generation marriage was a "natural path, and almost everyone had to marry whether or not the husband was suitable or the marriage would bring happiness. . . . Only being married was important." Likewise, Nhung said that for her mother and her grandmother getting married was a "default" (*một mặc định*) and an obligation (*một nghĩa vụ*). "Of course in my generation women still want a complete family (*gia đình trọn vẹn*), but they know to listen to what they themselves want and to follow that path, not to only follow the social norms society puts in front of them."[17] Following one's own path, admitted Linh and Nhung, was far more feasible for urban women than rural women with minimal education and resources. However, Oanh shared ideas about marriage similar to those of Linh and Nhung.[18] As Tuyết said, "Each person's situation is different, and that leads them on a different road and so they make different decisions."

Notably, by pointing to men's attitudes and behavior toward women, women reframed their own single status in terms of men's failings or unsuitability, not their own circumstances, as had women in the past. Men constitute the social problem, not single motherhood. The shift from considering oneself unsuitable for marriage to finding men wanting and therefore unsuitable is notable; it indicates a different way of assessing and valuing oneself and one's relationships. And it was also clear that Tuyết, Châu, Linh, and Nhung did not believe happiness hinged on being married. Together the women speak to alternative female subjectivities that derive not from an acknowledgment of one's shortcomings but rather from a positive assessment of who one is and who one wants to be.

The way Oanh, Tuyết, Châu, Linh, and Nhung discussed marriage (in terms of choice, the desire for a certain kind of marital relationship, and an unwillingness to subject themselves to unequal power relations inherent in the patrilineal patrilocal marriage kinship system) reflects a myriad of social and economic changes that had taken place since Đổi Mới, especially since the early 2000s. The previous generation did not reject the institution of marriage, but by helping make it acceptable for women to ask for a child, they created a space where the current rejection of marriage becomes possible.

MATERNAL RIGHTS, DESIRES, AND STRATEGIES

Having decided not to marry, how did the women go about satisfying their maternal desires? Why did they want children and what did they know about their maternal rights?

Maternal Rights

In the mid-1990s, the single mothers I spoke with who had asked for a child had been acutely aware of the 1986 Law on Family and Marriage and quite clear that it gave them the right to have their own child. Given the long history of the Vietnamese government's interest in single mothers' maternal desires, I expected contemporary women to view or understand their maternal rights in relation to the 1986 law or certainly to the more recent Decree #12. But this was not necessarily the case. For the most part, it was only when I asked them if they were familiar with the laws that they discussed them. In contrast to women a decade earlier, younger women took their maternal right for granted: in 2017, single women's right to a child was no longer part of the public discourse as it previously had been.

According to Tuyết, "A woman has the right to be a mother. She has the right to decide for herself to have a child. That is a natural and necessary right of all women." When I asked Tuyết if she was familiar with the laws that recognized single women's right to a child, she said no. Tuyết viewed her desire for a child as a private matter; the state had nothing to do with her decision. She hadn't known about the 1986 law or Decree #12. This may well have been because she took state legitimacy as a given.

Linh agreed with Tuyết: "The family is the foundation of society. . . . It is natural for women to give birth. And it is a necessity. And it is the right of each and every woman. When a woman decides not to marry, but to give birth to a child, it is her private decision. . . . Whatever her reason, it is justified because every woman has the right to become a mother." Linh had heard of the 1986 law and understood that she could register the child and her child would have the same rights as other children. But when I asked her if the law influenced her to have a child, she said, *"Hoàn toàn không"* (Absolutely not).

When Nhung spoke of her rights, she referred to the 1986 Law on Marriage and the Family, not to Decree #12. When I asked about the 1986 law, she said, "Yes, I know about the law. However, it does not specify the right of women to give birth, but states that children born within marriage or outside are equal." Nonetheless, Nhung referred to the 1986 law as granting her maternal rights, choosing to ignore the stipulation in Decree #12. When I asked her if she talked openly about her decision to ask for a child, she said, "Yes, I have, because I think that having a child does harm to no one; most of all it is my right, so I did not have to hide. Of course, I did not speak with those people who were opposed, because speaking would not change anything, so it is better not to talk."

A sociologist friend of mine explained Nhung's wariness. "Harriet, just because there is a law, that doesn't mean people accept this idea of single motherhood or that the majority think it is a good idea, or anyone wants their daughter to ask for a child. It is still quite difficult to do so. It is a difficult life. You must have a special character—to be strong and willing to brave public opinion."[19]

My friend's assertion helps explain the disparity between the social science and public discourses noted at the beginning of the chapter. The government felt a responsibility to single women who had dedicated their marriageable years to the nation during and after the American War. Having paid its debt by legitimating their reproductive agency, the state moved on; it does not bear responsibility for contemporary single women, for whom asking for a child is a matter of choice, not circumstance. Their reproductive agency therefore does not constitute a social problem the state needs to resolve. The government's earlier effort to create a new subject position (single mothers), however, did not generate universal public approval of this new kind of family. Continued social concerns, coupled with the new meaning of *xin con* as an implicit criticism of marriage, drive the public discourse.

Maternal Desires

Eschewing marriage, Oanh, Linh, Nhung, and Thị Mai each decided they wanted a child. Their reasons for wanting a child both resembled and differed from the previous generation of women who asked for a child. The key difference lay in how younger women viewed motherhood.

Oanh from Sóc Sơn said she wanted a child to have someone to take care of her in her old age.[20] On the other hand, Nhung, who is economically independent and works in Hà Nội, said, "I gave birth so that I could become a mother. I did not have a child so it would take care of me when I am old. . . . I have always loved children and wanted to raise children. . . . I think that for women, to have a child is extremely important. Being pregnant and breastfeeding a baby is an important part of being a woman, and I wanted those experiences, so I thought that bearing a child of my own blood would be one of the most special things a woman could undergo." Tuyết, who runs a shop out of her home, where she lives with her parents in Hà Nội, "wanted to experience the sensation of being pregnant." She wanted to give birth and care for a child, and she wanted a child to ensure she had someone to take care of her when she was old. Linh, a translator who is also from Hà Nội, wanted a child because "becoming a mother is the greatest happiness for a woman."

While Châu, who lives in Hà Nội with two female friends, considered the desire for a biological child to be natural, she disagreed that childbearing was requisite for all women. "Many people think it is a necessity, but I don't think so." Nhung's portrayal of motherhood as a choice and Châu's opinion that motherhood is not a natural desire that needed to be fulfilled differed from the previous generation. They did not need to justify their maternal desires in terms of an essentialist, homogenous female identity (discursively noted by the trope "all Vietnamese women") that linked being a woman to being a mother—as had women in the mid-1990s. This generational difference reveals a crack in the previous discursive framing of Vietnamese female subjectivity. It reflects a more diverse set of possible female gender identities made available as a result of Đổi Mới.

Rejecting the State's Path to Motherhood

Unlike women of the previous generation, Oanh, Châu, Yến, Nhung, and Linh could choose an alternative reproductive strategy by availing themselves of fertility treatment offered at the Bệnh Viện Phụ Sản Hà Nội (Obstetrics and Gynecology Hospital). Decree #12, in addition to legislating single women's right to bear their own child, specified a path forward by providing the means for single women to get pregnant by artificial insemination (AI). Ideologically, Decree #12 (the provision of AI) "privilege[s] . . . the womb as a site of kin relatedness" (Pashigian 2009a, 56) and thus acknowledges the "deeply seated importance of maternal kinship ties" (Luong 1984, 749) in Vietnam. The kinship ideals embedded in Decree #12 echo the way single women in the mid-1990s talked to me about pregnancy and motherhood. Examining Decree #12 is instructive— not just because the state implemented the means for single women to get pregnant, but because the techniques deployed to govern single women's reproduction did not in fact fully align with the women's own concerns.

Consistent with the actions comprising *xin con*, Decree #12 recognizes the concern of both the single woman and the biological father that the biological father's identity be kept secret. Paragraph 6 of Article 10 states that "medical officials shall have to: Keep secret all information on the names, ages, addresses, and images of sperm as well as ovum donors and recipients." Likewise, Article 21 reinforces women's assertion that the biological father should not and need not take any financial responsibility for the child. Article 21 states, "Children born by reproduction-supporting techniques shall not be entitled to claim the rights to inheritance and/or be nurtured from the sperm, ovum, or embryo donors."

The state's assumption, perhaps, was that single women, like infertile women, would willingly choose the state's alternative, newly available, technological route rather than asking for a child. For many single women, that assumption would prove questionable. More than a decade later (in 2013, 2015, and 2017) single women I spoke with in Hà Nội and Sóc Sơn were aware that AI was available for single women in Hà Nội but had chosen to ask for a child. Why? There are certainly aspects of AI that would be enticing to single women. But there are far more compelling reasons why women would choose not to follow the state's path. I explore women's decision-making in light of Decree #12 to examine what the ongoing dialogue between women and the state can tell us about *xin con* and subjectivity.

In 2013, I met with members of the Training and Scientific Study Division at the National Obstetrics and Gynecology Hospital in Hà Nội (Bệnh Viện Phụ Sản Hà Nội) to learn more about single women's access to AI. In contrast to a news report I had read about sperm availability, the team said there was plenty of sperm in Hà Nội but the demand was low. Whereas I had assumed that only wealthy urban women would be able to receive donor sperm, they said that the very small number of single women who did request donor sperm represented a cross-section of the Kinh population: they were rich, poor, rural, and urban.[21] Missing was data on women's sexuality. Availability, however, is not the same as access.[22] In 2013, to be considered as a candidate for artificial insemination, a woman had to be either a widow or over thirty-five.[23] This would not have been an issue for most of the women with whom I spoke, since they had gotten pregnant between the ages of thirty-one and thirty-nine. But it would have been for the women seeking to get pregnant when they were just past thirty. In addition to trying to define *when* single women could get pregnant, Decree #12 also stipulated three conditions at odds with the female agency inherent in the practice of *xin con*.

First, to be considered eligible for donor sperm a woman had to follow a number of official administrative procedures. She had to obtain a letter from a local authority (commune or hamlet) stating that she was a single woman who had never had a child. She had to write a personal statement expressing her desire for sperm donation and why she wanted a child. To make her case stronger, she should provide an explanation of her situation and an indication of family support. And she had to provide a health certificate, which she could get at the hospital, stating that she was fecund. As a result, a woman would be subject to governmental scrutiny and surveillance at multiple administrative levels that she would not be subjected to should she ask for a child.

Second, Paragraph 1 of Article 4, "Principles for the Application of Reproduction-Supporting Techniques," qualifies Article 2: "Infertile couples and single women shall be entitled to give birth to children by reproduction-supporting techniques on the prescription of specialized doctors." Women's access to sperm was controlled by and mediated through medical establishments that belonged to the government. Whereas women who asked for a child did so in secret, Decree #12 placed a private decision under the purview of local officials and doctors; it made a private intent public. Whereas *xin con* only involved two decision makers, Decree #12 placed the decision of whether a woman should get pregnant in the hands of a number of strangers—governmental authorities whose "expert" opinions would determine her reproductive future.

Third, should the medical authorities determine that she was eligible, the doctor would randomly choose which sperm to inseminate—randomly because the hospital did not collect data on sperm donors at that time. These requirements not only markedly constrained single women's agency by placing their reproductive decision-making in the hands of local officials and doctors, but they made it impossible for women to choose the biological father of their child. Artificial insemination, like many adoption situations in Vietnam, precluded knowing the biological father. Like women of the previous generation who asked for a child, single women in the 2000s and 2010s wanted to choose a man with whom they shared *tình cảm* (sympathy and understanding) and who they thought would be a good biological (though not social) father. While most women did not want the biological father to take any responsibility for the child, Nhung said, "I did not like the method of asking for sperm [*xin tinh trùng*] from just anyone or by in vitro [*bằng ống nghiệm*], so I thought I would have a child with someone with whom I have a little *tình cảm* so that later, when the child is eighteen years old, I could tell them who their father is." Women's desire for personal connection and the ability to discern whether an individual was a good person and perhaps what kind of family they came from was a clear rejection of the notion that data markers (generalized categorization of sperm) actually tell anything about a person (cf. Schmidt and Moore 2007).[24]

Theoretically, provision of AI increased single women's options for getting pregnant. But in fact, the three stipulations specified in Decree #12 do not align with the kind of reproductive agency indicative of *xin con*. Missing were recognition of women's self-determination in the execution of *xin con*, a preference for having some sort of personal connection to and knowledge of the biological father and the ability to choose who he would be, and an intense concern for privacy. Women who ask for a child do not have to advocate for themselves to government officials in order to get pregnant. Single women rejected AI because it did not align with the manner in which they wanted to bring their child into the world.

A compassionate act, Decree #12 nonetheless represented a new form of biopower, one that linked single women's maternal rights to the means to get pregnant. In doing so it sought to tie single women's reproduction to the state by making women objects of management and surveillance. However, it was not a very successful exercise of power.

Reproductive Strategies

If single women didn't use AI, how did they get pregnant? They did what the single women before them had done and what women whose husbands were infertile had done in the past: they got pregnant with a man they did not intend to marry. Other elements of single women's strategies were also similar to the previous generation of women who asked for a child: they rejected adoption, they chose men with whom they had *tình cảm* to get them pregnant, they planned in advance to get pregnant, they claimed and took full responsibility for the child, and they had minimal contact with the man after getting pregnant.

Akin to the previous generations, younger women stressed the importance of shared blood and for this reason would not consider adopting a child. Tuyết said she felt a bit badly about her opinions on adoption: "I am principally a little old-fashioned because I think adopting a child is complicated. Since you don't know where the child is from, you don't know about its health, maybe it could have some problems." She had also heard about cases in which adopted children had left home as adults because they knew their adoptive parents were not their biological parents. "They were a *little* ungrateful," Tuyết remarked. Nhung shared similar feelings: "I want my own child. I don't want someone else's, and I feel it would be extremely painful when one day my child goes to find their blood mother and father." Thị Mai concurred with Tuyết and Linh and stressed the importance of the link between shared blood and *tình cảm*: the shared understanding and sympathy between mother and child. Tuyết and Nhung's beliefs about adoption were not unique: a friend in Hà Nội who had adopted a child shook his head in dismay at what he considered to be entrenched pejorative ideas about adopted children that were all too common.

A notable difference between the two generations, however, was the open-ness with which contemporary single women approached family members and friends about their plan to get pregnant. In 1996, all but Bích told me they kept their intentions secret; they portrayed it as an entirely private matter. In contrast, in the 2000s and 2010s, Oanh, Tuyết, Linh, and Nhung told me they consulted with a family member or friend about getting pregnant. For Oanh, getting pregnant was a family affair; her mother, her sister-in-law, her brother, and relatives in a different province all helped her achieve her goal.

Tuyết didn't so much consult her parents as told them what she wanted to do and asked for their support. "When my marriage ended, I decided to have a baby right away." Her parents tried to discourage her; they wanted her to marry again. But Tuyết didn't want to wait. She was already thirty-three years old and feared that if she waited until she met someone new she would not be able to have a child. "I told my parents, 'I very much want to have a child. I would very much like that. Now at this moment I have you, but when you are no longer with me, then I want to have a child for comfort.' . . . I said, 'My child will not wait for anything at all.'" When her father saw she was resolute, he agreed. Her mother followed suit.[25] "My father was more supportive than my mother. He said, 'Since you have decided to do this, I also agree. You do not need to worry about anything.' So when I decided to do this, truly it was easy for me because my father supported me. There was no disagreement." At age thirty-four, Tuyết gave birth to a baby girl. She did not tell anyone how she got pregnant and did not want to talk about it. Since the birth, she has had no relationship with the biological father. "This means that I was determined to have a baby, to have a child. I took the initiative for everything, *tất tần tật* [including everything all together]. Me, only I wanted to have a child and to be completely independent, to worry and care for the child all by myself. I don't want anyone to be involved."[26]

Both Linh and Nhung spoke with their mothers and close friends before getting pregnant. A few of Linh's friends tried to discourage her because they thought being a single mother would be quite difficult, but after Linh gave birth (at age thirty-one in 2013), they supported her decision. Friends also advised Nhung against having a child out of wedlock, but she chose not to talk to people who opposed her. "The decision to have a baby was my decision. Other people's thoughts were irrelevant," she said. "I only cared to know what my parents thought, and it was lucky for me they agreed." In 2009, at age thirty-six, Nhung gave birth.

A single mother chats with the author about "asking for a child." Hà Nội, 2013. Photograph by the author.

The women's decision to discuss their desire for a child ahead of time demonstrates a level of familial and social support that was not as forthcoming in the 1980s and 1990s. At the same time the support was uneven; Linh and Nhung only talked to people who were supportive. Châu, by contrast, chose not to confide in anyone, especially her family. She said her parents would not have supported her decision, as "they are from the countryside; they are conservative." But when I asked Châu who went with her to the hospital and cared for her and the child after the birth, she answered, "My mother and sister of course." In 2012, at age thirty-four, Châu gave birth to a baby girl; they share an apartment with two other single women who had migrated to Hà Nội to work and attend school.

Discussing their desire for a child ahead of time with family members and friends did not mean telling them how or with whom they would get pregnant. Only Oanh's family knew who the man was. Châu, for example, had two single female friends who also got pregnant out of wedlock, but she did not know the circumstances of their pregnancies; they did not ask one another how they got pregnant. "These are private circumstances," she said. Her comment echoed the attitude of the previous generation of women toward their pregnancies. Indeed, in 2013, when I was talking to a good friend in Hà Nội about this secrecy, she realized she also had a single friend who had a child but did not know the circumstances; it had never occurred to her to ask.

REFRAMING *XIN CON*

In 1996, all of the single women with whom I spoke used the phrase *xin con* (asking for a child) or *kiếm con* (finding a child) to describe their decision to intentionally get pregnant; most used the phrase *xin con*. Social scientists and journalists referring to older single women used it as well. Initially, the phrase *xin con* signified a postwar reproductive strategy undertaken by *thanh niên xung phong* (youth brigade: youth who volunteered for the war effort) and other older women considered past marriageable age. The phrase was then adopted by the next generation of single women, who also found it difficult to find suitable men to marry but wanted a child. Over time, *xin con* became a socially recognized term for a socially intelligible reproductive strategy; the term conferred legitimacy and recognition on older single women's maternal desires.

The framing and strategies used by the newer generation were more variable. Oanh made it clear that she asked for a child. For her and her family *xin con* was a legitimate reproductive strategy that would enable Oanh to make sure she had a child to take care of her in her old age. So they found a child (*kiếm con*) for her. That was in 2005. Seven years later, in 2012, Châu at age thirty-four also asked for a child (*xin con*). Châu's use of the phrase *xin con* was her way of signaling that she had intended to get pregnant. It was not an accident. It was important that I knew this. Her use of *xin con* provided that distinction. Tuyết did not want to talk about the circumstances of getting pregnant at all. She did want me to know, however, that she took the initiative (*chủ động*) to have a child. At age thirty-six, Thị Mai found herself pregnant and decided to keep the child. While Thị Mai didn't exactly ask for a child, her decision to keep the child was similar to older single women of the previous generation who had found themselves in similar situations. However, Thị Mai knows other women her age who say they no longer want to marry but want to "ask for a child to raise" (*xin đứa con về nuôi*) or "go looking for a child to raise" (*đi kiếm đứa con về nuôi*).

Linh and Nhung each knew the phrase *xin con* but did not want to use it to refer to their situations. Linh had gotten pregnant with a single male friend with whom she remains friends. When I asked Linh whether she had asked for a child (*xin con*), she responded, "Although it is essentially correct in that I did ask someone, I would not describe it to other people that way. I would not say, 'I just asked for a child' [*tôi vừa xin con*], but I would say that I 'just gave birth to a baby or just had a child' [*tôi vừa sinh con hoặc vừa có con*]. Because I feel that when I am speaking to someone, the 'please' [*xin*] in the phrase suggests that my child deserves compassion or pity, like it is not respectable. I, like a lot of other women who choose to have children without husbands, made this decision very seriously, thoughtfully, and carefully. So I do not like it when people look at our children and feel sorry for them because they lack a father's care. Society has now moved from criticizing and scorning single mothers to pitying a child who does not have a father."

Linh's association of *xin con* with pity marks a shift in how contemporary single women thought about their relationship with the man whose sperm they used and how they thought of themselves. By using the language of the market economy—that of choice (*chọn*)—Linh is redefining *xin con*. Her notion of choice represents one of several options; it was her intention to get pregnant, but it was also a lifestyle choice—there are many ways she could choose to live her life. This is in contrast to single women in the mid-1990s who intentionally chose to get pregnant out of wedlock but did not envision their choice in terms of a range of lifestyle options. Social justification for their choice rested on the assertion that asking for a child was a necessity created by their circumstances in the aftermath of war.[27]

At the same time, Linh's frustration with pity was reminicent of the women in Phú Lương who, in the mid-1990s, had told the Women's Union official that they would only meet with me if I didn't pity them. Then, older single women were the ones being pitied because of their circumstances as single women and single mothers. But now, it is not the mother but the child who, according to Linh, is pitied. The shift to focusing on the child is evident in the state's concern with population quality. At the end of the discussion, Linh added, "The moment I first saw my son, I realized that while I had made many wrong decisions in life, my decision not to marry and to have a child were the right decisions. And I will never be sorry about this. I love life as it is." "Becoming a *single mum* [*việc trở thành single mum*] was completely my initiative," said Linh. "This was my choice. It is my life [*Đây là lựa chọn của tôi là cuộc sống của tôi*]."

Shifts in Meaning

Women's evolving strategies signal significant shifts in the meaning of *xin con*. The general context in which women practice *xin con* is broader than it was in the past. The fact that women discussed their plans with family or friends demonstrates that they hoped to benefit from the support of those close to them, an expectation neither assumed nor expressed by the previous generation of women. The women themselves are able to be more outspoken and forthcoming about their desires. Willingness to reach out to others (and the responses they received) indicates that the norms, values, and institutions through which agency becomes available and is constituted have changed.

The physiological logistics for single women to get pregnant have expanded. Asking for a child is no longer the only way to get pregnant outside of marriage. There are more opportunities to find men for sexual relations without having to "ask." After Nhung decided she did not want to get married and wanted a child, she stopped using contraception with her boyfriend. After she gave birth to her child, which she attributed to fate and a gift from God, she broke off relations with her boyfriend. She added, "I know many other women who hide their pregnancy from the man because they don't want him or his family to know about the child. They keep quiet." (She knew five women who had children on their own.) As a result, the younger generation's cultural project is a less constricted form of reproductive agency—one that is constituted by potential options and shaped by a different context of social intelligibility.[28]

Xin con no longer signals a singular discursive formation; it means distinct things to different women depending on their experiences with love, men, and marriage. And it means something singularly different to figures of authority who had worked so hard to support postwar single women's reproductive rights and legitimacy. Social scientists, Lê Thi in particular, do not consider the current manifestation of becoming a single mother (*làm mẹ đơn thân*) to be the same practice as the previous generation's reproductive strategy of asking for a child. For the previous generation, *xin con* signified a strategy born out of necessity through sacrifice to the nation. For many contemporary women, on the other hand, single motherhood is a choice that has been created by increased autonomy and relative economic prosperity—the very opposite of sacrifice.

The 1986 Law on Marriage and the Family was designed to address postwar single women's struggles. By the time Decree #12 was passed in 2003, two generations of postwar single women had already asked for a child. Given the vastly different socioeconomic, historical, and legal contexts, *xin con* came to signify a different kind of reproductive practice. While the actions are similar, the women who engaged in it think, feel, live, and experience the world quite differently than the previous generation of women. As the anthropologists João Biehl, Byron Good, and Arthur Kleinman (2007, 3) point out, subjectivity "becomes the ground on which a long series of historical changes and moral apparatuses coalesce."

Now that it is well established that single women have the right to a child, women no longer need to justify becoming a single mother. It is no longer important, for example, to say they were unlucky in love. The conversation on intentional single motherhood has shifted. It no longer focuses on the reasons and justification for *xin con*, or why women want a child, but on helping single women raise their children well. The focus is now on the child. Indeed, it was I who was asking the questions about single women's reproductive desires, rights, and strategies—not Vietnamese social scientists.

PUBLIC DISCOURSE: THE "SINGLE MUM MOVEMENT"

Promotion of the Manzi Art Space discussion suggested that women's choice to intentionally get pregnant out of wedlock was a sufficiently wide phenomenon to warrant public discussion. The internet, full of such conversations, demonstrates that the topic of intentional single motherhood remains salient.[29] As I analyzed this discourse, it became clear that how people talked about intentional single motherhood had shifted significantly since the mid-1990s. There are three prominent generational differences, each mirroring what I learned from the single mothers with whom I spoke. First, rather than depicting single motherhood as a social problem, people ask what single women's decision to become a mother signifies about marriage and Vietnamese men. Now men appear to be the social problem, not the women. Second, rather than focus on legitimizing or excusing *xin con*, people discuss what it is like being a single mother, how to become a single mother, and how to help single mothers raise their children well. Third, rather than a single discourse framed by political and academic elites, the contemporary discourse includes numerous, nonunified voices.

The discussion at the Manzi Art Space on "love in the time of cholera" focused on the anxiety the single mum movement has generated about marriage and men. An advertisement for the talk show posted on the website Hà Nội Grapevine tried to entice participants by posing a series of questions: "What has happened to love and marriage in Vietnam today? 'Single mum' movement has become a phenomenon! Vietnamese women keep spreading the words 'Don't marry Vietnamese men'! Fast-food divorce is getting more and more popular among the younger generation! Have men been left behind in this modern society or have women forgotten their female vocations and their traditional values? Could 'Mars' and 'Venus' fly together? Come and join us!"[30]

To whom were the moderators referring? Who are these single mums?[31] On the one hand, they were referring to Vietnamese celebrities who decided not to marry but to become single mums.[32] But in the swirl of excitement about celebrities in the news, there are other clear, strong voices, those of single women in their thirties and forties, both urban and rural women with access to the internet, who are quick to point out that single motherhood was their choice and their right; it was not an accident—they had planned their pregnancies. In addition to celebrities, these single mothers aroused concern and curiosity, becoming the subject of the talk show *Right or Wrong?*

While there is a history of ambivalence about the institution of marriage in Vietnam, an attitude reflected in Vietnamese literature at least since the late eighteenth century, perhaps the sharp rise in the divorce rate beginning in the early 2000s indicates a decisive unwillingness to put up with a bad marriage or to put up with Vietnamese men in general (Tran Thi Minh Thi 2011, 2012). As was the case with the women of the previous generation, "rather than marry at any cost, they wish to marry well" (Bélanger and Khuất 2002; cf. Thanh 2018).

The stories women shared on the internet, online blogs, Facebook, and TV talk shows reveal wariness about men. Vietnamese women seem exhausted, tired, frustrated, hurt, humiliated, angered, and "bored with Vietnamese husbands" (*chán chồng Việt*).[33] Circulating on the internet in 2013 was a list of ten bad habits, or *kinh hoàng* (horrors), of Vietnamese men that was posted by a married woman who wanted her readers to know she loved her husband.[34] According to her, married men disregard women, believe housework is only women's work, demonstrate no obligation to their wives' parents, let their wives do all the childcare, criticize their wives for being jealous, routinely engage in adultery, are brutish, drink indulgently, buy flowers on special days but ignore their wives the rest of the time, and lie.[35] While this wife's account could easily be dismissed as a partisan rant similar to those circulating in the popular media in the United States, her list aligns with discussions taking place around Hà Nội and rural areas (Grillot 2012). Probably the most evocative description of marriage I heard was in the documentary *By Choice or by Chance*, in which one of the three single mothers featured said men used to be like trees, the pillar (*trụ cột*) of the house, but then compared her former husband to a "bonsai tree in the house—it is beautiful but does nothing."[36] Thus, the public discourse of single motherhood shifted from the lack of *available* men to the lack of *desirable* men.

In the 1980s and 1990s, married women's letters to the editor indicated they were upset and concerned that the practice of *xin con* depended on their husbands' having extramarital relations. Journalists and social scientists responded by calling attention to gendered notions of sexuality, which held that men were capable of engaging in sexual intercourse solely for the purpose of bringing happiness to an older single woman who wanted a child; while it may bring a moment of unhappiness, it won't ruin overall family happiness. In 2013–17 it was Vietnamese men's extramarital proclivities, their character, and their authoritarian nature that prompted women to consider and possibly choose single motherhood. Men's assumed propensity for extramarital sex had switched from serving as an enabling factor to being a causative rationale for single motherhood.

The second focus of the discourse in the media was on single motherhood itself. The increase in single mothers led to a number of talk shows in which single women explain why they divorced or never married and the challenges and joys of raising children on their own.[37] Women can also find advice from fellow single women and single mothers on the internet. The following questions provide some examples of single women's concerns: "Should I ask for a child [*xin con*] from my old lover?" "Should I ask for a child [*xin con*] from a man who does not plan to marry me?" "How do you apply for sperm to become a single mother?" "Is it a good idea to use sperm from the hospital?" "Is it foolish to become a single mother [*làm mẹ đơn thân*]?" "My husband came home the other night and told me a single woman in his office asked him for a child [*xin chồng tôi một đứa con*]. He is considering it. I am not so sure what I think about this—what do you think?" Significantly, the responses and advice vary: there is no single voice. However, what does not change is the advice single mothers give to single women considering becoming a single mother: a single mother must have a strong character, she must have the means to raise a child on her own, and she should plan her pregnancy. One woman wrote, "You must have a specific plan. . . . The most natural method is to find a partner [*đối tác*], but this method can develop into troublesome complications. . . . You should be circumspect."[38] Other posts indicate that being a single mother is not easy; one woman wrote that she was suffering as a single mother and needed advice. And on December 5, 2012, Lê Hoàng, producer of the *Late Night Show* (Chuyện đêm muộn) on Vietnam TV3 (VNTV), hosted a discussion on how to "Stop the cruelty to single mothers" (*đừng ác với bà mẹ đơn thân*).[39]

But the most prevalent discussions focused not on whether or how to have a child but on how single women should raise their child to become a healthy, happy, intelligent person; it is a discourse of logistics and techniques. For example, in an interview with the model Xuân Lan, who was single and clearly pregnant at age thirty-five, the interviewer did not focus on why she had a child, but on Xuân Lan's thoughts on being a mother and on motherhood.[40] Only at the very end of the interview was Xuân Lan asked why she did not have a husband. The interview focused on how to help single mothers become good mothers and how to raise a child. The internet is full of articles on how single mothers can be good mothers, discussions that mirror the government's Population Quality Campaign. One can find an array of postings online regarding upcoming gatherings for single mum support groups and other events where women receive advice from social workers, psychologists, and educators, to women's magazines providing single mothers with advice on how to nurture and raise their children properly.

The third striking difference in the contemporary public discourse is the variety of voices represented. In the late 1980s and 1990s, the dominant public discourse about women who asked for a child had been largely generated and shaped by government-employed social scientists and Women's Union officials. Regardless of any individual concerns or misgivings, they presented a single unified voice, one of expertise and authority. They disseminated their messages through print media, newspapers and magazines, and at local Women's Union official gatherings. (The five major newspapers were all controlled by the state; there were no international cable networks and no internet.) Their overarching objective was to justify and provide legitimacy for older single women's decision to ask for a child and to change social opinion about single mothers. They did so by invoking themes of sympathy and sacrifice and by labeling older single mothers a "social problem" (vấn đề xã hội) that needed the government's attention.

The discourse on single mothers has since become far more multivoiced and multifaceted. "The production of ideology is no longer just [the] purview of the state. For the first time in decades, the generation of symbolic meanings for society has now also become part of the domain of a commercially viable popular culture" (Nguyễn-Võ 2008, xiv). Single women and single mothers, celebrities, social workers, psychologists, doctors, and TV hosts, in addition to government officials (Women's Union officials and journalists employed at state-run news organizations), generate news, give advice on blogs, and shape the discussion on single motherhood. In contrast to the 1980s and 1990s, the discussion is disseminated through a wide variety of media venues (print, internet, Facebook, YouTube, TV, and radio), which are not subject to the same degree of government surveillance as in the past. The discourse is also no longer bound by Vietnamese voices but incorporates opinions, advice, and examples from various parts of the world.

Evident in the public discourse are different kinds of subjectivities, different ideas of what it means to be a single mother, and different senses of what women experience, feel, and think about. Indeed, when I talked to a Hà Nội sociologist about contemporary people's attitudes toward women who asked for a child in the past or women from the younger generation who are choosing not to marry but to have children, she responded the same way Tuyết had:

> People have begun to move away from asserting essentialist notions of womanhood. Today people see and understand that there are people whose private lives are quite different from their own. This makes it more difficult for them to judge or interfere in other people's lives— compared to the past, when people's lives were more similar to one another. People no longer judge a woman based on how she *should* behave or think—on some general notion of what all Vietnamese women should be. Rather, they judge her as a person, as someone with her own individual character. So sometimes people are not sure what they think about intentional single motherhood, but they all know that a woman has a right to a child. You can see here that the discourse has shifted from a reliance on a unitary and essentialist notion of women to one that recognizes there are many voices, many different ideas, and many different ways of living one's life.

CONCLUSION

Fieldnotes: Sóc Sơn, July 2013:

There was a flurry of activity as we approached Chi's house. It was a different house than the one she lived in when I first met her in 1986. A man wearing a green army hat, blue jeans, and a white long-sleeved shirt splattered with white paint crossed the courtyard in front of us, picked up a bucket of paint, and headed inside the house. Chi's son, a tall, skinny young man dressed in a black V-neck T-shirt and white-washed blue jeans hurried out of the house and got on his cell phone. He didn't notice us and he certainly did not recognize me; the last time I saw him he was five years old. When Phương called out to him, he greeted us, went inside to call his mother, then came back outside and got on his Yamaha. Then a young woman wearing tight black jeans with gold-trimmed pocket zippers, a white short-sleeved blouse, and a wide red hair ribbon came out of the house and joined him on the motorbike. Pausing just long enough to smile and pose for a photo, they sped off. Chi came out and invited us inside as she pointed to the man covered in paint, to the back rooms where painting was clearly in progress, and to a meter-tall dreamy photograph hung on a newly painted wall. It was a prenuptial wedding photograph of her son and his fiancée, who had just left. The wedding would take place on Friday—in six days; the aqua blue that covered interior and exterior walls needed to be painted white. Preparations for the wedding were underway. There was a lot to do.

Chi, like other women of her generation who had asked for a child, did not reject the institution of marriage, but rather tried to reproduce the social institution by mimicking it (as best she could) and to reproduce it for her son. Chi would not be able to follow traditional wedding rituals such as having a husband symbolically stand next to her during the ceremony. She had invited the biological father but did not know if he would show; she said she wasn't particularly concerned one way or another.[41] Chi had invited married couples for good luck, and the neighbors had already offered to help with preparations.

The women of Chi's generation, some of whom happily told me their children were now married, had not set out to change the institution of marriage or society. But in fact their reproductive agency transformed both themselves and society. Their maternal desires were driven in part by the common belief that being pregnant and bearing and raising a child were transformative—physiologically, psychologically, and socially. Nonetheless, when I asked them at a group gathering if and how they themselves had changed as a result of being mothers, they just laughed, shook their heads, and proceeded to tell me how incredibly difficult it had been to be a single mother—especially when their children were little.

Yet their decision to ask for a child led to them becoming noticed, not just by gossiping neighbors and angry relatives, but by sympathetic neighbors, members of the Women's Union, government officials running state enterprises, and foreign NGOs. Agency has unintended consequences; *xin con* was transformative: it opened up alternative futures, ones they could not have anticipated. This was not the "natural" course taken by their mothers; they had charted a new path, working hard to raise their children and give them as good a life as they could. With the help of the Women's Union and foreign NGOs, they met other single mothers like themselves, enabling them to make friends and to create a unique social network all their own.

Their act of *xin con*, and the state's response, also opened up alternative futures and subject positions for the next generation of women in ways that they did not or could not anticipate. The same was true for the state: its exercise of governmentality had unintended consequences. In contrast to Chi, Mai, and Thủy, the next generation—Linh, Nhung, Thị Mai, Oanh, and Châu—seems to have little interest in reproducing a social structure (marriage) that limits or oppresses women. And the broader social and economic possibilities open to women mean they no longer have to become wives or even mothers to fit into society. *Xin con*, an act that looks fairly similar at the individual level and from one generation to the next, was in fact not the same. As my Vietnamese friends often said to me, when they explained a social norm or practice, "Same same, but different." Because agency presupposes an always-complex subjectivity, the meaning of this reproductive act has shifted, as has the significance people attribute to it. No longer viewed as a means to solve a "social problem," it is now considered indicative of a choice responsive to a different "social problem": that of men's treatment of women and unequal gendered dynamics inherent in existing patrilineal, patrilocal marital practices.

Also unlike the previous generation, contemporary single mothers readily articulated a more self-reflective transformative effect that their decisions may have on themselves and on society. Perhaps Thủy's daughter put it best when she learned, after her own marriage, that yet another man had proposed to Thủy. "Mother, you have not depended on anyone for a long time. You go out with your friends; no one manages your time. If you marry, then you must return home to him. If your friends call you on the phone, then he will be become more jealous of you, especially if you don't come home at a suitable time." When Thủy recounted this story to me, she said she realized that her "psychological" (*tâm lý*) makeup had changed. "Perhaps it is fate that I never marry," she said with a big grin on her face.

Conclusion

IN 1993 MY VIETNAMESE LANGUAGE TEACHER ENCOURAGED ME TO RESEARCH *xin con* because, he said, "it is remarkable." At the time I had found *xin con* surprising; I did not fully comprehend the significance of single women's decision to ask for a child. Since then, I have come to see not only how it was remarkable at the time but also how it remains so today.

The purpose of this book has been to explore and explicate the shifting meanings and implications of *xin con* over time. Examining *xin con* from different theoretical angles provides a progression of explanations, each of which illuminates the preceding analysis. Consideration of the larger sociocultural and political environment within which single women asked for a child proves inadequate by itself for fully appreciating *xin con* and its evolution. Further analyzing *xin con* in terms of agency, governmentality, and subjectivity not only helps explicate this unique reproductive practice but broadens our understandings of these theoretical lenses.

AGENCY

As a form of agency, *xin con* is a gendered cultural project in which single women drew on Vietnamese ideologies of love and sexuality and alternative reproductive strategies, navigated conventional yet malleable moral parameters surrounding reproduction, and devised rules of conduct in order to become mothers and chart their own future. In the mid-1980s it was an unconventional assertion of agency. Twenty years later, *xin con* had become recognized as a socially intelligible and legitimate reproductive strategy for older single women considered past marriageable age. In the intervening years, the sociocultural, economic, and political context had dramatically changed. Driven by the same desires for biological motherhood, women's exercises of agency in the 2000s and 2010s refracted a changed society and thus signified something different. Examining *xin con* over the long-term cautions against attributing the same meaning to similar acts over time.

In the 1980s and 1990s *xin con* was a practical form of kinship. Years later, as these single mothers celebrated their own children's marriages, it became clear that their pioneering practices had not resulted in a rejection of the institution of marriage, but rather stood as a testament to it. Their agency was relational; they benefited from the compassion and support of men, neighbors, government officials, and relatives. This support was based on postwar concerns regarding the plight of single women who had devoted their youth to the nation and whose marital prospects had been severely limited as a result of high male mortality during the American War, and by gendered socialist labor practices after the war. Engaging in an unorthodox reproductive strategy in order to achieve the traditional role of mother, single women who asked for a child conceptually and pragmatically separated reproduction from marriage in a novel way. By doing so, they, together with social scientists, instigated a social and political process that has contributed to the broadening of Vietnamese notions of gender, personhood, and kinship today.

In the 2000s and 2010s, single women's decision to ask for a child derived from similar maternal desires, but their agency signified something new. For some it was a rejection of the gendered inequality inherent in conjugal relationships. For others it was a rejection of the roles and responsibilities that would be required of them as daughters-in-law. For many it was a response to the emotional distress they had already experienced in nonmarital romantic relationships. For all, *xin con* was an act of freedom—not from their friends and relatives, but from an institution that would structure their lives and limit their ability to chart their own future.

The emergence of *xin con* in Vietnam and its continued practice also point to the historical and cultural specificities of agency. Single women's decision to bear children out of wedlock in the United States and recently in China, Japan, Taiwan, South Korea, and China might signal that intentional single motherhood is a global trend.[1] It would be tempting, for example, to argue that it is similar because contemporary single women around the globe have become more economically independent and cosmopolitan from living in a world in which ideas, people, and things are increasingly mobile. This is certainly the case, though the experience of similar social and economic processes does not mean their agency is identical. Just as demographics constituted a ground but not an explanation for *xin con* in Vietnam, global gender trends are meaningful in local but not universal terms. Agency is a cultural project.

GOVERNMENTALITY

Women's reproduction is always embedded in relations of power. In the modern era, single women's reproduction has typically been the target of social opprobrium and governmental condemnation. Only in a few countries, such as Israel, Romania, Russia, and South Korea, have governments formally recognized single women's maternal desire or encouraged their reproduction (Bucher 2000; Kahn 2000; Kligman 1995). In these cases the governments' tactics aim to increase the fertility rate amid declining population growth or to serve other nationalistic pronatalist agendas. Since Đổi Mới, the Vietnamese government has been interested in intentional single motherhood for other reasons, leading to a different kind of reproductive governance.

The question that arose in the mid-1980s for the Vietnamese government was not how to preserve or encourage a return to the "traditional" Vietnamese family but how to facilitate its ongoing transformation (Donzelot 1977) so Vietnamese households could successfully compete in the global market economy. When it became evident that older single women had been asking for a child, government officials chose to recognize and legitimize their reproductive agency rather than condemn it. Choosing to sidestep or justify as best they could the fact that women were mostly asking married men to get them pregnant, the state focused instead on the sacrifices that they, along with other widowed mothers, had made to the war effort (losing their youth, sons, husbands, fathers, and other men they loved). Discursively encompassing single women who asked for a child into a larger group of single mothers enabled the state to direct attention to what really mattered to the state: their children, the future of the nation.

In 1986 the government passed a new Law on Marriage and the Family that people broadly interpreted as granting all women the right to have a child. The law provided this right not directly but in terms of the needs of their children. Focusing on the child was consistent with the party's philosophy and goal of creating a new socialist society through the successive improvement of each generation. Focusing on the child rather than on the essential right of a woman to bear a child, the law empowered the state to regulate women's maternal behavior more effectively than it could have otherwise. Had the state failed to bestow upon single women the right to a child, the state would have no governing role. Single mothers, in particular those who asked for a child, subsequently became objects of interest, research, and public and official discourse, as well as subject to new state efforts to govern families.

The 1986 law and efforts to embrace rather than reject intentional single mothers constituted a unique form of governmentality. It was historically, politically, and economically specific, shaped on the one hand by the government's ongoing "larger national narrative of the forward march of history toward socialism" (Harms 2011, 104) and on the other by the devastation of war and the failure of the command economy, which ultimately led to the decision to enter the global market economy. The inclusivity shown to single mothers was necessary for the success of the nation. Marginalizing single mothers would not serve the state because it would not enable women to recognize that their own maternal desires aligned with the goals of the state and the nation. At the same time, this was a personal form of reproductive governance. It was intimate, not just because the personal is political but because it also issued from the desires of Women's Union governmental officials, some of whom themselves had asked for a child or wanted to do so.

The 1986 Law on Marriage and the Family, as well as subsequent efforts and policies, worked to improve single mothers' lives. These efforts are remarkable for helping render *xin con* discursively orthodox, producing a new subject position—that of intentionally single mothers—and working to normalize a new type of family: single female–headed households. These efforts gradually affected general social perceptions of single mothers and their children, as well as how single mothers perceived themselves.[2] The success of these efforts was in part due to their responsiveness to single women's reproductive agency and the way in which government actors created a public dialogue that incorporated different voices and concerns rather than simply imposing top-down regulations.

Ironically, recognition of single women's reproduction and the production of a new subject position unintentionally created new subjects (a decade later) who chose single motherhood not because of lingering effects of war and gendered socialist labor practices, but because they desired the individual freedom to create families outside the bounds of the patriarchal family. Having promoted a sense of autonomy through subsequent laws on marriage and the family (calling upon women to create Happy Families in which women focus on domestic duties and develop the skills to create economically sustainable households), the state has contributed to constructing female subjects with their own ideas about the kind of lives they want to live—which the state must again figure out how to govern.

To catch up with contemporary single women's reproduction, the government issued Decree #12 in 2003, which granted single women both the right and the means to get pregnant. In doing so, it directly linked women's reproduction to state management and surveillance. Decree #12, like the 1986 Law on Marriage and the Family, was a pragmatic recognition that single women were already getting pregnant on their own. Both the law and the decree opened up and created new legal reproductive spaces for single women. However, in contrast to the 1986 law, which derived from research that portrayed single women's need to ask for a child as a social problem that cried out for recognition and sympathy, no such social problem existed for the cohort of women coming of marital age in 2003. This younger cohort had not sacrificed their youth and marriageable years to the nation, and there was no longer an imbalanced sex ratio of women and men of marriageable age. Nor did single women appear to have trouble finding men to get them pregnant.

Decree #12 was a different form of governance than the 1986 law. It governed more through administration than through freedom of opportunity: for instance, the stipulations for accessing sperm conflicted with the actual practice of *xin con*. Choosing to be impregnated by men they knew, the next generation of single women rejected artificial insemination but did embrace the Population Quality Campaign enacted around the same time.[3] This is because the campaign focused not on how women got pregnant but on the child—as did the 1986 Law on Marriage and the Family. Indeed, the Population Quality Campaign was a mode of governance that both reinscribed women's desires and incited them to birth and raise quality children for the benefit of all: the children, the family, and the nation. The more recent decriminalization of gay marriage falls within this same mode of governing. The focus isn't so much on how people form families as on guiding them to raise productive members of society.

The ongoing dialogue between women's reproductive agency and the Vietnamese state's efforts to govern the population through reproduction—its continuing efforts to catch up with women's reproductive agency, to support it while also managing and legislating it—provides insight into Vietnamese modes of governmentality beginning with the Đổi Mới reforms in 1986, and onward as Vietnam became increasingly integrated into the global market economy. It is worth emphasizing that through this ongoing dialogue, reproductive governance not only produces new kinds of subjects; it also changes the state itself, which must respond to the changes it has instigated by shifting its techniques of governmentality.

SUBJECTIVITIES

In the mid-1980s and 1990s, single women drew on cultural narratives that discursively framed Vietnamese women in essentialist terms to explain why they asked for a child. "All Vietnamese women" want to become mothers, they repeatedly told me. Being a real woman, they pointed out, meant being a mother. They were not interested in changing society; they just wanted a child to love and care for. Because they believed that the physiological process of birth is transformative and that biological children are more likely to care for aging parents, single women eschewed adoption. Asking for a child enabled them to experience maternal love, a love they (and many other women) considered to be the quintessential kind of love, far more sustaining than conjugal love. They talked about their personal desires in terms of "all Vietnamese women," not as unique to themselves as individuals. What differentiated them from married women was not their hopes and desires but the circumstances that led them to ask for a child.

By the 2010s, the way these same women (who asked for a child two decades earlier) perceived themselves had changed. Some of them had contributed to the Women's Museum exhibit in Hà Nội, speaking frankly about their lives, the choices they had made, and their struggles as single mothers. Rejecting former representations that portrayed them as women to be pitied, they now constructed their personas as single mothers who worked hard to raise their children and who were fully capable of surviving, if not necessarily thriving, in the new economy. These changes in subjectivity were in large part enabled by the Vietnamese state's decision to support single women's reproductive agency and the ongoing socioeconomic and cultural shifts instigated by Đổi Mới.

It was in this new socioeconomic and cultural context—forged in part by the practice of *xin con*—that the next generation of single women chose to ask for a child. They too desired the love of a child and wanted someone to care for them when they were too old to care for themselves. However, contemporary single women are engaged in a different cultural project than their predecessors. Having grown up in a very different milieu, they are interested in charting their own paths, in making choices consonant with their own sense of self. They do not want to subject themselves to the unequal gender and kinship relations that structured the marriages in which their mothers and friends seemed confined. A fundamental reason they were able to think about choice was that they had rejected the essentialist narratives of Vietnamese womanhood that the previous generation had held on to in order to justify asking for a child. No longer needing to justify having a child out of wedlock, contemporary single women focused on other concerns, such as what kind of person they were and what kind of life they wanted to live. In contrast to the previous generation, they attributed their single status not to circumstance but to their own sense of whether or not they were suited to marriage. In many ways, contemporary single mothers' subjectivities exemplify the consumer market economy they had become accustomed to. As Tuyết said, "This was my choice. It is my life."

MAI REDUX

Let's return to Mai, whose story opens this book, and reexamine it in light of the analytic lenses I have pursued. The account provided above depicts key elements of Mai's life experiences leading up to her decision to ask for a child. Her life was forged amid revolution, war, socialist labor practices, and a shift from a command to a market-based economy. Mai's story also gestures to affective experiences with love, children, and family, as well as personal, material, and sociocultural changes.

One way of examining Mai's decision to bear a child out of wedlock is to look at the sociocultural and political milieu in which she lived, the larger structural factors: state socialist policies drew her out of her home and provided her with education, employment, and housing, eliminating her need to rely on her family or a husband. But by relocating her boyfriend, the state also rendered Mai's personal relationship a casualty of nation-building. Skewed sex ratios due to wartime mortality made it difficult to find another suitable man her age to marry, exacerbating her feelings of betrayal. Unwilling to marry either a younger man or a widower whose children she would have to "pamper," Mai decided she was better off single. This is the ground upon which Mai asked for a child, but it does not fully explain why or how she did so. Social structures shaped but did not determine her behavior. It is, therefore, helpful to consider Mai's decision to ask for a child in terms of agency and its predicate, subjectivity.

Analyzing *xin con* in terms of agency entails examining how *xin con* is constituted and made available by gendered social norms, reproductive practices, and various institutions. Attending to subjectivity focuses our attention on how Mai, as a single woman, perceived and engaged with her local world, still largely structured by patriarchal kinship ideologies. Conventional gender ideologies continued to render women's need to bear a child essential. In most ways Mai's desire for a child was no different than that of married women, but she did not recognize herself in them. Instead, she identified with the *thanh niên xung phong* (youth brigade volunteers), whose decision to ask for a child after the American War had prompted the state, in 1986, to grant all women the right to a child. Had they not exerted their novel reproductive agency, the state would not have been incentivized to reach out to them. "Everyone was talking about it. It was on the radio and in the newspapers." Mai engaged with her own fate and identity as a single woman and intentionally got pregnant with a man she had come to know. "Mostly, I had a child because I knew it would make me happy when I got older; on my own I would be sad."

Mai's parents and brothers were not happy when they learned Mai was pregnant. They did not come to terms with Mai's decision until her sister reasoned with them. It was not simply the context within which she made a choice that prompted her to ask for a child, but her initiative to change her own circumstances, which constituted the very possibility of her choice. The consequence of her actions was that she became an intentional single mother. Mai's subjectivity, her sense of self (itself mediated by cultural and institutional norms), was now that of a single mother.

Mai's reproductive agency was embraced, not rejected, by the state (a hallmark of governmentality). The army enterprise where Mai worked and lived provided childcare for her infant son. Later, after Mai resigned to move closer to her family, the local Women's Union (a state organization) asked her to join a microcredit program for single mothers. Mai benefited from participating in the program. She borrowed money for animal husbandry and seeds for her garden. In addition to cultivating rice for her pigs, corn, and sweet potatoes, she grew and sold at a profit pomelos, cassava, and pumpkins. Through the credit program, Mai grew close with other single mothers who shared their life's difficulties; they became one another's support group. Eventually, Mai made enough money to build a new two-story house, complete with a new bathroom and kitchen, for herself and her son, who was away at engineering school. "My situation as a single mother is a lot easier than it was for the youth brigade volunteers. I had help from my neighbors. And people no longer gossip about older single mothers, only young girls who got pregnant by mistake."

Having exerted her agency and enacted her subjectivity, Mai became part of a larger and longer sociopolitical process, initiated by state actors, that embraced and enfolded single women's reproductive agency in its own terms and for its own agenda of managing the population. The 1986 law and the microcredit program were governmental tactics deployed to improve the lives of all single mothers. So were the efforts of the Women's Union to educate the public and garner sympathy for single mothers and their children. Together, these efforts, along with the kindness of neighbors and relatives, helped Mai improve her living conditions and changed how she experienced and lived in the world.

Given Mai's choice to remain single and ask for a child, we could surmise that she would identify with contemporary single women who have made similar decisions. Their cultural projects align, but they also diverge in significant ways. Đổi Mới policies led to a series of unanticipated gendered consequences that prompted women such as Oanh, Nhung, and Linh to experience and react to their social worlds in new ways. Their decision to embrace the now-orthodox strategy of *xin con* was motivated by different sociocultural and gender power dynamics and was made for diverse reasons. Through their actions, *xin con* has been given a new meaning that reflects the cultural context within which it is performed. At the same time the change in *xin con* demonstrates that the interaction among an individual's sociocultural and political environment, their exercise of agency, and the governmental response is dynamic, continually leading to new gendered subjectivities and cultural change.

NOTES

PREFACE

1   My research on *xin con* has unfolded over many years and has contributed to journal articles and book chapters, some of which I draw on in this book. Chapter 1 includes revised material from an article published in the *Asian Pacific Journal of Anthropology*. Chapter 2 includes revised material from an article in *positions: east asia cultures critique* and content from *The World Book of Love*. Chapter 5 includes content from my chapter in *The Secret: Love, Marriage and HIV* and from a coauthored article in *Critical Medical Anthropology*.

2   I had intended to conduct research in rural state forestry farms but was unable to secure permission. My research sponsor said it was *"rất phức tạp"* (very complicated)—too difficult to make happen.

3   I conducted research in Sóc Sơn District, forty-five minutes north of Hà Nội. The women's primary economic activity was agriculture (rice, sweet potatoes, corn, cassava, peanuts, beans, and sesame). At the time, farmers traded their produce at the District Market of Sóc Sơn, five to six kilometers away. Sóc Sơn District, the home of the old airport and many army bases, had been heavily bombed during the American War.

4   My research assistant Trinh, a history major who had written her thesis on Thanh Liệt, conducted the interviews in Thanh Liệt because local officials had denied my request to do so. Trinh interviewed women farmers, Women's Union employees, and women engaged in small businesses, most of whom had studied up to but not beyond seventh grade.

5   Phú Lương was thirty minutes by car north of Thái Nguyên, which in 1996 was the provincial capital of Bắc Thái Province. Bắc Thái, one of the country's metallurgy, machinery, manufacturing, and mining centers, was heavily bombed during the American War. Among the women I interviewed in Trân Dù were a schoolteacher, a seamstress, and a cement factory worker. With the exception of the teacher, none had received a formal education beyond seventh grade; most had left school after second or third grade.

6 The women in Hà Nội had a higher educational level (secondary or beyond) than the women in rural areas. Three had white-collar office jobs and one was a guard.

7 The discourse analysis I conducted for this time period is largely based on articles from the following newspapers: *Báo Phụ nữ Thủ đô* (Capital city women's news); *Báo Phụ nữ Việt Nam* (Vietnamese women's news); *Báo Tiền phong* (Vanguard news); *Báo Pháp luật* (Legal news); *Báo Tuổi trẻ* (Youth news); and *Báo Nhân Dân* (People's news). The articles include news reports, short stories, poems, legal clarifications, and letters to and response from the editors.

8 Of the single women I interviewed, Oanh (born in 1979) lives in Sóc Sơn; Tuyết (born in 1979), Nhung (born in 1973), and Thị Mai (born in 1972) were born and raised in Hà Nội; and Châu (born in 1978) and Linh (born in 1982) were each born in Thanh Hóa Province but now reside in Hà Nội (they are not acquainted). Oanh was a farmer. Thị Mai and Tuyết each ran small businesses (hairdressing and a coffee shop, respectively). Nhung worked as translator for a Vietnamese company, Châu was a governmental employee in a communications department, and Linh worked for an international NGO. Each of the women was financially self-sufficient, though their incomes varied widely. These names are pseudonyms.

9 My discourse analysis for this time period is based on the following online forums and news websites: afamily.vn; bacgiang.net; baomoi.com; danviet.vn; giadinh.net .vn; giaoducduhoc.nld.com.vn; lily.vn; luatminhkhue.vn; news.zing.vn; ngoisao.vn; phunutoday.vn; singlemum.vn; talkvietnam.com; thanhnien.com.vn; tinmoi.vn; tintuconline.com; tuoitre.vn; us.eva.vn; vietnamnet.vn; vietnambreakingnews .com; vietnamonline.com; vnexpress.net; yeutre.vn; webthro.com.

INTRODUCTION

1 All research participants' names in this book are pseudonyms unless otherwise specified.

2 It was also the case that children born out of wedlock were given to a relative to raise or a single woman became a concubine or a second wife to the man who impregnated her.

3 The Vietnam Women's Union (Hội Liên hiệp Phụ nữ Việt Nam) is a mass state organization with branches throughout the country at all administrative levels, from the central to provincial, district, commune, and hamlet levels. It is responsible for educating, mobilizing, and representing women and has played a significant role shaping gender and kinship ideals. See L. A. Hoang 2020; Pettus 2003; Rydström 2016; Schuler et al. 2006; Waibel and Glück 2013.

4 My references to "the state" refer to the party-state, an assemblage that comprises the Communist Party of Vietnam (CPV) and the government.

MAI

1 Đoàn Thị Tuyến, an anthropologist at the Institute for Cultural Studies in Hà Nội, accompanied me on a number of trips to Sóc Sơn.

CHAPTER 1. MATERNAL DESIRE

1 Hồng Liên, "Chúng tôi mong muốn được làm mẹ!," *Báo Phụ nữ Việt Nam*, December 14, 1988.

2 Prior narratives linking childbearing to women's physical and psychological balance are evident in 1930s French-influenced Vietnamese publications (T. L. Nguyen 2016).

3 While *tình cảm* is often translated in English as "sympathy," this does not fully convey its cultural meaning. *Tình cảm* means shared sentiments, emotions, feelings, and understandings. A person who has *tình cảm* demonstrates a certain kind of affectual connection and recognition of and perhaps responsibility to others by behaving in appropriate ways and engaging in certain practices, such as caring for an elderly parent.

4 For research on care for the elderly, changes in coresidence patterns, and the role of daughters caring for parents, see Bùi et al. 1999; Barbieri 2009; Vietnam National Committee on Aging 2012; T. T. D. Ngo 2013; Bousquet 2016; and Thai 2012.

5 Manifestations of filial piety remain ubiquitous—from women lighting incense at family altars or giving offerings to the dead so they will be content in the spirit world, to family members gathering to wash the bones of their deceased relatives a year after their death, to young couples postponing their weddings should a relative die, and to the young speaking deferentially to elders.

6 Less commonly, a single woman could live with a sister's family or with other relatives (Bui et al. 1999).

7 Consider the Confucian proverb "A brother is like your hands and legs, a spouse is like a dress" (*Anh em như chân tay, vợ chồng như quần áo*).

8 For a historical discussion of this practice, see N. T. Tran (2018).

9 One couple living in a village near Hà Nội said there were not many orphans to adopt in the mid-1970s. Because the war was principally fought in the south and central regions of the country, children in the north were rarely orphaned due to war. If they were, a relative would raise the child. See Dana Sachs (2010) for a comparison on adoption and orphans in the south during the mid-1970s. For a colonial era comparison, see T. L. Nguyen (2016).

10 This practice is a form of "child circulation," a common family strategy in many parts of the world characterized by "co-residence, a physical closeness coupled with sharing the daily tasks of the home" (Leinaweaver 2008, 3, 81–104).

11 In 1988 the National Council on Population and Family Planning announced the one- to two-child policy and began to devote resources to policy implementation and contraceptive provision. The campaign promoted later age at marriage and longer birth spacing, with penalties for policy violations, cash incentives for sterilization, and free contraceptives and abortions. Billboards throughout the country promoted the new policy (Haughton 1997).

12 In 2017 a social scientist countered that regardless of the overall drop in fertility, there were always children available to adopt because rural relatives continued to have lots of children.

13 For a historical account, see Vinadia, "Rước voi về giày mả tổ," accessed August 7, 2020, http://www.vinadia.org/to-quoc-an-nan-nguyen-gia-kieng/to-quoc-an-nan-ruoc-voi-ve-day-ma-to/.

14 "Con nuôi có được thừa kế di sản của cha mẹ nuôi không?," *Báo Lao động*, January 30, 1986; Nguyễn Bạch, "Hỏi," *Báo Pháp luật*, January 17, 1989.

15 Vietnamese distinguish between biological mothers (*mẹ đẻ*), adoptive mothers (*mẹ nuôi*), and stepmothers (*mẹ ghẻ*).

16 If a woman adopted the child from a relative as an infant, she might never tell the child he or she was adopted. The child would then call the adoptive mother "mother" and its biological mother "aunt."

17 This was the case for a young man in his mid-thirties I met in 2017 who had been adopted when he was seven months old. Because the two families kept in touch and he lived in the next village, he maintained close ties to his natal family. When he was a teenager he secretly visited his natal family to hang out with his siblings. He demonstrates filial loyalty to his adoptive parents but feels pulled in two directions.

18 In Sóc Sơn and Phú Lương, if a family was unable or unwilling to give their single daughter a small plot of land, she could buy some (if she had the money) or the cooperative would give her land—usually of poor quality and in remote fields (Lê Thi 2005, 84; also see Bélanger and Khuất 2002). Land allocation to single mothers derived from an amendment to Resolution No. 10 (Contract 10 or Khóan Mười), issued in 1988 to decollectivize the farming system and revitalize the peasant household economy (Kerkvliet 2005; Phan Huy Lê 2006; Kirk and Nguyen 2009). Initially, single mothers were not given land under Resolution 10, but "with the support of the Women's Union, single women . . . obtained the right to access leased land along criteria applied to a family" (Truong 1996, 11).

19 Single women were not the only ones reproved for adopting outside the family. An elderly couple I met in 2017 who lived on the outskirts of Hà Nội recounted how, in the mid-1970s, the husband's younger brothers pressured them to return the infant boy they had adopted from outside the family in order to have a son to carry on the family lineage. The brothers contended that one of their sons should do so.

20 Vietnamese historians depicted prerevolutionary Vietnamese families as nuclear families embedded within a larger extended family (Huynh 1994). The family, not the individual, had legal status. Individual concerns were secondary. "There is no free individual; every facet of his life is bound up with the family," wrote Mai Huy Bích (1991, 50).

21 Nguyễn Thị Mai, "Nuôi con nuôi như thế nào? (Trao đổi kinh nghiệm)," *Báo Phụ nữ Thủ đô*, January 29, 1996.

22 Merav Shohet's (2013, 206) ethnographic research in central Vietnam indicates that mothers begin to "cultivate in their children the moral dispositions to *hy sinh* [sacrifice] when the children are quite young." Having observed a mother instruct her child on proper comportment, such as how to kowtow to a grandmother, Shohet remarks, "The toddler is developing a basic, embodied understanding of

the moral values and enacted symbols of her world even before she has full conscious and verbal command of what her actions entail" (211). I also witnessed such early childhood socialization in northern Vietnam; mothers instructed their children upon entering a house to respectfully greet all elderly people using appropriate kinship terms, such as *Bà* (Grandmother) and *Ông* (Grandfather), before running off to play. In addition to learning correct comportment, children were taught to memorize proverbs such as "The debt we owe our father is as great as Mount Thai; the debt we owe our mother is as inexhaustible as the streams that flow down from the mountains" (*Công cha như núi Thái Sơn Nghĩa mẹ như nước trong nguồn chảy ra*) or "When you eat the fruit, remember the person who planted it" (*Ăn quả nhớ người trồng cây*).

23 Hà Phương, "Hạnh phúc được làm mẹ," *Báo Tuổi trẻ*, April 25, 1996.

24 An entirely other issue is whether the parents of an adopted child will try to retrieve the child in the future. Such was the case for a female worker in the Vĩnh Phú forestry enterprise who had adopted a six-month-old girl (Nguyễn Thị Khoa 1993)

25 Also see Nguyễn Thị Khoa's (1993, 46) reference to the proverb "Different blood makes the heart stink."

26 "Khác máu tanh long," accessed November 30, 2020, https://www.youtube.com /watch?v=FUZYlrhuBuE; "Khác máu tanh long," accessed August 7, 2020, https:// www.webtretho.com/f/sach-truyen-tho/khac-mau-tanh-long-2410191; "Mẹ ơi, khác máu thanh lòng," accessed June 15, 2017, http://mevabe.vn/tam-su--tu -van/tam-su/me-oi-khac-mau-tanh-long-.html.

27 In 2017, when I inquired further about the phrase *khác máu tanh lòng*, no one I talked to recognized it. However, one person noted the use of *người tanh*, which translates as a fishy person: someone with such a negative nature that it can't be overcome and causes feelings of displeasure.

28 In 2014, the Vietnamese government lifted its ban on surrogacy, making it permissible for female relatives to be a surrogate. While placing less significance on maternal uterine identity, it preserves the importance of shared blood.

29 See also "Nuôi con bằng sữa mẹ: Trách nhiệm của cộng đồng," *Báo Tiền phong*, August 1, 1996.

30 Despite the film's portrayal of fatherly affinity toward his daughter, stories circulated around Hà Nội about children who sought out their biological fathers, only to be rebuked.

31 Thảo Mai, "Về việc chấm dứt việc nuôi con nuôi," *Báo Pháp luật*, November 15, 1994.

32 Hoài Xuân, "Cô Thanh Tâm thân mên," *Báo Phụ nữ Trung Ương*, January 29, 1996; Lê Thị Phương, "Hòm thư bạn gái," *Báo Phụ nữ Việt Nam*, July 13, 1992; Nguyễn Tiên Dâm, "Em muốn biết sự thật," *Báo Phụ nữ Việt Nam*, December 28, 1992.

CHAPTER 2. "WHEN WILL YOU GIVE OUT SWEETS?"

1 For the effects of differential recruitment policies during the American War and war mortality, see Merli 2000; Fitzgerald 1989; Guillemot 2009; Teerawichitchainan 2009.

2   The success of the DRV's call for youth to delay love is undermined by numerous accounts of wartime loves such as Nguyen Van Hai's (2012) *Women Driving the Hồ Chí Minh Trail*.

3   The three Trưng sisters (Hai Bà Trưng) were famous female heroes venerated for building and defending the Vietnamese nation against foreign aggressors. Appealing to female spirits that were considered "quintessentially" Vietnamese, mobilization efforts sought to bring together people from different walks of life to join the effort to reunite the nation (S. Taylor 1999, 386). The youth brigades, despite being disbanded after fighting the French, quickly reorganized to help in reconstruction of the DRV (Guillemot 2009).

4   Mortality estimates indicate that by the end of the Indochina wars, 10–20 percent of men and women who attempted the journey down the Hồ Chí Minh Trail died en route to the south as a result of bombing, malaria, tigers, bears, snake bites, poisonous mushrooms, drowning, or starvation (Guillemot 2009).

5   See Mai and Lê 1978; S. Taylor 1999; Turner 1998.

6   Murray Hiebert, "Single Mothers: Women in Men-Short Vietnam Are Having Children out of Wedlock," *Far East Economic Review*, February 24, 1994, 60.

7   Many of the women who headed to these northern forestry stations were from Thái Bình, Nam Định, or Hà Tây provinces. Most of the men from these Red River Delta regions had joined the fight against the Americans (Lê Thi 1987, 2005; Lê Thi, "Chăm sóc điều kiện sống và lao động của nữ công nhân lâm nghiệp," *Báo Nhân Dân*, April 6, 1987). Also see Dror 2018.

8   See Fforde 1987; Lê Ngọc Lân 1987, 1991, 1992; Liljeström 1987; and Ohlsson 1987.

9   Hiebert, "Single Mothers," 60.

10 Personal communications (1996) with social scientists at the Institute for Family and Gender Studies / Vietnam Academy of Social Sciences (previously Center for Scientific Research on Women and the Family) and female researchers at the Hà Nội Women's Union.

11 Kevin Doyle, "Vietnam's Forgotten Cambodian War," *BBC News*, September 14, 2014, https://www.bbc.com/news/world-asia-29106034. Also see Thayer 2019.

12 Michael Sullivan, "Ask the Vietnamese about War, and They Think China, Not the U.S.," *NPR*, May 1, 2015, https://www.npr.org/sections/parallels/2015/05/01/402572349/ask-the-vietnamese-about-war-and-they-think-china-not-the-u-s; cf. Merli 2000.

13 The "marriage squeeze" was strongest for the female cohort born between 1945 and 1950 (Goodkind 1997, 111).

14 The state's policy of *phân công* persisted into the 1990s for certain types of employment. Female elementary and secondary school teachers of Kinh ethnicity were assigned posts in remote rural areas of the country, in particular the mountainous highlands, to teach Vietnamese culture and language, as well as socialist ideals, to the children of minority peoples (Turner 1998). As a result, their opportunities for meeting potential and desirable spouses were extremely limited. Many saw their marriageable years slip away (Trần Kim Hương, "Hòm thư bạn gái," *Báo Phụ nữ Việt Nam*, July 15, 1991; Lê Anh Hoài, "Nỗi khó cô giáo vùng cao,"

Báo Phụ nữ Việt Nam, November 18, 1991; Lê Diễn, "Số phận các cô gái đồng bằng trên miền núi," *Báo Phụ nữ Việt Nam*, March 25, 1991).

15 *Hộ khẩu* remain indispensable for identification purposes: ID cards, passports, travel cards, birth and marriage and death certificates.

16 Research conducted in the northern part of the delta indicated that in the late 1990s, rural girls around age twenty-three were regarded as too old to marry. There were "100–200 girls of that age in every village. To get married, 'many rural girls [had] no choice but to either unconditionally accept marriage with men who [had] houses in the cities or move to cities to find jobs in hopes of building a family'" (Ha and Ha 2001, 59). In contrast, single women in southern Vietnam married transnationally in hopes of finding a suitable spouse (Thai 2008).

17 For example, *em* (younger sister), *chị* (older sister), *cháu* (niece), and *bà* (grand-mother) all translate the English pronoun "she." The terms are not gender specific for those younger than oneself; *em* and *cháu* are also used for males.

18 Thắm's attitude toward the appropriate ages for husbands and wives is also expressed by the proverb "An old husband and a young wife form a blessed couple, a young man and an old woman form an unfortunate match" (*Chồng già vợ trẻ là tiên, vợ già chồng trẻ là duyên nợ nần*).

19 David Lamb, "Vietnam's Women of War," *Los Angeles Times*, January 10, 2003.

20 Lamb, "Vietnam's Women of War."

21 War veteran Ngô Ngọc Bội's 1992 short story "Những mảnh vụn" (A blanket of scraps) depicts the effects of war and illnesses (e.g., malaria) on women's bodies (K. Werner 2017).

22 Thường Tín, "Một đời lặng lẽ yêu thương," *Báo Tiền Phong*, April 3, 1996.

23 H.L., "Hạnh phúc ấy quá mong manh" (That fragile happiness), *Báo Phụ nữ Việt Nam*, June 18, 1990.

24 This discussion on syncretic love is quoted from Phinney and Khuất (2013, 312–13).

25 For an extended discussion on the history of the politics of love in the north, see Phinney (2008).

26 The outlawing of polygamy eliminated a socially prescribed role that women in the past, perhaps grudgingly, had assumed. Despite its illegality, men have con-tinued to take a second wife either to have a son or if their wife is infertile (Luong 1989; Pashigian 2009a).

27 Engels saw the monogamous family as a form of exploitation, akin to the exploitation of the proletariat class by the bourgeoisie. Extrapolating, Engels aligned women with the proletariat, subject to the control of men, the bourgeoisie ([1884] 1995).

28 Article 11 requires that all marriages be recognized and registered with the state and declares all other marital unions or ceremonies invalid.

29 Compare Potter's discussion of legal marriage reform in China in 1953 and 1981. Although it became illegal to require someone to marry without consent, the laws in China did not specify romantic love as a necessary component of spousal choice. Rather, a marriage was to be based on "good feelings," which are those of "social responsibility and altruism" (Potter 1990, 190).

30 For in-depth discussions of Vietnamese concepts of fate, see Schafer (2010) and Gammeltoft (2014).

31 Clearly missing from this discussion is whether women "desired" men in the first place. In 1995 and 1996, I had tried to tease out whether women's reasons for not marrying might be because they preferred women. My queries were readily dismissed, though I was told a story about two women living together in Hà Nội under the pretense of being friends.

CÀ MAU

1 During the American War, Xóm Mũi was an important battlefield and was heavily bombed.

2 Note that he merely alludes to sexual relations but does not explicitly state that the women asked men for sex. Before the 1990s, when referring to sex, the Vietnamese media (and elderly people) "used formal words like relationship (quan hệ), intimate relationships (quan hệ luyến ái) or symbolic, euphemistic phrases such as rain and clouds (chuyện mây mưa), bedroom matter (chuyện phòng the), or mattress matter (chuyện giường chiếu)" (Khuat, Le, and Nguyen 2009, 33). The professor who told me this story was in his late sixties when I talked with him, and therefore old enough to have experienced this shift.

CHAPTER 3. *XIN CON*, "ASKING FOR A CHILD"

1 There were many reasons older single women who wanted a biological child did not ask for a child. I was often told that you had to be a certain kind of woman, one who was tough enough to withstand social opinion, the likelihood of being scorned, and the knowledge that your fatherless child might be teased at school. You also had to have the mental and physical strength to care for a child on your own.

2 When I asked women who had given birth if they would marry should the opportunity arise, they said they would not. Minh (born in 1958), who rejected a marriage proposal after she asked for a child, said, "I wanted to reserve all of my love for my child." She echoed many women's feelings that men could not adequately love and care for a child who was not their own biological child.

3 Determining intent structured my research methodology: I was able to identify women who had asked for a child based on their age, marital status, and age at first birth. If women gave birth after what was considered marriageable age, then it was likely they had asked for a child. Having identified women with whom to speak, I then clarified in our discussions that they in fact had asked for a child after they considered themselves to be past marriageable age.

4 Note that the women appealed to the state and to their rights after the passing of the new 1986 Law on Marriage and the Family, which was widely interpreted as recognizing all women's right to have a biological child.

5 For research on the differences between women initiating, joking, and talking about sex, see Khuất, Lê, and Nguyễn (2009).

6 "During the war, because these [tứ đức] precepts were inconsistent with ideas of the 'new socialist woman,' the Party sought to modify them in order to mobilize women for the war. During the war women were praised for enacting what were considered to be more masculine qualities such as being 'heroic, indomitable, loyal, and resourceful.' After the war, these characteristics were gradually replaced in public discourse with 'loyal, gentle, elegant, tactful and resourceful'" (T. N. B. Ngo 2004, 52–53). Nonetheless, girls were still taught to embody (tu duc) precepts (Rydström 1998).

7 In vitro fertilization (IVF) first became available in Hồ Chí Minh City in 1997, and the first IVF birth was in 1998. The first sperm bank opened in Hà Nội in 2002; I was told that married women had priority due to the limited supply of sperm.

8 Women's Union officials corroborated Bích's assertion by explaining that if men were going to look for someone to have sex with, it would not have been older women; they preferred younger women.

9 Another well-educated Hà Nội woman I met, also from a family of high social standing and working for a state agency, encountered similar difficulties; her parents advised her to get married and be done with it so she could have a child.

10 A child needs a birth certificate to enroll in primary school, take exams, work, apply for social insurance, and prove her right to inheritance, as well as for basic legal protection.

11 Vợ hai is distinguished from vợ kế, which is a second legitimate (legal) wife by a later marriage (the man having been widowed or divorced). The nineteenth-century Gia Long Legal Code distinguished between vợ cả (first wife and legal spouse), vợ hai (second wife), and vợ lẽ (concubine). A ceremony took place recognizing the rank of a second wife, who was chosen not by her husband but by the first wife. A concubine was brought into the house without any formal ritual (Pashigian 2009a). Given that taking a second wife has been illegal since 1959, it is not clear whether this prior moral distinction between second wives and concubines remains; otherwise why would a woman refer to herself as a concubine?

12 Having "married" for the purposes of entering what they may have felt to be a more socially acceptable or financially secure relationship, the women nonetheless would be unable to secure the support of the state should the man abandon his responsibilities. Women's Union advice columnists and cadres worried that a man who wanted a boy would take advantage of older single women. This was considered especially true of men whose wives were infertile (Minh Phương, "Chị Thanh Tâm kính mến," Báo Phụ nữ Việt Nam, August 26, 1993).

13 Where do second wives or concubines live? Anthropologist Hy Van Luong's research indicates that in the early 1900s a man kept his "surviving wives and sons living with him under one household," but fifty years later, when polygyny was no longer legal, a man would "set up separate households upon getting married" (Luong 1989, 744). This latter residence pattern remains evident today, though it is not

recognized by the state as a legitimate marriage; the extent to which people do warrants further research. How does a man find a second wife? Practices have varied. In some cases, a man asked his wife to find him a second wife. In other cases, a wife went looking herself or told her husband to do so. Single women who asked for a child benefited from these culturally recognized polygamous kinship practices.

14 Years later, with the advent of IVF, Melissa Pashigian (2009a, 40) would write that married women secretly use donor sperm if they suspect their husbands are infertile. It is a "generally well-kept secret between a woman and her doctor."

15 For discussion of Agent Orange, see Black 2019; Gammeltoft 2014; Rydström 2010; Ariel Garfinkel, "Vietnam '67: The Vietnam War Is Over; The Bombs Remain," *New York Times*, March 20, 2018.

16 These stories of infertile men stand in stark contrast to the stories of infertile women I was told in the mid-1990s. As in Ngọc's case, some wives encouraged their husbands to take a second wife. In other instances, wives suffered their husband's decision to take a second wife. In some cases, men asked their wives for a divorce so they could remarry. I was told a story about a woman whose husband's family offered her $1,000 to divorce their son so that he could marry someone else and have children. She agreed to the divorce but not the money. Although her former in-laws watched after her, she regretted her decision to divorce. Not all men, however, decide that childbearing is more important than being with their wife and refuse to divorce or take a second wife.

17 Evelyn Blackwood (2005), critiquing the concept of the "absent presence" of the "patriarchal man," points out that even a man's absence structures the narrative around men and in so doing maintains heteronormativity.

18 For the same reason, women in other communes and provinces cut off relations with the man who got them pregnant (Lê Nhâm 1994; Nguyễn Thị Khoa 1993; Lê Thi 1993).

19 Lê Thi's (2005, 10) research, conducted between 1988 and 1990 in forestry stations in the northern provinces, found that "some men had fallen deeply in love and continued the affair, providing support to [the] single women and their children. In some cases, the man's wife and relatives paid visits to the woman and offered additional support. This was especially likely to occur if the woman gave birth to a boy who the man's family expected to take and raise as one of their own. In this case, the [single] woman had a luckier fate than most."

20 Reproductive choices are often embedded in and informed by unequally stratified social and economic relations (Colen 1995; Geronimus 2003; Ginsburg and Rapp 1995b). Older Vietnamese women who wanted to ask for a child were limited in their mobility, their resources, and the available men whom they could or wanted to ask. It would be misleading to portray women's agency in terms of unfettered reproductive autonomy; it obviously required men's consent and the ability to locate men, and the time and space necessary to have enough sexual encounters to get pregnant.

21 For this reason (that women would not reveal the identity of the man who got them pregnant), I was unable to interview any of the biological fathers.

22 Having agreed to take full responsibility for the child and promising not to reveal the man's identity, women had to decide what *họ* (family name) to give their child and to list on the child's birth registration (*khai sinh*). In Vietnam, when a woman marries she becomes part of her husband's family but retains her father's *họ*, while her children are given her husband's *họ*. They belong to his family, not hers. Single women, not bound by convention, could give their child their own father's *họ* or that of the biological father; it was their choice. Given that there are only about a hundred Kinh surnames in Vietnam (with Nguyễn by far the most common), many people share the same last name, so naming the child was not an issue. Women who intended to maintain relations with the father, such as Quỳnh or more commonly those who became a concubine or second wife, chose to give their child the biological father's name. In cases where a man had a second wife in the hope she would give birth to a boy, the boy certainly would be given the biological father's *họ* so he could pass down the man's lineage. Other than these situations, there was no discernible pattern in women's naming decisions. There was no correlation between *họ* and the sex of the child. There was no correlation between *họ* and the man's residence: whether he lived nearby or elsewhere. Nor was there a correlation between *họ* and whether women asked for a child before or after the 1986 Law on Marriage and the Family. In some cases it did not matter because the woman and the man shared the same *họ*.

23 Anthropologist Martha Kahn's (2000, 44) remarks regarding single women's use of artificial insemination in Israel during the mid-1990s more or less align with Vietnamese women who asked for a child: "Unmarried Israeli women who have children through artificial insemination are not necessarily motivated by a desire to undermine traditional family ideologies or to raise their children outside regular, informal childcare networks; nor do they necessarily understand their reproductive agency as a threat to these ideologies or networks" (cf. Weston 1991).

24 A social science researcher from VASS recounted in 2017 that when she was younger, rural villagers with whom she conducted research encouraged her to ask for a child. She declined to do so but felt that the frequency with which she received this advice indicated that *xin con* was considered an acceptable means for older single women in rural areas to have a child.

25 One of the best-known examples, other than state enterprises, where there are large concentrations of women who are raising children without men is the village of Làng Lôi, in central Vietnam (Julie Cohn, "A Tiny Village Where Women Choose to Be Single Mothers," *New York Times*, February 14, 2013).

26 Other women who worked for the Women's Union also sought approval from their superiors or from the district authority in charge of spiritual and cultural affairs prior to getting pregnant. Prior to Đổi Mới, state employees' personal and professional lives were circumscribed by the dictates of the *công đoàn* (trade union). Women who were familiar with military life (especially *thanh niên xung phong*) were in the habit of informing (*báo cáo*) their superiors about their plans. By 1996 the *công đoàn* still existed but no longer had the same responsibilities and control over its employees' lives as it had in the past.

27 Hồng Minh, "Bạn gái thân mên," *Báo Phụ nữ Việt Nam*, July 19, 1993; Thanh Hông, "Chị Thanh Tâm kính mến," *Báo Phụ nữ Việt Nam*, March 12, 1990.

28 One of the two social developments Winter highlights is the creation of "fictive kinships": alternative kinship networks that enabled people to deal with bereavement. Heonik Kwon (2008, 84) writes that Winter's "account of 'fictive kinship' shows not only how the destructive event of war shatters the integrity of intimate human communal lives but also how the morality of kinship . . . may extend to a wider normative horizon of civil solidarity and human kinship." The gradual acceptance of *xin con* may well illustrate a similar social process.

29 For example, to enable women to participate in the revolution, the government established crèches and primary and secondary education for children, thereby reducing women's childcare duties. The development of the massive state sector since the 1960s created the conditions for women to enter training programs, work, reside, and create networking communities with people outside their extended family networks. During the 1980s state agencies provided collective housing for their staff. Working for the state also enabled women to earn a stable income, albeit small. Earning one's own income and living in state cooperative housing provided single women a bit of independence from their families.

30 See Nhung Tuyet Tran's (2018) historical analysis of how women in early modern Vietnam drew on and subverted patriarchal laws and cultural practices to their own advantage.

CHAPTER 4. GOVERNING *XIN CON*

1 CSRW was initially named the Center for Women's Studies, itself the successor to the Programme of Social Research on Women established in 1985. Lê Thi was director of CSRW from 1987 to 1997. The name was subsequently changed to the Institute for Family and Gender Studies (IFGS) and is part of the Vietnamese Academy of Social Sciences (VASS). Given the time period, I refer to it as CSRW.

2 The tale of Bà Đế has since been written down. The story line varies depending on the website but now portrays the encounter between the king and the girl as a love story, which was not how I heard Lê Thi recount the tale to me in 1996 (see Thành Văn, "Chuyện tình bi thương giữa chúa Trịnh và cô gái cắt cỏ," *Người Đưa tin*, December 28, 2012, https://www.nguoiduatin.vn/chuyen-tinh-bi-thuong-giua-chua-trinh-va-co-gai-cat-co-a14297.html). In 2017 the old Bà Đế temple was no longer visible, but a new, elaborate temple complex dedicated to Bà Đế had been built. Families travel to the temple to pray for assistance for family members who have fallen victim to unfortunate circumstances. It is also promoted as a tourist destination. Đồ Sơn was once a poor fishing village, nowadays it is in Ngọc Hải Ward, Đồ Sơn District, in the city of Hải Phòng.

3 And yet it is necessary to recognize that "the forms of self-cultivation emergent in the context of late socialism mean new things when situated in a dramatically transformed context" (Harms 2012, 412).

4 Nguyễn Thị Định, "Vấn đề bảo vệ quyền lợi phụ nữ trong Luật Hôn Nhân và Gia Đình," *Báo Nhân Dân*, August 13, 1986; Thế Lan, "Chính sách bảo vệ bà mẹ và trẻ em trong dự thảo Luật Hôn Nhân và Gia Đình," *Báo Nhân Dân*, August 27, 1986; "Có những vấn đề gì đặt ra trong hôn nhân và gia đình?," *Báo Nhân Dân*, March 7, 1986; "Xây dựng gia đình hạnh phúc, dân chủ và hòa thuận," *Báo Nhân Dân*, June 27, 1986.

5 The 1959 law had six chapters and thirty-five legal articles, whereas the 1986 law had ten chapters and fifty-seven legal articles. For a detailed explication of the changes embodied in the 1986 law, see Nguyễn Hữu Minh 2009; Nguyễn Thanh Tâm 1991; Nguyễn Thị Định, "Vấn đề bảo vệ quyền lợi phụ nữ trong Luật Hôn Nhân và Gia Đình," *Báo Nhân Dân*, August 13, 1986; Nguyễn Thế Giai 1993; "Có những vấn đề gì đặt ra trong hôn nhân và gia đình?," *Báo Nhân Dân*, March 7, 1986; "Xây dựng gia đình hạnh phúc, dân chủ và hòa thuận," *Báo Nhân Dân*, June 27, 1986; Dư Huệ Liên, "Về Vấn đề hôn nhân và gia đình," *Báo Nhân Dân*, January 12, 1987; Nguyễn Thế Giai, "Pháp luật: Hình mẫu gia đình xã hội chủ nghĩa qua Luật Hôn Nhân và Gia Đình," *Báo Nhân Dân*, January 23, 1987.

6 "Chính sách bảo vệ bà mẹ và trẻ em trong dự thảo Luật Hôn Nhân và Gia Đình," *Báo Nhân Dân*, August 27, 1986.

7 "Có những vấn đề gì đặt ra trong hôn nhân và gia đình?," *Báo Nhân Dân*, March 7, 1986.

8 "Vấn đề bảo vệ quyền lợi phụ nữ trong Luật Hôn Nhân và Gia Đình," *Báo Nhân Dân*, August 13, 1986, 2.

9 Võ Xuân Phong, "Chị Thanh Tâm kính mến," *Báo Phụ nữ Việt Nam*, February 12, 1990; Hồng Dương, "Bàn thêm về các trường hợp: Con ngoài giá thú," *Báo Pháp luật* (Số Đặc Biệt), January 1991.

10 Lê Thị Nhâm Tuyết wondered what problems asking for a child would cause for married couples and whether it would contribute to a rise in polygnous marriages, widely viewed as a "feudal" practice (quoted in Tran and Le 1997, 175). Her concern is in contradistinction to advocates for the law who worried that *not* providing single women with maternal rights would prompt them to become second wives. A lawyer working on the 2014 Law on Marriage and the Family stated that while the government may see the necessity of enacting a new law (such as gay marriage), they hold off until they feel society is ready for such a law. Indeed, the government took incremental steps from that point on to lift the ban on same-sex marriage in 2015.

11 Hoàng Hương, "Người đàn bà không chồng," *Báo Phụ nữ Thủ đô*, December 15, 1993.

12 It is illuminating to compare the Vietnamese government's response to another postwar predicament in which there was high male mortality, leaving women without men to marry. In post-WWII Russia the demographic sex imbalance, declining fertility rates, and negative population growth prompted the Soviet leadership to implement pronatalist policies that encouraged all women, married and single, to have children (Bucher 2000). To increase the population, Soviet officials "encouraged all women to bear children. . . . [I]t encouraged men to impregnate unmarried women, or at least encouraged men to sire more children than they could afford to support" (Utrata 2015, 26). The Vietnamese 1986 Law on

Marriage and the Family was not a pronatalist policy in the sense that it sought to encourage women to have more children. The concomitant Happy Family Campaign encouraged married couples to have just two children. Despite high male mortality during the war with the Americans, the fertility rate had not dropped.

13 Nguyễn Thị Định, "Vấn đề bảo vệ quyền lợi phụ nữ trong Luật Hôn Nhân và Gia Đình," *Báo Nhân Dân*, August 13, 1986, 2.

14 See Nguyễn Thị Khoa 1993; Nguyễn Thanh Tâm 1991; Thế Lan, "Chính sách bảo vệ bà mẹ và trẻ em trong dự thảo Luật Hôn Nhân và Gia Đình," *Báo Nhân Dân*, August 27, 1986.

15 The 1959 Law on Marriage and the Family also had provisions on determining parentage under Chapter IV ("Relations between Parents and their Children"), Articles 21, 22, 23. In 1961 a circular stating that all children born out of wedlock could be registered at birth without stating the father's identity was instituted as an addition to existing clauses relating to children born out of wedlock (Thanh Tú, "Cần có điều kiện gì để khai sinh cho con ngoài thú?," *Báo Pháp luật*, September 26, 1989).

16 Prior to the August 1945 Revolution, neither Vietnamese nor French colonial law gave children born out of wedlock the right to ask for recognition of their father or mother before the courts (Nguyễn Thế Giai 1993, 97).

17 Promulgation of the articles reflected the poor familial and social living conditions children without fathers suffered. Newspaper articles I collected from the mid-1980s to the mid-1990s portrayed maltreatment of fatherless children. Phong Huyền wrote a short story, "Loang loáng ánh trăng" (The diffuse light of the moon), about the miserable life of a child whose father died during the war (*Báo Tiên Phong*, September 3, 1991). The parents had fallen in love but did not have a chance to marry due to the war. The woman got pregnant, but her boyfriend died before he knew he was going to be the father of a child. The woman raised the child, but the child was incessantly teased as a "bastard" (*con hoang*). Mai Thanh Thủy wrote the short story "Đứa trẻ và biển xanh" (The child and the green sea), portraying the similar situation of a girl who suffered severely from criticism by people around her because she did not have a father (*Báo Tiên Phong*, April 2, 1991). And in 1994, Pham Xuân Đào wrote an account of the unjust behavior people directed toward a girl who did not have a father. Unable to bear this constant burden, the girl committed suicide. Pham Xuân Đào's article, titled "Đừng khía vào vết thương lòng..." (Don't cut deep into a wounded heart...), evoked the misery fatherless children experienced (*Báo Tiên Phong*, September 20, 1994). Publication of journalistic accounts and short stories was meant, I was told, to encourage society to look more carefully at its inhumane treatment of fatherless children in the hope that people would develop sympathy for them and incorporate them into social life.

18 Increased state control is also evident in "Articles Protecting Mothers and Children," which adds a number of regulations specifying mothers', fathers', and children's duties and rights. It also differentiates between different kinds of children.

19 "Trả lời: Giải đáp pháp luật—Sinh con ngoài giá thú có bị buộc thôi việc không?," *Báo Phụ nữ Việt Nam*, March 23, 1992, 3.

20 "Có những vấn đề gì đặt ra trong hôn nhân và gia đình?," *Báo Nhân Dân*, March 7, 1986; "Xây dựng gia đình hạnh phúc, dân chủ và hòa thuận," *Báo Nhân Dân*, June 27, 1986. One of the fundamental functions of the Women's Union since its inception in 1946 has been to help women organize family life. Over time, it has launched numerous political movements to orient and organize women for specific political and social ends. At the Fourth Women's Union Congress in 1974, the union considered "the molding of the new socialist woman" as its "fundamental task" (Vietnam Women's Union and Center for Women's Studies 1989, 174). Specifically, it resolved to "educate mothers to realize their great responsibilities in the ideological and cultural revolution and in the formation of future generations, show them how to bring up children according to scientific methods and encourage them to set good examples to their children in the family and in society" (175). "Women must be helped to organize their family affairs in a scientific way, to lead lives that conform with the general situation in the country, to create conditions for everyone to discharge . . . their responsibility to society" (180).

21 CSRW worked closely with SIDA (Swedish International Development Agency) to conduct research in state enterprises where the Swedish government had provided developmental assistance.

22 While governments enact laws to set conditions and define parameters, they do not control how the law is interpreted, nor its effects. For some single mothers, the 1986 law helped ease relationships with family members. For others, it meant no longer being treated with disdain or criticism, but rather being acknowledged for having made the right decision. For Quỳnh and Lý, the law prompted them to go ahead and ask for a child. But many single mothers still suffered from social condemnation.

23 "An important cautionary note that Foucault introduces in all his work is that elements of a strategy cannot be functionally reduced to the overall strategy in which they end up participating" (Ransom 1997, 70). The cautionary remark I made in chapter 3 with regard to single women's intention to ask for a child holds true here. "There is no single, all-encompassing rationality that determines the shape and content of historical objects. Rather, different rationalities meet in a determinate historical landscape and establish coalitions for the pursuit of aims that, for a time at least, complement one another" (70).

24 In 1995 and 1996, friends and acquaintances working for NGOs would occasionally return from field site visits relaying stories confirming that Women's Union cadres and leaders had asked for a child. Also see Lê Nhâm (1994).

25 This statement and the ensuing discussion regarding the newspaper editors' motives and reasons surrounding Chị Thanh Tâm and the newspaper discussion forums are based on private discussions I had with one of the editors of *Báo Phụ nữ Việt Nam* in 1996.

26 Articles targeting a female audience were published in newspapers such as *Báo Phụ nữ Việt Nam* (Vietnamese women's newspaper), the official newspaper of the National Women's Union, and *Báo Phụ nữ Thủ đô* (Capital city women's newspaper), the official newspaper of the Hà Nội Women's Union. Articles targeting

a broader audience, including men, appeared in *Báo Pháp luật* (Legal news) and *Báo Tuổi trẻ* (Youth news).

27 *Báo Phụ nữ Thủ đô*, October 20, 1990.

28 "Hạnh phúc của những người phụ nữ cô đơn," *Báo Phụ nữ Việt Nam*, March 9, 1992.

29 "Chia sẻ sự đồng cảm với những phụ nữ đơn thân," *Báo Pháp luật*, March 2, 1993.

30 A second line of discussion emerged in newspapers that countered the idea that single women could not be happy living alone, as well as an insidious notion that they were alone because they were not good people (Hồng Liên, "Chúng tôi mong muốn được làm mẹ!," *Báo Phụ nữ Việt Nam*, December 14, 1988; Lưu Đình Triều and Hữu Thiện, "Hạnh phúc một mình?," *Báo Tuổi trẻ*, July 13, 1992; Giang Thu, "Lại nói về những người phụ nữ cô đơn," *Báo Phụ nữ Việt Nam*, April 1, 1991; Thanh Dám, "Khi hôn nhân không với tới," *Báo Phụ nữ Việt Nam*, September 30, 1991; Lê Nguyên Ngữ, "Nắng muộn," *Báo Phụ nư Việt Nam*, July 13, 1992; Phạm Hà, "Những mảnh đời cô đơn," *Báo Phụ nư Việt Nam*, April 8, 1996; Nguyễn Châu Khanh, "Một vài ý kiến về 'Những mảnh đời cô đơn,'" *Báo Phụ nữ Việt Nam*, May 13, 1996). According to the author of "Duyên muộn" (Late love), an opinion piece published in *Báo Phụ nữ Việt Nam* on April 9, 1990, many people had the misperception that single women were somehow bad people who had committed a sin or a crime, that they had some sort of psychological problem. Vân Thanh (1992) called attention to the abuse older single women endured, mostly from men. She asked, "What can be done to stop the hatred and resentment" of "women who live alone"?

31 Khuất Thu Hồng (1998, 25) describes the situation during the 1960s and 1970s as follows:

> Society struggled for free love between men and women Yet, at the same time, it sharply condemned extra-marital sexual relations, regarding it as a serious crime. . . . If discovered, people would be severely punished and, as a result, they could never recover their social standing and dignity in the eyes of others. If they were Party members or members of the Youth Union, they would be expelled. If they were local leaders, they would be demoted. Rank and file employees and workers faced enormous danger of being fired and sent back to their home village. These penalties do not begin to tell of the public scorn and the loss of friends, and sometimes families. In rural areas, the consequences of an "illegitimate" love were much more serious, particularly for women.

32 Cơ Quan Y Bắc Thái, "Chị Thanh Tâm kính mến," *Báo Phụ nữ Việt Nam*, May 3, 1989. Office Y was not the real name of the office but an alias.

33 Ngọc Văn, "Bàn về vấn đề con ngoài giá thú," *Báo Phụ nữ Việt Nam*, June 28, 1989.

34 The accounts I refer to are as follows: In 1989, a girl who had moved to Hà Nội to live with her female teacher wrote asking Chị Thanh Tâm's advice regarding the relationship between her teacher and her father (Cháu của cô Quốc Hải, "Cô Thanh Tám kính mến," *Báo Phụ nữ Việt Nam*, August 25, 1989). The teacher told the girl that she had asked the girl's father for a child. The girl, disheartened and mortified that her father had had adulterous relations with her teacher, wanted

to know what to do: should she inform her mother and move out of the teacher's house? Chị Thanh Tâm reminded the girl that the teacher has a right to have a child to take care of her in her old age, but the teacher does not have the right to bring prejudice or harm to another person's family. Chị Thanh Tâm stated that "clearly the father lacked good judgment" by establishing a relationship with a woman with whom his daughter resided. Nor did he have the right to betray his wife and child by continuing the relationship. She stressed that it was the father's responsibility to terminate the relationship with the teacher and go back to his own family. However, the girl should not turn her back on the teacher because the teacher now had a child and was happy.

In 1990 Võ Xuân Phong wrote to Chị Thanh Tâm explaining that his wife had recently found out that he helped a single woman get pregnant ("Chị Thanh Tâm kính mến," *Báo Phụ nữ Việt Nam*, February 12, 1990). Phong had met the woman a long time earlier in the Trường Sơn Mountains; she loved him then and still did, so she asked him for a child. Hesitant at first, he eventually agreed because she was lonely and just living with her mother, who was getting old. Then his wife found out. Phong regretted his action and wanted to know how he should explain himself to his wife. Chị Thanh Tâm responded that if Phong's wife was a good person, if she had "heartfelt sympathy," then she would understand another woman's "eager need to become a mother." Chị Thanh Tâm explained that the "need to be a mother is a woman's instinct, it is natural [*thiên bẩm*]." "Now after many years of dedicating their youth to strengthening the country," many single women are "sad, feel self-pity, and are miserable because they cannot build a family and become a mother." Therefore, Chị Thanh Tâm advised Phong to explain the situation to his wife and his children. He should explain that his relationship with the woman was not a love affair and remind them that they "have many riches and the single woman has few." She then advised him to decide how he planned to help the child he begat, and when he did, to tell everyone so it was out in the open.

In 1991, Hoàng Văn wrote to Chị Thanh Tâm for advice ("Chị Thanh Tâm kính mến," *Báo Phụ nữ Việt Nam*, September 14, 1991). Văn began his letter by stating that he had married for love and continued to love his wife and four girls very much. But his parents wanted a son to pass down the lineage. When he heard about a single woman in his village who was "too ugly" to marry but wanted a child, he approached her. She gave birth to a boy. Afterward, everyone in the village, including his wife, claimed that the child must be his because it looked just like him. What should he do? Chị Thanh Tâm responded that it was clear he was a good husband and a responsible father. She advised him to tell his wife the truth; if he was open and honest with his wife, she would sympathize with the single woman and trust her husband more. "You need to make her realize that the other woman does not want to steal you away. Tell your wife the situation so she can understand. She will have sympathy with Cô N. Later you can decide if you want to recognize the child."

35 Hồng Liên's article "Hai phụ nữ" (Two women) related the story of a wife who learned her husband had agreed to impregnate an older single woman (*Báo Phụ*

nữ Việt Nam, August 9, 1989). After giving birth to a boy, the single woman asked for a work transfer in order to move away from the man and his family. The wife searched for the woman so she could learn more about her. Having found her, the wife realized that the single woman was a good person and developed admiration for her. There the story ends.

36 "Chị Thanh Tâm thân mến," *Báo Phụ nữ Việt Nam*, June 7, 1989.

37 Notably, I did not find any newspaper articles from 1986–96 in which wives accused their husbands of being led by lust rather than sympathy and charity. What should I make of the absence of such discussions? Perhaps it represents a form of biopower that extends to both wives and husbands: wives *should* respond sympathetically to single women's desires, whereas husbands are more lightly subjectified, their desires merely channeled in a more proper direction.

38 "In his 1982 essay 'The subject and power' Foucault affirms . . . that power is only power (rather than physical force or violence) when addressed to individuals who are free to act one way or another. Power is defined as 'actions on other's actions'; that is, it presupposes rather than annuls their capacity as agents; it acts upon, and through, an open set of practical and ethical possibilities" (Gordon 1991, 5).

39 It would be a mistake to paint American policy regarding single motherhood in static terms; it is far more mercurial, subject to who is in control of Congress and the White House. Despite American programs and policies designed to stem the tide of single motherhood, in 2005 "one out of every three children [were] born to an unmarried mother" (Hertz 2006, xv). This suggests that punitive approaches have not effectively governed the desires of the populace.

40 It would be naive to glamorize or romanticize the Vietnamese government's population agenda. I certainly would not argue that every policy or even every population policy has been based on its citizens' desires. Indeed, prior to the early 2000s the government implemented a top-down approach to population control that limited couples to bearing two children—leading in some provinces to extremely high abortion rates and use of IUDs. Single mothers were subject to this same policy.

41 Opposition to Confucian orthodoxy and calls for leniency are evident throughout Vietnamese literature. The most famous example is the eighteenth-century poetess Hồ Xuân Hương, who wrote a number of poems defending "unmarried mothers at a time when society violently disapproved any illegal union" (Nguyen Khac Vien and Huu Ngoc n.d., 327). In the mid-1990s, the writer Hồ Anh Thái portrayed and critiqued the cruel, callous prejudices to which unmarried pregnant women were subjected in his novel *Người đàn bà trên đảo* (The women on the island), first published in Vietnamese in 1988, reissued as *Vot mai mot ngon roi* (Whittling the point of the whip) in 1996, and made into an audio book in 2017.

42 Lan's decision to emulate a more senior Women's Union official is telling given that Women's Union officials were supposed to be models for the rest of society. During the collectivist era, "all party members shared a special responsibility to serve as 'models' (*gương mẫu*) for other residents to follow. Drawing on the Confucian principle of '*ching giao*,' party members had to provide lived examples of the

new morality and customs," signified by the slogan "'Party members go first, the nation follows' (*Đảng viên đi trước, làng nước theo sau*)" (Malarney 2002, 64). This is an example of Vietnamese governmentality at this moment in time; instead of repressing single women's maternal desires, government authority figures embraced the women's agency and in doing so modeled social change.

43 A younger woman's refusal to do so was considered foolish, and her love for her boyfriend portrayed as innocent and naive. Such women were treated harshly by their parents, looked down upon by their communities, and only grudgingly provided assistance. Two women I interviewed in 1996 spoke of such treatment. Hằng was thrown out of her house and disowned by her family after she unintentionally got pregnant by a boyfriend who would not marry her. Điệp, single and pregnant at age twenty-five, was told she could not give birth in her parents' house. She had to find another villager willing to let her do so. Her family did not help at all but did eventually develop *tình cảm* for her child.

44 At the same time as government authorities acknowledged older single women's reproductive space, the boundaries of permissibility they drew delineated and constructed a new social problem and, in doing so, another identity group: teenage mothers. Whereas an unmarried teen mother (and by extension her family) would likely have been the subject of gossip in the past, she too is now researched. Her identity congeals as it becomes specified and defined, part of another population discourse in which young unmarried women were pressured to get an abortion (cf. Nguyen, Shiu, and Farber 2016). The opening up of reproductive space for older women was thus linked to the creation of a new category of person.

45 The book is a compilation of articles based on collaborative research that investigated the status of different types of families: workers, farmers, intellectuals, young couples, and ethnic minorities in north, central, and southern Vietnam (Lê Thị 1991).

46 *Cô đơn* can be translated as either "alone" or "lonely"; depending on the context, if people are alone they may be considered to be lonely. This was the attitude of women I spoke with in the mid-1990s. More contemporary usages of *cô đơn* might not assume women living alone would be lonely.

47 "Toàn bộ những yếu tố trên đã bổ sung cho xã hội gương mặt gia đình mới: Gia đình chỉ bao gồm người mẹ và đứa con sống với nhau mà chúng ta tạm gọi là những gia đình thiếu, vắng chồng."

48 This is a direct translation provided by a native Vietnamese speaker.

49 In the 1996 volume Lê Thị first presents an overview of the situations of women who were lacking or missing husbands in northern Vietnam. Nguyễn Thị Khoa's chapter, "Tình cảnh *éo le* của những gia *đình* phụ nữ không chồng có con" (The awkward/tragic situation of women without husbands who have a child), provides an in-depth discussion of the situation of women who had borne children out of wedlock, with a particular focus on older women who had asked for a child. The discussion was based on research conducted in Tuyên Quang, Vĩnh Phú, Nam Hà, and Bắc Thái Provinces. The women she discusses were predominantly the

thanh niên xung phong who overcame their single status to enjoy the "happiness of being a mother" (Nguyễn Thị Khoa 1996, 129).

50 The book was translated into English in 2005 and published by Thế Giới Publishers. In the English translation, Lê Thi argues for single mothers' maternal rights by situating them within the larger international discourse on human rights and gender equality (Lê Thi 2005, 14–15).

51 Based on my attendance at the International Workshop on Vietnamese Families in the Context of Industrialization, Modernization and Integration in Comparative Perspective organized by the Institute for Family and Gender Studies in Hà Nội in 2013, at which Lê Thi was present, I think it would be fair to assert that Lê Thi would not encourage women to become single mothers. However, once they have done so, they and their children should be treated in a respectful manner.

52 Foucault states that "there are two meanings of the word 'subject': subject to someone else by control and dependence, and tied to his own identity by a conscience or self-knowledge. Both meanings suggest a form of power that subjugates and makes subject to" (Foucault 2000, 331).

53 There were earlier and ongoing calls for the state to improve the social lives of the large number of still marriageable women living in isolated rural areas. Suggestions included relocating women to less isolated areas, encouraging them to submit personal ads in the newspaper (some women did find husbands this way), and organizing social events and clubs for women to meet men (Lê Thị, "Chăm sóc điều kiện sống và lao động của nữ công nhân lâm nghiệp," *Báo Nhân dân*, April 6, 1987; Mỹ Hằng and Trầng Đức Thắng, "Một vấn để xã hội bước đầu được giải quyết," *Báo Lao động*, March 5, 1987; Kỷ An, "Cầu vồng hạnh phúc," *Báo Tiền Phong*, April 14, 1987; Kiều Thư, "Quá lứa, lỡ thì dười tuổi 30(?!)," *Báo Tiền Phong*, December 11, 1990; Đỗ Minh Cương, "Hội độc thân," *Báo Tiền Phong*, October 23, 1990; Đỗ Minh Cương, "Về những 'Hội độc thân,'" *Báo Tiên Phong*, December 18, 1990).

54 Women borrowed money to raise pigs or chickens, buy a sewing machine, renovate the house, buy fertilizer, or pay medical expenses.

55 The Vietnamese Bank of Agriculture (VBA) operated a poverty alleviation program through the commune People's Committee, but few people received a loan. In Sóc Sơn, there was an informal system for providing one another credit in times of difficulty. According to DEVAID (1996), poor farmers and single women received little help from their neighbors or relatives. Cash could be borrowed from local moneylenders at a high interest rate. There were also cases of revolving funds where five or six women, usually close friends or relatives, formed a group. Yet these were generally women who were married or widowed.

56 Personal communication, Women's Union employee.

57 For a current image of *Me Viet Nam*, see the museum website: https://baotangphunu .org.vn/gioi-thieu/.

58 In the 1960s and 1970s women were criticized "for wearing lipstick and make-up and for having clothes or hairstyles similar to Western women, [and] behavior [that] was seen as representing the lazy, carefree lifestyle of the exploitative

classes. . . . Women's interest in fashion was regarded as 'sexual provocation' while sexual desire was considered base and animal-like" (Khuất 1998, 24).

59 Mai Uyen Linh, "Women's Place," *Vietnam Investment Review*, February 19, 1996, 34.

60 According to Althusser, "Ideology 'acts' or 'functions' in such a way that it 'recruits' subjects among the individuals . . . or 'transforms' the individuals into subjects (it transforms them all) by that very precise operation which I have called interpellation or hailing" (Althusser 1971, 174). Interpellation, a process of subjectification, assumes a monolithic or totalistic understanding of state power in which women unknowingly internalize dominant societal norms (cf. Kuan 2015). However, as single women who asked for a child demonstrate, ideological projects are never hegemonic; even if there are points of recognition in an encounter of being hailed, there is potential for a "variety of unpredictable effects" (England 2019, 19).

61 For analyses of efforts to forge a relationship between motherhood and the nation from the colonial era to the mid-twenty-first century, see Tai 1992; Mai and Lê 1978; Marr 1981; Pelly 2002; Pettus 2003; T.L. Nguyen 2016; Womack 1996.

62 The book is online at http://baotangphunu.org.vn/Tin-tuc/277/chuyen-nhung-ba -me-don-than.

63 Three themes structure the women's stories. In "The Context of Their Lives" the women explain how they came to be single mothers and briefly tell of their personal and financial struggles. In "Points We'd Like to Make" they focus their discussion of family life on how they earn a living. And in "A Community Shares" fellow neighbors and villagers discuss how their understanding of and attitudes toward single mothers have changed.

CHAPTER 5. "THIS WAS MY CHOICE. IT IS MY LIFE."

1 The show's name derives from Gabriel García Márquez's 1985 novel, *Love in the Time of Cholera*. On a basic level, the novel explores various aspects of love, such as whether being lovesick makes you physically sick (unhealthy) or whether one can be plagued by love (like cholera). The questions García Márquez raises about marriage based on economic and social security versus marriage based on passion and romance provided an apt starting point for a talk show concerned with contemporary social issues. See https://hanoigrapevine.com/2013/11/talk-show-love -time-cholera/0; httpp://www.vietnamplus.vn/cung-mo-xe-tinh-yeu-thoi-tho-ta -voi-cac-chuyen-gia/230600.vnp.

2 See Lainez 2012; Martin 2010; P. A. Nguyen 2007; Tran Thi Minh Thi 2011, 2012.

3 See Padilla et al. (2007) for ethnographically based analyses of how global forces shape intimacy, love, and marriage in different cultural contexts.

4 *diaCRITICS*, "Same-Sex Marriage Rights in Viet Nam—the Conversation Begins," August 9, 2012, diacritics.org/2012/08/same-sex-marriage-rights-in-viet-nam -the-conversation-begins/.

5 Men I interviewed in 2004 regarding men's extramarital sex felt that as long as they provided for their family economically, they were being faithful to their wives.

6 The 2000 law, like the 1996 law, recognized women's rights to a biological child via the rights of the child. An associate professor of jurisprudence in Hà Nội told me in 2013, "The law stands behind the children."

7 By 2005, having stabilized population growth, the government sought to align itself with international trends emphasizing reproductive health rights, development, and poverty reduction. This shift is reflected in the 2010–20 Population Strategy; during the first five years of the program, efforts were stepped up to improve the "quality of the race" (*chất lượng giống nòi*) (Phinney et al. 2014).

8 The Chinese government had previously developed a population campaign to improve the quality (*sushi*) of the Chinese population (Anagnost 1995; Kipnis 2006; Yan 2003). However, in China "*sushi* largely refers to a project of cultivating individual quality. . . . Families provide the resources to support children in this process" (Leshkowich 2012, 502). The Vietnamese goal is to raise the quality of the family unit itself because the family, as reproducer of the nation and the basic unit of economic production—not the individual—is considered central to Vietnamese cultural life (Rydström 2010).

9 It is markedly similar to the colonial era, when Vietnamese physicians promoted "scientific motherhood" in order to "prevent the degeneration of the race," subjecting mothers to "greater state intervention that included maternity teaching, infant care consultations, and regulations in breastfeeding and wet nursing" (T. L. Nguyen 2016, 144–45). Similarly, in 1984 the state proclaimed, "State bodies must pay adequate attention to the physical and physiological conditions of women and their motherhood duties" (Vietnam Women's Union and the Center for Women's Studies 1989, 76). The 1986 law further incorporated motherhood into the legal framework, placing maternal desire for children directly under the influence of the state.

10 Article 2 of Decree #12 states, "This Decree shall apply to infertile couples and single women wishing to give birth to children by reproduction-supporting techniques; sperm donors, recipients and depositors; ovum donors and recipients; embryo donors and recipients; sperm- and embryo-storing establishments; and medical establishments which are permitted by the Health Ministry to apply reproduction-supporting techniques for childbirth (hereinafter referred to as medical establishment)." Socialist Republic of Vietnam, Decree No. 12/2003/ND-CP of February 12, 2003 on Childbirth by Scientific Methods (2003).

11 Oanh was the only single mother from Sóc Sơn who had asked for a child since 2000 that I was able to interview. Phương from the local Women's Union said there were not as many single women in Sóc Sơn who ask for a child as there had been in the 1990s because they were far more mobile, and those who could moved to Hà Nội to work.

12 Shohet's research on love in Đà Nẵng in 2007–8 indicates that women who did not want to become too old to marry would weigh their marital prospects in terms of the kind of love or *tình cảm* they could expect to share or develop with a potential husband. One woman in particular assessed the value of marrying a man based on the fact that he (and she) would be free of patrilineal kinship

obligations. Like the single women I interviewed, "their love involves at once morally acting, sensing, feeling, and reasoning in the world—a world of affective ties with others" (Shohet 2017, 557–58).

13 For a discussion on married women's struggles, see Kwiatkowski (2008).

14 For a discussion on companionate marriage in different cultural contexts, see Hirsch et al. 2010; Hirsch and Wardlow 2006.

15 I asked the single mothers I interviewed in the 2000s whether they desired women and not men. I also asked about their friends who were choosing to get pregnant out of wedlock. All answered that, no, they did not desire women.

16 Women's decision to remain single has been evident for some time in other East and Southeast Asian countries ("Asian Demography: The Flight from Marriage," Briefing, *Economist*, August 20, 2011; Fincher 2014; Jones 2010; "Marriage in Japan: 'I Don't,'" *Economist*, September 1, 2016; Situmorang 2007; Tey 2007; T. H. Kwon 2007).

17 See the art historian Nora Taylor's (2007) discussion of women artists from Vietnam who chose not to marry or decided to divorce in order to have freedom to follow their own creative artistic paths. This does not mean, however, that artists depict Vietnamese women as free from social constraints. Also see Duong (2017, 3) regarding changes in the Vietnamese educational examination system that illustrate broader social changes in Vietnam such as "freedom of choice and individuality."

18 See L. Williams (2009) for attitudes on marriage; Earl (2014) on gender and the new middle class; Kwiatkowski (2008) regarding men's preferences for marrying women with lower educational and professional achievements; "Vietnam's Working Women Opting to Stay Single," *Straits Times Asia*, April 29, 2017, https://www.straitstimes.com/asia/vietnams-working-women-opting-to-stay-single.

19 When I returned to Sóc Sơn in 2015, I asked single mothers I had met in the mid-1990s how their lives had changed since the early 2000s. All agreed that, in general, people are "more open-minded" and thus more accepting of single mothers. But stigma remains; another friend told me, "In Hà Nội some people won't invite single mothers to their children's wedding, fearing they will bring bad luck."

20 The adage "Youth depend on parents, elderly depend on children" (*Trẻ cậy cha, già cậy con*) still holds. While the government is working to address Vietnam's aging population, there are still few government facilities that care for the elderly (Vietnam National Committee on Ageing 2019).

21 Although they did not keep data on the numbers of single women seeking donated sperm, one doctor estimated that less than 10 percent of all IUI (intrauterine inseminations) a year were for single women.

22 Paragraphs 2 and 3 of Article 9 restrict single women's access to reproductive technology: ovum and embryo recipients must be wives undergoing infertility treatment. In other words, single women only have access to sperm.

23 As was the case with the 1986 Law on Marriage and the Family, the decree was not meant to encourage younger women (of marriageable age) to become single mothers.

24 Nhung and other contemporary Vietnamese single women's preference for getting pregnant with someone they knew personally and with whom they shared *tình cảm* stands in stark contrast to single women who turn to artificial insemination because it is anonymous and impersonal (Hertz 2006).

25 It was not easy for Tuyết to recount the story of her divorce and her efforts to convince her parents she needed to have a child. The first time we met, she was tired and a little sick, and as she spoke about her husband, she began to cry. She apologized. I felt horrible and suggested we stop talking, call off the discussion, meet another time, but only if she wanted. She said she wanted to tell me her story. She had never recounted it to anyone; she did so as a favor for me. She pulled herself together, and as she veered away from the tragedy of her marriage to talk about her desire for a child, her convictions gave her the strength to carry on. This "ethnographic moment" was by no means the first time I questioned my profession while conducting fieldwork. Tuyết's willingness to carry on, to tell me her story, no matter how difficult, reminded me of my obligation to all of the single women who had shared their stories with me over the years. Two years later when we met again, Tuyết and I focused our conversation on what it was like to raise a child as a single mother.

26 "Tức là em xác định có em bé, có con, là em chủ động hết, 'tất tần tật.' Em thì bản thân em chỉ muốn em có một đứa con và em tự lập hết, em tự lo lắng và nuôi con em hết, em không có gì dính dáng."

27 It is worth noting that choice, like agency, is not *completely* free. It is limited by material constraints, and it operates in relation to gendered hierarchies of power within a specific sociocultural milieu.

28 It would be a mistake to construe women's options as if they were shopping in a grocery store, as if they could pick and choose. None of the women talked about their choices in this way. My portrayal of women who might want to ask for a child as women who have options will be readily countered by those who claim that these women are too ugly or too old to find men who will have sex with them. When I heard this assertion in the 2010s, I noted that I had heard the same comment in the mid-1990s.

29 See the preface, which discusses my research methodology, for a list of the online forums and websites I examined. Due to the number of online posts regarding single motherhood and the fact that many URLs no longer work or direct the researcher to different or more recent articles on the same topic, I only provide cites for a few stable links. A number of articles and posts were picked up and circulated by many other websites. A quick internet search will reveal that these conversations are ongoing and the concerns and advice dynamic.

30 See Zhang (2010) for a discussion on how Chinese women's "shifting notions of self-worth and modes of valuation reconfigure[d] the intimate realm of heterosexual love and marriage" among the middle class, evident in public debates in China.

31 For an extended discussion on the lives of single mothers in Hà Nội compared to single mothers in Korea, see Nguyễn Thị Thu Vân 2015.

32 "Những ông bố 'vô hình' của showbiz Việt," Tin Tức Online, April 30, 2014, https:// tintuconline.com.vn/sao/nhung-ong-bo-vo-hinh-cua-showbiz-viet-n-187635.html; "Những "bà mẹ đơn thân" đáng khâm phục của showbiz Việt," Phunutoday, May 2, 2014, https://phunutoday.vn/nhung-ba-me-don-than-dang-kham-phuc-cua -showbiz-viet-d40304.html; "Ngo Thái Uyên: Ai bảo có chồng mới được có con?," Người Đưa Tin, December 27, 2012, https://www.nguoiduatin.vn/ngo-thai-uyen -ai-bao-co-chong-moi-duoc-co-con-a16299.html.

33 "Chán chồng Việt, tôi đi xin con trai Tây," Eva.vn, accessed February 20, 2014, http:// us.eva.vn/eva-tam/chan-chong-viet-toi-di-xin-con-trai tay-c66a164151.html.

34 "10 tật xấu 'kinh hoàng' của đàn ông Việt," VietNamNet, October 15, 2013, https:// vietnamnet.vn/vn/doi-song/10-tat-xau-kinh-hoang-cua-dan-ong-viet-149470 .html. Often one article was picked up and circulated by a number of different platforms, such as vnexpress.net. Also see Grillot (2012).

35 We should also add domestic abuse to this list (Kwiatkowski 2008, 2011; Vung et al. 2008; Thuy Linh, "Chained to Chores: Vietnamese Women Remain Unequal to Men—Study," *Thanh Nien News*, March 8, 2016, http://www.thanhniennews .com/society/chained-to-chores-vietnamese-women-remain-unequal-to-men -study-60012.html.

36 In 2012, Peter J. de Vries produced the documentary *By Choice or by Chance* by Marijn Poels, which premiered in Hà Nội on March 8, 2013, International Women's Day. The documentary follows three single mothers living in Hà Nội. The goal of the documentary was to generate funds for single mothers and to make their struggles known. *By Choice or Chance*, Netherlands, https://www.youtube.com /watch?v=EkP8rz1X-ZA.

37 "Làm mẹ đơn thân Part I," Gia Đình Online, May 29, 2012, https://www.youtube .com/watch?v=L9l54BfImkc; "Làm mẹ đơn thân Part II," Gia Đình Online, May 29, 2012, https://www.youtube.com/watch?v=Ygb9avAbXts; "Mẹ đơn thân," Sài Gòn 21, October 9, 2013, https://www.youtube.com/watch?v=YF2FBUGcKxU.

38 The URL (eva.vn) for this quote is no longer valid.

39 Some TV talk show moderators provide a neutral stance regarding the increase in single motherhood with the aim of understanding single mothers' challenges. Other moderators aim to dissuade single women from becoming single mothers.

40 "Xuân Lan lóng ngóng trong lần đầu mang thai," VN Express, July 16, 2013, https:// vnexpress.net/xuan-lan-long-ngong-trong-lan-dau-mang-thai-2849796.html.

41 Over the years Chi had managed to put food on the table and pay her son's school fees. She worked long hours first as a brick maker and later as a cement maker; in addition, she farmed the two *sao* allotted by the hamlet. Now that her son had a job fixing electronic devices, he was able to contribute to the family income.

CONCLUSION

1 May Masangkay, "'Single Mothers by Choice' Fight Stigma, Seek to Change Perceptions in Japan," *Kyodo News*, June 2, 2017; Mandy Zuo, "Single Mum in Legal Fight for China's Unmarried Mothers," *South China Morning Post*, September 14, 2019.

2 As was the case for the previous generation, government officials supported single women considered past marriageable age, not young marriageable women who got pregnant.

3 It is interesting to note that in 2015 and again in 2017, the Vietnamese Ministry of Health announced that artificial insemination was now available for single women at the National Obstetrics and Gynecology Hospital in Hà Nội. I found the announcement curious given that AI was, in fact, first decreed in 2003, and in 2015 I had spoken with hospital employees who had briefed me on the stipulations for accessing sperm. These press releases may signal an ongoing effort to encourage single women to use (and pay for) these services rather than to ask for a child.

BIBLIOGRAPHY

Abu-Lughod, Lila. 1990. "The Romance of Resistance: Tracing Transformations of Power through Bedouin Women." *American Ethnologist* 17 (1): 41–55.

Ahearn, Laura M. 2001. "Language and Agency." *Annual Review of Anthropology* 30:109–37.

Althusser, Louis. 1971. *"Lenin and Philosophy" and Other Essays*. Translated by Ben Brewster. New York: Monthly Review Press.

Anagnost, Ann. 1995. "A Surfeit of Bodies: Population and the Rationality of the State in Post-Mao China." In Ginsburg and Rapp 1995a, 22–41.

———. 1997. *National Past-Times: Narrative, Representation, and Power in Modern China.* Durham, NC: Duke University Press.

Balaban, John, trans. 2000. *Spring Essence: The Poetry of Ho Xuan Huong.* Port Townsend, WA: Copper Canyon Press.

Barbieri, Magali. 2009. "Doi Moi and Older Adults: Intergenerational Support under the Constraints of Reform." In *Reconfiguring Families in Contemporary Vietnam*, edited by Magali Barbieri and Danièle Bélanger, 133–68. Stanford, CA: Stanford University Press.

Bélanger, Danièle. 2004. "Single and Childless Women of Vietnam: Contesting and Negotiating Female Identity." In Drummond and Rydström 2004, 96–116.

Bélanger, Danièle, and Khuat Thu Hong. 1996. "Marriage and the Family in Urban North Vietnam, 1965–1993." *Journal of Population* 2 (1): 83–111.

———. 2002. "Too Late to Marry: Failure, Fate or Fortune? Female Singlehood in Rural North Việt Nam." In Werner and Bélanger 2002a, 89–110.

Biehl, João, Byron Good, and Arthur Kleinman. 2007. "Introduction: Rethinking Subjectivity." In *Subjectivity*, edited by João Biehl, Byron Good, and Arthur Kleinman, 1–24. Berkeley: University of California Press.

Black, George. 2019. "Fifty Years After, a Daunting Cleanup of Vietnam's Toxic Legacy." *YaleEnvironment360*, May 13, 2019. https://e360.yale.edu/features/fifty-years-after-a-daunting-cleanup-of-vietnam-toxic-legacy-dioxin-agent-orange.

Blackwood, Evelyn. 2005. "Wedding Bell Blues: Marriage, Missing Men, and Matrifocal Follies." *American Ethnologist* 32 (1): 3–19.

Bledsoe, Caroline H. 2002. *Contingent Lives: Fertility, Timing, and Aging in West Africa*. Chicago: University of Chicago Press.

Bousquet, Gisele. 2016. *Urbanization in Vietnam*. New York: Routledge.

Bradley, Mark P. 2009. *Vietnam at War*. Berkeley: University of California Press.

Briggs, Laura. 2017. *How All Politics Became Reproductive Politics: From Welfare Reform to Foreclosure to Trump*. Oakland: University of California Press.

Browner, Carole H., and Carolyn F. Sargent, eds. 2012. *Reproduction, Globalization, and the State*. Durham, NC: Duke University Press.

Bucher, Greta. 2000. "Struggling to Survive: Soviet Women in the Post-War Years." *Journal of Women's History* 12, no. 1 (Spring): 137–59.

Bùi, Thế Cương, Trương Sĩ Anh, Daniel Goodkind, John Knodel, and Jed Friedman. 1999. *Vietnamese Elderly Amidst Transformations in Social Welfare Policy*. Research Report No. 99-436. Ann Arbor: University of Michigan Population Studies Center.

Burchell, Graham, Colin Gordon, and Peter Miller, eds. 1991. *The Foucault Effect: Studies in Governmentality*. Chicago: University of Chicago Press.

Butler, Judith. 1990. *Gender Trouble: Feminism and the Subversion of Identity*. New York: Routledge.

Carsten, Janet. 2013, "Introduction: Blood Will Out." In *Blood Will Out: Essays on Liquid Transfers and Flows*, edited by Janet Carsten, 1–23. Hoboken, NJ: Wiley-Blackwell.

Chanoff, David, and Doan Van Toai. 1996. *"Vietnam": A Portrait of Its People at War*. New York: I. B. Tauris.

Colen, Shellee. 1995. "'Like a Mother to Them': Stratified Reproduction and West Indian Childcare Workers and Employers in New York." In Ginsburg and Rapp 1995a, 78–102.

Craig, David. 2002. *Familiar Medicine: Everyday Health Knowledge and Practice in Today's Vietnam*. Honolulu: University of Hawai'i Press.

Dang, Nguyen Anh. 2000. "Women's Migration and Urban Integration in the Context of Đổi Mới." *Vietnam's Socio-Economic Development: A Quarterly Review* 23 (Autumn).

Das, Veena. 1995. "National Honor and Practical Kinship: Unwanted Women and Children." In Ginsburg and Rapp 1995a, 212–33.

Davis-Floyd, Robbie E. 2003. *Birth as an American Right of Passage*. Berkeley: University of California Press.

DEVAID. 1996. *Project Report: Savings and Credit Project Sites*. September 1996. Hà Nội: DEVAID.

Doan, Mau Diep, Nolwen Henaff, and Trinh Khac Tham. 1998. "Patterns of Rural-Urban Migration and Solutions to the Problem: A Case Study of Hanoi." In *International Seminar on Internal Migration: Implications for Migration Policy in Vietnam*. Population Council Vietnam Research Report No. 9. New York: Population Council.

Donzelot, Jacques. 1977. *The Policing of Families*. Translated by Robert Hurley. Baltimore: Johns Hopkins University Press.

Dorow, Sara, and Amy Swiffen. 2009. "Blood and Desire: The Secret of Heteronormativity in Adoption Narratives of Culture." *American Ethnologist* 36 (3): 563–73.

Dror, Olga. 2018. *Making Two Vietnams: War and Youth Identities, 1976–1975*. Cambridge: Cambridge University Press.

Drummond, Lisa B. Welch. 2012. "Middle Class Landscapes in a Transforming City: Hanoi in the 21st Century." In Nguyen-Marshall, Drummond, and Bélanger 2012, 79–93.

Drummond, Lisa, and Helle Rydström, eds. 2004. *Gender Practices in Contemporary Vietnam*. Singapore: NIAS Press.

Duong, Phuoc M. 2017. "Unpredictable Agency: An Analysis of Youth and Educational Practice in Times of Political and Economic Precarity in Contemporary Đà Nẵng City, Việt Nam." PhD diss., University of California Riverside. https://escholarship.org/uc/item/28w4q8wh.

Dutton, George. 2012. "Advertising, Modernity, and Consumer Culture in Colonial Vietnam." In Nguyen-Marshall, Drummond, and Bélanger 2012, 21–42.

Earl, Catherine. 2014. *Vietnam's New Middle Class: Gender, Career, City*. Denmark: Nordic Institute of Asian Studies.

Engels, Friedrich. (1884) 1995. *The Origin of the Family, Private Property and the State*. London: Penguin.

England, Christopher. 2019. "Hegemony, Ideology, Governmentality: Theorizing State Power after Weber." *SPECTRA* 7 (1): 13–23.

Evans, Grant. 1985. "Vietnamese Communist Anthropology." *Canberra Anthropology* 8 (1–2): 116–47.

Fforde, Adam. 1987. *Vietnam—Historical Background and Macro Analysis: Forestry Workers in Vietnam, a Study on the Living and Working Conditions*. Stockholm: Swedish International Development Authority.

Fincher, Leta Hong. 2014. *Leftover Women: The Resurgence of Gender Inequality in China*. London: Zed Books.

Fitzgerald, D. M. 1989. *The Vietnamese People's Army: Regularization of Command, 1975–1988*. Canberra Papers on Strategy and Defense No. 46. Canberra: Australian National University.

Foucault, Michel. 1978. *The History of Sexuality*. Vol. 1, *An Introduction*. Translated by Robert Hurley. New York: Pantheon.

———. 1991a. "Politics and the Study of Discourse." In Burchell, Gordon, and Miller 1991, 52–72.

———. 1991b. "Governmentality." In Burchell, Gordon, and Miller 1991, 87–104.

———. 2000. "The Subject and Power." In *Michel Foucault: Power*, edited by James D. Faubion, 326–48. New York: New Press.

Gainsborough, Martin. 2010. "Present but Not Powerful: Neoliberalism, the State, and Development in Vietnam." *Globalizations* 7 (4): 475–88.

Gammeltoft, Tine. 2014. *Haunting Images: A Cultural Account of Selective Reproduction in Vietnam*. Berkeley: University of California Press.

Geronimus, A. T. 2003. "Damned if You Do: Culture, Identity, Privilege, and Teenage Childbearing in the U.S." *Social Science and Medicine* 57:881–93.

Giddens, Anthony. 1979. *Central Problems in Social Theory: Action, Structure, and Contradiction in Social Analysis*. Berkeley: University of California Press.

Ginsburg, Faye D., and Rayna Rapp, eds. 1995a. *Conceiving the New World Order: The Global Politics of Reproduction*. Berkeley: University of California Press.

———. 1995b. "Introduction." In Ginsburg and Rapp 1995a, 1–17.

Goodkind, Daniel. 1997. "The Vietnamese Double Marriage Squeeze." *International Migration Review* 31 (1): 108–27.

Gordon, Colin. 1991. "Governmental Rationality: An Introduction." In Burchell, Gordon, and Miller 1991, 1–51.

Grillot, Caroline. 2012. "Between Bitterness and Sweet, When Bodies Say It All: Chinese Border Perspectives on Vietnamese Women in a Border Space." *Journal of Vietnamese Studies* 7 (1): 106–48.

Guillemot, Francois. 2009. "Death and Suffering at First Hand: Youth Shock Brigades during the Vietnam War (1950–1975)." *Journal of Vietnamese Studies* 4 (3): 17–60.

Ha Thi Phuong Tien and Ha Quang Ngoc. 2001. *Female Labour Migration: Rural-Urban*. Hà Nội: Women's Publishing House.

Hakkarainen, Minna. 2015. "Navigating between Ideas of Democracy and Gendered Local Practices in Vietnam: A Bakhtinian Reading of Development Aid Practice." PhD diss., University of Helsinki.

Hardy, Andrew. 2001. "Rules and Resources: Negotiating the Household Registration System in Vietnam under Reform." *Sojourn* 16 (2): 187–212.

———. 2003. *Red Hills: Migrants and the State in the Highlands of Vietnam*. Singapore: NIAS Press.

Harms, Erik. 2011. *Saigon's Edge: On the Margins of Ho Chi Minh City*. Minneapolis: University of Minnesota Press.

———. 2012. "Neo-Geomancy and Real Estate Fever in Post-Reform Vietnam." *positions* 20 (2): 404–34.

Haughton, Jonathan. 1997. "Falling Fertility in Vietnam." *Population Studies* 51 (2): 203–21.

Hertz, Rosanna. 2006. *Single by Chance, Mothers by Choice: How Women Are Choosing Parenthood without Marriage and Creating the New American Family*. Oxford: Oxford University Press.

Hiebert, Murray. 1994. "Single Mothers: Women in Men-Short Vietnam Are Having Children out of Wedlock." *Far East Economic Review*, February 24, 1994.

Hirsch, Jennifer S. 2003. *A Courtship after Marriage: Sexuality and Love in Mexican Transnational Families*. Berkeley: University of California Press.

Hirsch, Jennifer S., and Holly Wardlow, eds. 2006. *Modern Loves: The Anthropology of Romantic Courtship and Companionate Marriage*. Ann Arbor: University of Michigan Press.

Hirsch, Jennifer S., Holly Wardlow, Daniel Jordan Smith, Harriet M. Phinney, Shanti Parikh, and Constance A. Nathanson. 2010. *The Secret: Love, Marriage, and HIV*. Nashville, TN: Vanderbilt University Press.

Hirschman, Charles, S. H. Preston, and Vu Manh Loi. 1995. "Vietnamese Casualties during the American War: A New Estimate." *Population and Development Review* 21:782–812.

Hồ Anh Thái. 1988. *Người Đàn Bà Trên Đảo*. Hà Nội: Nhà Xuât Bản Lao Động.

Hoang, Lan Anh. 2020. "The Vietnamese Women's Union and the Contradictions of a Socialist Gender Regime." *Journal of Asian Studies Review* 44 (2): 297–314.

Hoang, Thi Lich. 1999. "Contemporary Housing in Urban Hanoi." In *Women's Rights to House and Land: China and Vietnam*, edited by Irene Tinker and Gale Summerfield, 77–94. Boulder, CO: Lynne Rienner.

Howell, Signe. 2009. "Adoption of the Unrelated Child: Some Challenges to the Anthropological Study of Kinship." *Annual Review of Anthropology* 38: 149–66. Berkeley: University of California Press.

Huynh, Dinh Te. 1994. "Introduction to Vietnamese Culture." In *Introduction to Indochinese Cultures*, edited by San Diego State University Multifunctional Resource Center. San Diego: Southeast Asia Community Resource Center.

Jamieson, Neil. 1986. "The Traditional Family in Vietnam." *Vietnam Forum* (Summer–Fall): 91–150.

Jayakody, Rukmalie, and Vu Tuan Huy. 2009. "Family Change in Vietnam's Red River Delta: From War, to Reunification, to Renovation." In *Reconfiguring Families in Contemporary Vietnam*, edited by Magali Barbieri and Danièle Bélanger, 203–36. Stanford, CA: Stanford University Press.

Jellema, Kate. 2007. "Everywhere Incense Burning: Remembering Ancestors in Đổi Mới." *Journal of Southeast Asian Studies* 38 (3): 467–92.

Jones, Gavin W. 2010. *Changing Marriage Patterns in Asia*. Asia Research Institute (ARI) Working Paper Series No. 131. Singapore: National University of Singapore.

Kahn, Susan Martha. 2000. *Reproducing Jews: A Cultural Account of Assisted Conception in Israel*. Durham, NC: Duke University Press.

Kerkvliet, Benedict J. Tria. 2005. *The Power of Everyday Politics: How Vietnamese Peasants Transformed National Policy*. Ithaca, NY: Cornell University Press.

Kerkvliet, Melinda Tria, and Le Van Sinh. 1997. "Life Stories of Retired Factory Workers in Hanoi." Paper prepared for EUROVIET III, Bi-Annual Conference, Amsterdam, July 2–4, 1997.

Khuất Thu Hồng. 1998. *Study on Sexuality in Vietnam: The Known and Unknown Issues*. Population Council South and East Asia Regional Working Papers No. 11. New York: Population Council. DOI: 10.13140/RG.2.2.15215.84640.

Khuất Thu Hồng, Lê Bạch Dương, and Nguyễn Ngọc Hương. 2009. *Sexuality in Contemporary Vietnam: Easy to Joke About but Hard to Talk About*. Hà Nội: Institute for Development Studies (ISDS) Knowledge Publishing House.

Kipnis, Andrew B. 2006. "Neoliberalism Reified: *Suzhi* Discourse and Tropes of Neoliberalism in the People's Republic of China." *Journal of the Royal Anthropological Institute* 13:383–400.

———. 2008. "Audit Cultures: Neoliberal Governmentality, Socialist Legacies, or Technologies of Governing?" *American Ethnologist* 35 (2): 275–89.

Kirk, Michael, and Nguyen Do Anh Tuan. 2009. *Land-Tenure Policy Reforms: Decollectivization and the Đổi Mới System in Vietnam*. IFPRI Discussion Paper 00927. Washington, DC: International Food Policy Research Institute.

Kleinman, Arthur, and Erin Fitz-Henry. 2007. "The Experiential Basis of Subjectivity: How Individuals Change in the Context of Societal Transformation." In

Subjectivity, edited by João Biehl, Byron Good, and Arthur Kleinman, 52–65. Berkeley: University of California Press.

Kligman, Gail. 1995. "Political Demography: The Banning of Abortion in Ceausescu's Romania." In Ginsburg and Rapp 1995a, 234–55.

Kuan, Teresa. 2015. *Love's Uncertainty: The Politics and Ethics of Child Rearing in Contemporary China*. Berkeley: University of California Press.

Kwiatkowski, Lynn. 2008. "Political Economy and the Health and Vulnerability of Battered Women in Northern Vietnam." *The Economics of Health and Wellness: Anthropological Perspectives* 26:199–226.

———. 2011. "Domestic Violence and the 'Happy Family' in Northern Vietnam." *Anthropology Now* 3, no. 3 (December): 20–28.

Kwon, Heonik. 2008. *Ghosts of War in Vietnam*. Cambridge: Cambridge University Press.

Kwon, T. H. 2007. "Trends and Implications of Delayed and Non-Marriage in Korea." *Asian Population Studies* 3 (3): 223–41.

Lainez, Nicolas. 2012. "Commodified Sexuality and Mother-Daughter Power Dynamics in the Mekong Delta." *Journal of Vietnamese Studies* 7 (1): 149–80.

Lalu, P. 2000. The Grammar of Domination and the Subjection of Agency: Colonial Texts and Modes of Evidence. *History and Theory* 39 (4): 45–68.

Lê Bạch Dương and Khuất Thu Hồng. 2008. "An Historical Political Economy of Migration in Vietnam." In *Market Transformation, Migration, and Social Protection in a Transitioning Vietnam*, edited by Lê Bạch Dương and Khuất Thu Hồng, 25–55. Hà Nội: The Gioi.

Le Bach Duong, Truong Thanh-Dam, and Khuat Thu Hong. 2014. "Transnational Marriage." In *Migration, Gender and Social Justice: Perspectives on Human Insecurity*, edited by Thanh-Dam Truong, Des Gasper, Jeff Handmaker, and Sylvia J. Bergh, 87–103. New York: Springer.

Lê Ngọc Lân. 1987. "Đời sống văn hoá tinh thần của gia đình công nhân lâm trường." In *Kỷ yếu hội thảo khoa học về điều kiện lao động và đời sống của nữ công nhân lâm trường nguyên liệu giấy Tỉnh Hà Tuyên*. Hà Nội: Trung Tâm Nghiên Cứu Phụ nữ Thuộc Uỷ Ban Khoa Học Xã Hội Việt Nam.

———. 1991. "Gia đình phụ nữ thiếu vắng chồng, Một vấn đề xã hội cần quan tâm." *Khoa học về Phụ nữ* 3 (5): 22–25.

———. 1992. "Vấn đề gia đình đối với những phụ nữ lỡ thì ở nông thôn." *Khoa học về Phụ nữ* 1 (7): 28–30.

Lê Nhâm [Lê Thị Nhâm Tuyết]. 1994. "'Asking for a Child' Practice in An Hiệp Commune." *Vietnam Social Sciences* 1 (39): 103–9.

Lê Thi. 1987. "Báo cáo tổng hợp kết quả đợt khảo sát về điều kiện lao động và sinh hoạt của nữ công nhân các lâm trường vùng nguyên liệu giấy (Hà Tuyên)." In *Kỷ yếu hội thảo khoa học về điều kiện lao động sống của nữ công lâm trường nguyên liệu giấy Tỉnh Hà Tuyên*. Hà Nội: Trung Tâm Nghiên Cứu Phụ nữ Thuộc Ủy Ban Khoa Học Xã Hội Việt Nam.

———. 1990. *Gia đình phụ nữ thiếu vắng chồng: Các bản phỏng vấn sâu tại Ca Đình Vĩnh Phú*. Hà Nội: Trung Tâm Nghiên Cứu Khoa Học Về Gia Đình và Phụ nữ.

———, ed. 1991. *Người phụ nữ và gia đình Việt Nam hiện nay.* Hà Nội: Nhà Xuất Bản Khoa Học Xã Hội.

———. 1993. "Women, Marriage, Family, and Gender Equality." *Vietnam Social Sciences* 2:21–33.

———. 1995. "Vietnamese Women during the Past Ten Years: Progress and Problems." Special Issue: Vietnamese Women Today. *Vietnam Social Sciences* 1/45: 11–17.

———. 1996. "Đời sống gia đình phụ nữ thiếu vắng chồng ở một số vùng miền Bắc Việt Nam." In *Gia đình phụ nữ thiếu vắng chồng,* edited by Lê Thi, 15–63. Hà Nội: Nhà Xuất Bản Khoa Học Xã Hội.

———, ed. 1996. *Gia đình phụ nữ thiếu vắng chồng.* Hà Nội: Nhà Xuất Bản Khoa Xã Hội.

———. 2002. *Cuộc sống của phụ nữ đơn thân ở Việt Nam.* Hà Nội: Nhà Xuất Bản Thế Giới.

———. 2005. *Single Women in Việt Nam.* Translated by Trần Quốc Năm. Hà Nội: Thế Giới.

Lê Thị Nhâm Tuyết. 1975. *Phụ nữ Việt Nam qua các thời đại.* Hà Nội: Nhà Xuất Bản Kho Học Xã Hội.

———. 1993. "'Demand for Children' in An Hiep Village." *Vietnamese Studies* 3:60–66.

———. 1995. "Chính sách xã hôi với người phụ nữ cao tuổi cô đơn." *Khoa Học về Phụ nữ* 4:10–12.

Leinaweaver, Jessaca B. 2008. *The Circulation of Children: Kinship, Adoption, and Morality in Andean Peru.* Durham, NC: Duke University Press.

Lemke, Thomas. 2001. "'The Birth of Bio-Politics': Michel Foucault's Lecture at the College de France on Neo-liberal Governmentality." *Economy and Society* 30 (2): 190–207.

Leshkowich, Ann Marie. 2012. "Rendering Infant Abandonment Technical and Moral: Expertise, Neoliberal Logics, and Class Differentiation in Ho Chi Minh City." *positions* 20, no. 2 (Spring): 497–526.

Li, Tania Murray. 2005. "Beyond 'the State' and Failed Schemes." *American Anthropologist* 107 (3): 383–94.

———. 2007. *The Will to Improve: Governmentality, Development, and the Practice of Politics.* Durham, NC: Duke University Press.

Liljeström, Rita. 1987. "The Living Conditions of the Forestry Workers with Particular Attention to Women." Part 2 of *Forestry Workers in Vietnam: A Study on the Living and Working Conditions.* Göteborg: Swedish International Development Authority.

Liljeström, Rita, Adam Fforde, and Bo Ohlsson. 1987. "Main Report: The Living Conditions of the Forestry Workers Associated with Bai Bang Project." In *Forestry Workers in Vietnam: A Study on the Living and Working Conditions.* Göteborg: Swedish International Development Authority.

Liljeström, Rita, and Tương Lai, eds. 1991. *Sociological Studies on the Vietnamese Family.* Hà Nội: Social Sciences Publishing House.

Luker, Kristin. 1996. *Dubious Conceptions: The Politics of Teenage Pregnancy.* Cambridge, MA: Harvard University Press.

Luong, Hy Van. 1984. "'Brother' and 'Uncle': An Analysis of Rules, Structural Contradictions, and Meaning in Vietnamese Kinship." *American Anthropologist* 86:
290–315.

———. 1989. "Vietnamese Kinship: Structural Principles and the Socialist Transformation in Northern Vietnam." *Journal of Asian Studies* 48 (4): 741–56.

———. 2003. "Gender Relations: Ideologies, Kinship Practices, and Political Economy." In *Postwar Vietnam: Dynamics of a Transforming Society*, edited by Hy Van
Luong, 201–24. London: Rowman and Littlefield.

———. 2006. "Structure, Practice, and History: Contemporary Anthropological
Research on Vietnam." *Journal of Vietnamese Studies* 1 (1–2): 371–409.

Mahmood, Saba. 2005. *Politics of Piety: The Islamic Revival and the Feminist Subject.*
Princeton, NJ: Princeton University Press.

Mai Huy Bích. 1991. "A Distinctive Feature of the Meaning of Reproduction in Confucian Family Tradition in the Red River Delta." In Liljeström and Lai 1991, 49–56.

Mai Thị Tú and Lê Thị Nham Tuyết. 1978. *Women in Vietnam*. Hà Nội: Foreign Languages Publishing House.

Malarney, Shaun Kingsley. 2002. *Culture, Ritual and Revolution in Vietnam.* London:
Routledge Curzon.

Marr, David. 1981. *Vietnamese Tradition on Trial, 1920–1945*. Berkeley: University of California Press.

Martin, Philip. 2010. "'These Days Virginity Is Just a Feeling': Heterosexuality and
Change in Young Urban Vietnamese Men." *Culture, Health, and Sexuality* 12
(August): S5–S18.

Merli, M. G. 2000. "Socioeconomic Background and War Mortality during Vietnam's
Wars." *Demography* 37 (1): 1–15.

Mizoguchi, Nobuko. 2010. "The Effect of the Vietnam War on Marriage Patterns in
Vietnam: Measuring the Marriage Squeeze." Princeton University, Princeton, NJ.
http://paa2011.princeton.edu/papers/111781.

Morris, Stephen J. 1999. *Why Vietnam Invaded Cambodia: Political Culture and the Causes
of War.* Stanford, CA: Stanford University Press.

Mullings, Leith. 1995. "Households Headed by Women: The Politics of Race, Class,
and Gender." In Ginsburg and Rapp 1995a, 122–39.

Nathanson, Connie A. 1991. *Dangerous Passage: The Social Control of Women's Adoles-
cence.* Philadelphia: Temple University Press.

Newton, Natalie Nancy. 2012. "A Queer Political Economy of 'Community': Gender,
Space, and the Transnational Politics of Community for Vietnamese Lesbians
(les) in Saigon." PhD diss., University of California Irvine.

Ngo, Thi Nhan Binh. 2004. "The Confucian Four Feminine Virtues (Tu Duc): The Old
versus the New—Ke thua versus Phat huy." In Drummond and Rydström 2004,
47–73.

Ngo, Thi Tuan Dzung. 2013. "Elderly People in Vietnam: Some Issues of Concern from
a Family and Gender Perspective." Paper presented at AASSREC Forum on Ageing in Asia Pacific: Balancing State and Family, Cebu, Philippines, April 3–4, 2013.

Ngọc Văn. 1991. "Về những người phụ nữ cô đơn." *Khoa học về Phụ nữ* 4 (6): 30–32.

Nguyen, Huong, Chengshi Shiu, and Naomi Farber. 2016. "Prevalence and Factors Associated with Teen Pregnancy in Vietnam: Results from Two National Surveys." *Societies* 6 (17): 1–16.

Nguyễn Hữu Minh. 2009. *Vietnamese Marriage Patterns in the Red River Delta: Tradition and Change*. Hà Nội: Social Sciences Publishing House.

Nguyen Khac Vien. 1993. "Children and Families in Present Vietnamese Society." *Vietnamese Studies* 3:23.

Nguyen Khac Vien, and Huu Ngoc, eds. N.d. *Vietnamese Literature: Historical Background and Texts*. Translated by Mary Cowan, Carolyn Swetland, Dang The Binh, Paddy Farrington, Elizabeth Hodgkin, and Huu Ngoc. Hà Nội: Red River Foreign Languages Publishing House.

Nguyen, Phuong An. 2007. "'Relationships Based on Love and Relationships Based on Needs': Emerging Trends in Youth Sex Culture in Contemporary Urban Vietnam." *Modern Asian Studies* 41 (2): 287–313.

Nguyễn Quốc Tuấn. 1995. *Tìm hiểu các Qui định Pháp luật về Hôn nhân Và Gia đình*. Thành Phố Hồ Chí Minh: Nhà Xuất Bản Thành Phố Hồ Chí Minh.

Nguyen Thanh Binh. 2012. "Age at First Marriage in Recent Years in Vietnam." *Mediterranean Journal of Social Sciences* 3 (1): 491–96.

Nguyễn Thanh Tâm. 1990. "Gia đình nữ công nhân cô đơn làm chủ hộ ở một lâm trường phía bắc, những vấn đề đặt ra." *Khoa học Về Phụ nữ* 1 (6): 29–31.

———. 1991. "Về những gia đình phụ nữ cô đơn, thiếu chồng." In *Người phụ nữ và gia đình Việt Nam hiện nay*, edited by Lê Thi, 112–18. Hà Nội: Nhà Xuất Bản Khoa Xã Hội.

———. 1992. "Remarks on the Women Who Live without Husband." *Vietnam Social Sciences* 4:76–80.

———. 1994. "Hướng tới việc xây dựng hệ thống chính sách xã hội cho những gia định phụ nữ cô đơn." *Khoa học Về Phụ nữ* 1 (15): 19–22.

Nguyễn Thế Giai. 1993. *Luật Hôn Nhân và Gia Đình: Trả lời: 120 câu hỏi*. Hà Nội: Nhà Xuất Bản Chính Trị Quốc Gia.

Nguyễn Thị Bích Vân. 2011. *Chuyện Những Bà Mẹ Đơn Thân*. Hà Nội: Bảo Tàng Phụ nữ Việt Nam.

Nguyễn Thị Khoa. 1991. "Thực trạng gia đình công nhân lâm nghiệp và gia đình nông dân vùng nguyên liệu giấy phía bắc." In *Người phụ nữ và gia đình Việt Nam hiện nay*, edited by Lê Thi, 36–51. Hà Nội: Nhà Xuất Bản Xã Hội Học.

———. 1993. "The Single Mother." *Vietnamese Studies* 3:44–60.

———. 1996. "Tình cảnh éo le của những gia đình phụ nữ không chồng có con." In *Gia đình phụ nữ thiếu vắng chồng*, 125–55. Hà Nội: Nhà Xuất Bản Khoa Xã Hội.

Nguyễn Thị Thu Vân. 2015. "Vị Thế Của Người Mẹ Đơn Thân Trong Xã Hội Hàn Quốc Hiện Nay Và Liên Hệ Với Tực Tiễn Ở Việt Nam." Academic dissertation, Viện Hàn Lâm Khoa Học Xã Hội Việt Nam.

Nguyen, Thuy Linh. 2016. *Childbirth, Maternity, and Medical Pluralism in French Colonial Vietnam, 1880–1945*. Rochester, NY: University of Rochester Press.

Nguyen Van Hai. 2012. *Women Driving the Hồ Chí Minh Trail (Nữ chiến sĩ lái xe Trường Sơn)*. Hà Nội: Bảo Tăng Phụ Nữ Việt Nam.

Nguyen-Marshall, Van, Lisa B. Welch Drummond, and Danièle Bélanger, eds. 2012. *The Reinvention of Distinction: Modernity and the Middle Class in Urban Vietnam.* New York: Springer.

Nguyễn-Võ, Thu-Hương. 2008. *The Ironies of Freedom: Sex, Culture, and Neoliberal Governance in Vietnam.* Seattle: University of Washington Press.

Nhà Xuất Bản Phụ nữ. 2001. *Những quy định pháp luật về hôn nhân và gia đình.* Hà Nội: Nhà Xuất Bản Phụ nữ.

Obermeyer, Ziad, Christopher J. L. Murray, and Emmanuela Gakidou. 2008. "Fifty Years of Violent War Deaths from Vietnam to Bosnia: Analysis of Data from the World Health Survey Programme." *BMJ* 336:1482.

O'Harrow, Stephen. 1995. "Vietnamese Women and Confucianism." In *'Male' and 'Female' in Developing Southeast Asia,* edited by Wazir Jahan Karim, 161–81. Oxford: Berg.

Ohlsson, Bo. 1987. "Forestry Work and Rural Development Associated with the Bai Bang Project." In *Forestry Workers in Vietnam: A Study on Living and Working Conditions.* Götenborg: Swedish International Development Authority.

Ortner, Sherry B. 1995. "Resistance and the Problem of Ethnographic Refusal." *Comparative Studies in Society and History* 37 (1): 173–93.

———. 2006a. "Power and Projects: Reflections on Agency." In *Anthropological Theory: Culture, Power, and the Acting Subject,* 129–53. Durham, NC: Duke University Press.

———. 2006b. "Subjectivity and Cultural Critique." In *Anthropological Theory: Culture, Power, and the Acting Subject,* 107–128. Durham, NC: Duke University Press.

Padilla, Mark B., Jennifer S. Hirsch, Miguel Munoz-Laboy, Robert E. Sember, and Richard G. Parker, eds. 2007. *Love and Globalization: Transformations of Intimacy in the Contemporary World.* Nashville: Vanderbilt University Press.

Pashigian, Melissa. 2009a. "The Womb, Infertility, and the Vicissitudes of Kin-Relatedness in Vietnam." *Journal of Vietnamese Studies* 4 (2): 34–68.

———. 2009b. "Inappropriate Relations: The Ban on Surrogacy and In Vitro Fertilization and the Limits of State Renovation in Contemporary Vietnam." In *Assisting Reproduction, Testing Genes: Global Encounters with New Biotechnologies,* edited by Daphne Birenbaum-Carmeli and Marcia C. Inhorn, 164–88. New York: Berghahn.

Pelly, Patricia M. 2002. *Postcolonial Vietnam: New Histories of the National Past.* Durham, NC: Duke University Press.

Pettus, Ashley. 2003. *Between Sacrifice and Desire: National Identity and the Governing of Femininity in Vietnam.* London: Routledge.

Phan Huy Lê. 2006. "Research on the Vietnamese Village: Assessment and Perspectives." In *Vietnam: Borderless Histories,* edited by Nhung Tuyet Tran and Anthony Reid, 32–41. Madison: University of Wisconsin Press.

Phan Thanh Hảo. 2021. *Momentous Years in Vietnam: A Memoir.* Self-published.

Phinney, Harriet. 2005. "Asking for a Child: The Refashioning of Reproductive Space in Post-War Northern Vietnam. *Asia Pacific Journal of Anthropology* 6 (3): 215–30.

———. 2008. "Objects of Affection: Vietnamese Discourses on Love and Emancipation." *positions* 16 no. 2 (Fall): 329–58.

———. 2010. "'Eaten One's Fill and All Stirred Up': Doi Moi and the Reconfiguration of Masculine Sexual Risk and Men's Extramarital Sex in Vietnam." In *The Secret: Love, Marriage and HIV*, edited by Jennifer Hirsch, Holly Wardlow, Daniel J. Smith, Harriet Phinney, Shanti Parikh, and Connie Nathanson, 108–35. Nashville, TN: Vanderbilt University Press.

Phinney, Harriet, and Khuất Thu Hồng. 2013. "Love in Vietnam: Tình Cảm." In *The World Book of Love*, edited by Leo Bormans, 312–13. Tielt, Belgium: Lannoo.

Phinney, Harriet, Khuat Thu Hong, Vu Thi Thanh Nhan, Nguyen Thi Phuong Thao, and Jennifer S. Hirsch. 2014. "'Obstacles to the Cleanliness of Our Race': HIV, Reproductive Risk, Stratified Reproduction, and Population Quality in Hanoi, Vietnam." *Critical Public Health* 24 (4): 445–60.

Potter, Jack. 1990. "The Cultural Construction of Emotion in Rural Chinese Social Life." In *China's Peasants: The Anthropology of a Revolution*, edited by Jack Potter, 180–95. Cambridge: Cambridge University Press.

Ransom, John S. 1997. *Foucault's Discipline: The Politics of Subjectivity*. Durham, NC: Duke University Press.

Rigg, Jonathan. 2016. "Policies and Negotiated Everyday Living: A View from the Margins of Development in Thailand and Vietnam." In *The Everyday Political Economy of Southeast Asia*, edited by Juanita Elias and Lena Rethel, 27–48. Cambridge: Cambridge University Press.

Rydström, Helle. 1998. *Embodying Morality: Girls' Socialization in a North Vietnamese Commune*. Linkoping, Sweden: Linkoping University.

———. 2004. "Female and Male 'Characters': Images of Identification and Self-Identification for Rural Vietnamese Children and Adolescents." In Drummond and Rydström 2004, 74–95.

———. 2010. "Compromised Ideals: Family Life and the Recognition of Women in Vietnam." In *Gendered Inequalities in Asia: Configuring, Contesting and Recognizing Women and Men*, edited by Helle Rydström, 170–91. Singapore: NIAS Press.

———. 2012. "Gendered Corporeality and Bare Lives: Local Sacrifices and Sufferings during the Vietnam War." *Signs* 37, no. 2 (Winter): 275–99.

———. 2016. "Vietnam Women's Union and the Politics of Representation: Hegemonic Solidarity and a Heterosexual Family Regime." In *Gendered Citizenship and the Politics of Representation*, edited by Hilde Danielsen, Kari Jegerstedt, Ragnhild Muriaas, and Brita Ytre-Arne, 209–34. London: Palgrave Macmillan.

Rydström, Helle, and Lisa Drummond. 2004. "Introduction." In Drummond and Rydström 2004, 1–25.

Sachs, Dana. 2010. *The Life We Were Given: Operation Babylift, International Adoption, and the Children of War in Vietnam*. Boston: Beacon Press.

Schafer, John. 2010. "Lê Vân and Notions of Vietnamese Womanhood." *Journal of Vietnamese Studies* 5 (3): 129–91.

Schmidt, Matthew, and Lisa Jean Moore. 2007. "Constructing a 'Good Catch,' Picking a Winner: The Development of Technosemen and the Deconstruction of the Monolithic Male." In *Beyond the Body Proper: Reading the Anthropology of Material*

Life, edited by Margaret Lock and Judith Farquhar, 550–66. Durham, NC: Duke University Press.

Schuler, Sidney Ruth, Hoang Tu Anh, Vu Song Ha, Tran Hung Minh, Bui Thi Thanh Mai, and Pahm Vu Thien. 2006. "Constructions of Gender in Vietnam: In Pursuit of the 'Three Criteria.'" *Journal of Culture, Health and Sexuality* 8 (5): 383–94.

Schwenkel, Christina. 2014. "Rethinking Asian Mobilities: Socialist Migration and Post-Socialist Repatriation of Vietnamese Contract Workers in East Germany." *Critical Asian Studies* 46 (2): 235–58.

Shohet, Merav. 2013. "Everyday Sacrifice and Language Socialization in Vietnam: The Power of a Respect Particle." *American Anthropologist* 115 (2): 203–17.

———. 2017. "Troubling Love: Gender, Class, and Sideshadowing the 'Happy Family' in Vietnam." *Ethos* 45 (4): 555–76.

Sidel, Mark. 2009. *The Constitution of Vietnam: A Content Analysis*. Portland, OR: Hart Publishing.

Silva, Elizabeth Bortolaia. 1996. "Introduction." In *Good Enough Mothering? Feminist Perspectives on Lone Mothering*, edited by Elizabeth Silva, 1–9. London: Routledge.

Situmorang, Augustina. 2007. "Staying Single in a Married World: Never-Married Women in Yogyakarta and Medan." *Asian Population Studies* 3 (3): 287–304.

Slaughter, M. M. 1995. "The Legal Construction of 'Mother.'" In *Mothers in Law: Feminist Theory and the Legal Regulation of Motherhood*, edited by Martha A. Fineman and Isabel Karpin, 73–100. New York: Columbia University Press.

Solinger, Rickie. 2000. *Wake Up Little Susie: Single Pregnancy and Race before Roe v. Wade*. London: Routledge.

Tai, Hue-Tam Ho. 1992. *Radicalism and the Origins of the Vietnamese Revolution*. Cambridge, MA: Harvard University Press.

———. 2010. *Passion, Betrayal, and Revolution in Colonial Saigon: The Memoirs of Bao Luong*. Berkeley: University of California Press.

Taussig, Michael. T. 1999. *Defacement: Public Secrecy and the Labor of the Negative*. Stanford, CA: Stanford University Press.

Taylor, Nora, ed. 2007. *Changing Identity: Recent Works by Women Artists from Vietnam*. Washington, DC: International Arts and Artists.

Taylor, Sandra C. 1999. *Vietnamese Women at War: Fighting for Ho Chi Minh and the Revolution*. Lawrence: University Press of Kansas.

Teerawichitchainan, Bussarawan. 2009. "Trends in Military Service in Northern Vietnam, 1950–1995: A Sociodemographic Approach." *Journal of Vietnamese Studies* 4 (3): 61–97.

Tey, N. P. 2007. "Trends in Delayed and Non-Marriage in Peninsular Malaysia." *Asian Population Studies* 3 (3): 243–61.

Thai, Hung Cam. 2008. *For Better or for Worse: Vietnamese International Marriages in the New Global Economy*. New Brunswick, NJ: Rutgers University Press.

———. 2012. "The Dual Roles of Transnational Daughters and Transnational Wives: Monetary Intentions, Expectations, and Dilemmas." *Global Networks* 12 (2): 216–32.

Thanh Thi Vu. 2018. "Meanings of Marriage to Young People in Vietnam." *Journal of Marriage and Family Review* 54 (6): 531–48.

Thayer, Carlyle A. 2019. "China's Decade-Long Hybrid War against Vietnam, 1977–1987." In *Stealing a March: Chinese Hybrid Warfare in the Indo-Pacific: Issues and Options for Allied Defense Planners*, edited by Ross Babbage, 2:23–27. Washington: Center for Strategic and Budgetary Assessments. https://csbaonline.org/uploads/documents/Stealing_a_March_Annex_Final.pdf.

Thế Giới. 1993. *Fundamental Laws and Regulations of Vietnam*. Hà Nội: Thế Giới.

Tran Dinh Huou. 1991. "Traditional Families in Vietnam and the influence of Confucianism." In Liljeström and Lai 1991, 25–47.

Trần, Ngọc Angie. 2002. "Gender Expectations of Vietnamese Garment Workers: Việt Nam's Re-Integration into the World Economy." In Werner and Bélanger 2002a, 49–71.

Tran, Nhung Tuyet. 2018. *Familial Properties: Gender, State and Society in Early Modern Vietnam, 1463–1778*. Honolulu: University of Hawai'i Press.

Tran Thi Minh Thi. 2011. "Divorce in Rural Red River Delta: Individual and Traditional Factors and the Participation of Social Organization." *Vietnam Journal of Family and Gender Studies* 6 (1): 59–78.

———. 2012. "Prevalence and Patterns of Divorce in Vietnam 2000–2009." *Vietnam Journal of Family and Gender Studies* 7 (1): 55–79.

Tran Thi Van Anh and Le Ngoc Hung. 1997. *Women and Đổi Mới in Vietnam*. Hà Nội: Women's Publishing House.

Trinh Duy Luan. 2007. "Vietnamese Youth Participation in Their Society during 'Đổi Mới.'" *Vietnam Journal of Family and Gender Studies* (2) 1: 30–43.

Trinh Khac Tham 1998. "Characteristics of Rural-Urban Migration in Vietnam and Policies to Control It." In *International Seminar on Internal Migration: Implications for Migration Policy in Vietnam*. Population Council Vietnam Research Report no. 9. New York: Population Council.

Trinh, T. Minh-ha. 1992. *Framer Framed*. New York. Routledge.

Truong, Thanh-Dam. 1996. *Uncertain Horizons: The Women's Question in Viet Nam Revisited*. Working Paper Series no. 212. The Hague: Institute of Social Studies.

Turner, Karen. 1998. *Even the Women Must Fight*. Hoboken, NJ: John Wiley & Sons.

Utrata, Jennifer. 2015. *Women without Men: Single Mothers and Family Change in the New Russia*. Ithaca, NY: Cornell University Press.

Vân Thanh. 1992. "Nỗi dày vò của phụ nữ sống độc thân." *Khoa học Về Phụ nữ* 3 (9): 45.

Vietnam National Committee on Ageing. 2012. *Report Vietnamese 10 Years of Implementation of the Madrid International Plan of Action on Ageing (MIPAA, 2002–2012)*. Hà Nội. https://ageingasia.org/vietnamese-10-years-of-implementation-of-mipaa/.

———. 2019. *Toward a Comprehensive National Policy for the Ageing in Vietnam*. https://vietnam.unfpa.org/sites/default/files/pub-pdf/Toward%20a%20comprehensive%20ageing%20policy_ENG.pdf.

Vietnam Women's Union and the Centre for Women Studies, eds. 1989. *Vietnamese Women in the Eighties*. Hà Nội: Vietnam Women's Union and the Centre for Women Studies.

Vũ Mạnh Lợi. 1991. "The Gender Division of Labor in Rural Families in the Red River Delta." In Liljeström and Lai 1991, 149–64.

Vũ Mạnh Lợi, Vũ Tuấn Huy, Nguyễn Hồng Quang, Nguyễn Hồng Thái, Nguyễn Khánh Bích Trâm, và Đặng Vũ Hoa Thạch. 2002. "Những vấn đề xã hội của gia đình năm 2000." In *Phát triển xã hội ở Việt Nam: Một tổng quan xã hội học năm 2000*, edited by Trịnh Duy Luân, 123–52. Hà Nội: Nhà Xuá Bản Khoa học Xã hội.

Vung, N. D., P. Ostergren, and G. Krantz. 2008. "Intimate Partner Violence against Women in Rural Vietnam—Different Socio-Demographic Factors Are Associated with Different Forms of Violence: Need for New Intervention Guidelines?" *BMC Public Health* 8 (1): 55.

Wahlberg, Ayo. 2018. *Good Quality: The Routinization of Sperm Banking in China.* Berkeley: University of California Press.

Waibel, G., and S. Glück. 2013. "More than 13 Million: Mass Mobilization and Gender Politics in the Vietnam Women's Union." *Gender and Development* 21 (2): 343–61.

Walsh, Thomas J. 2011. "The Law of the Family in Vietnam: Assessing the Marriage and Family Law of Vietnam." *California Western International Law Journal* 42 (1): 61–122.

Walters, William. 2012. *Governmentality: Critical Encounters.* London: Routledge.

Werner, Jayne. 2002. "Gender, Household, and State: Renovation (Doi Moi) as Social Process in Viet Nam." In Werner and Bélanger 2002a, 29–48.

Werner, Jayne, and Danièle Bélanger, eds. 2002a. *Gender, Household, State: Đổi Mới in Viet Nam.* Ithaca, NY: Cornell University Southeast Asia Program Publications.

———. 2002b. "Introduction: Gender and Viet Nam Studies." In Werner and Bélanger 2002a, 13–28.

Werner, Karen. 2017. "A Vietnamese Woman Directs the War Story: Duc Hoan: 1937–2003." In *Gender, Sexuality and the Cold War: A Global Perspective*, edited by Phillip Mueklenburg, 204–33. Nashville, TN: Vanderbilt University Press.

Weston, Kath. 1991. *Families We Choose: Lesbians, Gays, Kinship.* New York: Columbia University Press.

Williams, Lindy. 2009. "Attitudes toward Marriage in Northern Vietnam: What Qualitative Data Reveal about Variations across Gender, Generation, and Geography." *Journal of Population Research* 26:285–304.

Williams, Raymond. 1977. "Structures of Feeling." In *Marxism and Literature*, 129–35. Oxford: Oxford University Press.

Wolf, Margery. 1972. *Women and Family in Rural Taiwan.* Stanford, CA: Stanford University Press.

Womack, Sarah. 1996. "The Remaking of a Legend: Women and Patriotism in the Hagiography of the Trung Sisters." *Crossroads* 9 (2): 31–50.

Yan, Yunxiang. 2003. *Private Life under Socialism: Love, Intimacy, and Family Change in a Chinese Village, 1949–1999.* Stanford, CA: Stanford University Press.

Young, Marilyn B. 1991. *The Vietnam Wars 1945–1990.* New York: Harper Perennial.

Zhang, Li. 2010. *In Search of Paradise: Middle-Class Living in a Chinese Metropolis.* Ithaca, NY: Cornell University Press.

INDEX

abortion, 117, 189nn43,44
adoption: abandonment concerns in, 37, 38, 174n17; author's fieldwork on, ix; and a child's character, 33–34; costs and availability of children, 32, 173n12; from inside and outside the family, 36, 174nn16,17, 174n19; non-blood mother-child relationships, 37–38, 149; from orphanages, 32–33, 173n9; perceived risks of, 19, 34, 37, 39, 175nn24,30; strategies for, 29–31; women's rejection of, 19, 34, 149, 167
adultery. *See* extramarital relations
age and marriageability: chronological age, 57–58, 177n16; gendered relational age, 57, 58–59; as parameter of *xin con*, 74; physiological age, 57, 59–60, 177n18
agency: and decision making, 10; fields of meaning of, 76; and free will, 77; and single women's use of AI, 147–49; and subjectivity, 161; Women's Union and politics of, 110
agency in *xin con*: ambiguous reproductive intent in, 83–85; as challenge to social norms, 89, 95; intentionality and, 74–75, 76–77, 185n23; marrying at an older age, 60–61; and maternity care, 92–94; and men's anonymity, 90–92, 180n21; navigation of moral constraints, 85–92; openness about decision to get pregnant, 150; and patrilineage, 86–87; and power, 76–77, 97; prior intent in, 78–81; and responsibility for the children, 87–89, 91, 180nn18,19; shift in public attitudes toward, 135; social and economic constraints, 180n20; summary of, 73–74, 94–97, 162–64; traditional intent in, 81–83,

179nn11–13; use of sperm banks, 89–90. *See also* autonomy and freedom; governmentality; subjectivity, women's
Agent Orange, 86
AI. *See* artificial insemination (AI)
Althusser, Louis, 191n60
American War: evacuation of families during, 48–49; male and female mortality during, 49–51, 163, 176n4; and motivation for *xin con*, 6; subjects' suffering from, xii; universal draft, 44; and Vietnam's demographic imbalance, xiv, 44, 49, 50–51, 57, 105, 117; women's responsibilities during, 44–45; *xin con* as creative development from, 95. *See also* governmentality; Vietnam
artificial insemination (AI): access compared to *xin con*, 166, 193nn21,22; availability of, 146–47, 196n3; eligibility compared to *xin con*, 147; impersonality of, 194n24; prescription needed for, 148. *See also* in vitro fertilization; sperm banks
asking for a child. See *xin con*
Âu Cơ, legend of, 65–66
autonomy and freedom: and children, 40; in decisions to have a child, 6, 152–53; desire for independence, 140–42, 161; Đổi Mới state's reinforcement of, 127; economic independence, 9; limits on choice, 194nn27,28; modernity's increase in, 137; and relational views of the self, 32; through having children, 25, 39; war effort's facilitation of, 47; of women exhibited in museum, 126; women's choice to be single, 193nn16,17; *xin con* as form of, 96, 163. *See also* subjectivity, women's

Bà Đế legend and temple, 98, 182n2
Bắc Thái forestry farm discussion forum on xin con, 112–15
Bãi Bằng Forestry Project, 113
Báo Nhân Dân on 1986 Law on Marriage and Family, 104
Báo Phụ nữ Thủ đô, 185n26
Báo Phụ nữ Việt Nam, 185n26; advice on *xin con*, 112–14; advice to women in, 111, 186–87n34; on age differences in marriage, 60; "Discussion on the Matter of Children Born out of Wedlock," 113; on single women, 186n30; and state intervention in intimate affairs, 115
Bélanger, Danièle, 102
Bích (interviewee): and father's involvement with the child, 88; on finding men for *xin con*, 78–79; intention to *xin con*, 78, 150; maternity care for, 92–93; specifics of *xin con* and support for, 79; support from family, 96; work in cement factory, 47; *xin con* experience of, 92
Bích Thủy (interviewee): on children and womanhood, 23
Biehl, João, 155
biopower, 101, 138, 149. *See also* Vietnamese socialist research
Blackwood, Evelyn, 180n17
blood relations: Confucian ideology of, 27, 173n7; as factor in decision to reproduce, 31, 35, 36, 39, 145; importance of shared blood, 149, 175n28; lure of, 37–38, 175n30; purity in, 4; and *tình cảm* (affective connection), 34–36, 37; in Vietnamese kinship practices, 28, 34–36, 149, 173n7; 175n28; and womanhood, 24
By Choice or by Chance (de Vries, documentary), 156, 195n36

Cà Mau, women's agency in, 71–72, 74–75, 76, 77, 178n2 (Cà Mau)
Cambodian war, 48, 50
Carsten, Janet, 36
cement factories: employees of, 16, 47, 78, 195n41; support for single mothers at, 79, 93, 94; women asking for a child at, 78–79, 92
censorship, xii
Center for Scientific Research on the Family and Women (CSRW): about, 182n1; Bà Đế legend and work of, 98; discourse on single motherhood, 116, 158; mission and findings

of, 109–10; *Người phụ nữ và gia đình Việt Nam hiện nay*, 118, 189n45; and normalization of single motherhood, 118–20; petition to the state for support for single mothers, 120; public education on *xin con*, 110–11, 113; strategies to improve lives of single mothers, 110; work with SIDA, 185n21
Châu (interviewee): about, 172n8; decision to get pregnant, 151; and marriage, 139, 140–41, 143; use of term *xin con*, 152; view of motherhood, 146
Chi (interviewee): decision to participate in *xin con*, 7; socioeconomic changes for, 195n41; and son's marriage, 159–60
Chị Tâm Giao, 38, 117
Chị Thanh Tâm, 33, 111, 112–14, 117, 186–87n34
childbearing: and aging, 59; as marital and economic security, 19; pregnancy and gestation, 36–37, 39–40; significance in Vietnam of, 19; and social interaction, 21; and sons, 94, 179n12; as transformational, 20; value of having a biological child, 19; Vietnamese customs for, 92; women's right to bear children, 104, 192n6. *See also* maternal desire; maternal rights
childless women, 23–24, 40
children: education of, 82, 120, 179n10; illegitimate children, 107, 184n15, 184n17; and poverty in families without fathers, 184n17; socialization of, 174n22; as source of happiness, 111–12; state's focus on, 138, 153, 155, 157–58, 164, 166
children's rights, 104, 107, 108, 113, 184nn16,18, 192n6
CIDSE (Coopération Internationale pour le Développement et la Solidarité), 121
Cô gái mang tên một dòng sông (film), 37–38, 175n30
Comaroff, John and Jean, 76
Committee for Social Sciences of Vietnam, 109
Communist Party of Vietnam (CPV), xii, 43, 99, 112, 172n4
Communist Youth Organization, 109
concubinage, 82, 103, 172n2, 179n11,13, 181n22
Confucian heritage: alignment with Communist ideology, 9, 11; blood relations in, 173n7; and childbearing, 19, 100; and collective responsibility, 27; as driver of Vietnam's *xin con* governmentality, 99; and

filial piety, 19, 27, 39, 173n5, 174n22; Four Virtues, 75, 91; loosening influence of, 137; opposition to orthodoxy of, 188n41; and responsibility to be a model, 188n42; Three Submissions, 32, 58, 75, 91; young women's break with, 43. *See also* patriarchal ideologies; Vietnamese kinship values and practices

Craig, David, x

CSRW. *See* Center for Scientific Research on the Family and Women (CSRW)

Đặng Thị To Ngân, 123

Đào (interviewee): about, 172n8; family's treatment of, 172n8; on marriage and remaining single, 64, 65; personal transformation of, 121–22

Decree #12 "On Childbirth by Scientific Methods": and access to reproductive technologies, 146, 148, 193nn22,23; beneficiaries of, 192n10; compared to 1986 Law, 166; conditions stipulated in, 147–48; as form of biopower, 149; and men's anonymity, 146; passage of, 138–39, 154; women's knowledge of, 144

Democratic Republic of Vietnam (DRV). *See* Vietnam

DEVAID, 121

divorce, 101, 103, 137, 138, 156

Đoàn Thị Tuyến, 172n1 (Mai)

Đổi Mới policies: and author's fieldwork, x; description of, 6, 8–9; as driver of *xin con* governmentality, 99–100; economic responsibility of households, 121, 127; emphasis on women's reproduction, 100; gendered effects of, 136; the Happy Family campaign, 100–103; mobility under, 55, 91; and new roles for the press, 110–11; and population management, 11; and resituating women in the home, 40; socioeconomic changes from, xiii, 135, 137, 167

Đúng hay sai? (Right or Wrong? talk show), 134, 156, 191n1

Dương Bích Hạnh, xi

elderly. *See* old-age support

Embassy of Finland, 125

emulation campaigns, 44–45

Engels, Friedrich, 63, 177n27

ethnographic research of author: challenges to, 194n25; and changes in Vietnam, xii–xiii; observation of, xi; permissions for, x;

xiii; publications from, xiv, 171nn1,2; purposes of, ix, 40; subjects and materials in, xii, 172nn6–8

extramarital relations: adultery, 115, 156; advice concerning, 112–14; and changed attitudes toward men, 157; government response to *xin con* and, 112; increase in, 101, 137–38; legal regulation of, 138; research on, 91–92; unacceptability of, 93–94, 186n31; Vietnamese men on, 191n5

families: alternative models of, 118, 137, 138, 165; assumption of responsibility by, 101, 103, 107, 121; family separations, 48, 52–53, 66, 67; incomplete families, 118–19; Model Vietnamese Family designation, 122; *xin con* and happiness of, 114

fertility: addressing infertility, 85–86, 180n16; effects of war on, 59; and nations' populations, 164; treatments for, 146

filial piety: childbearing as demonstration of, 19; devotion and sacrifice in, 39, 174n22; manifestations of, 173n5; and security for mothers, 27

films: depicting lure of blood relations, 37–38, 175n30; *Thương nhớ đồng quê* (Đặng Nhật Minh, 1996), 56

forestry farms, 45–47, 67, 113, 176n7

Foucault, Michel, 99, 101, 185n23, 190n52; "The Subject and Power," 188n38

García Márquez, Gabriel, 191n1

gender equality, 63–64, 141, 143, 161, 163, 167

gender performance, 97

Giddens, Anthony, 76

Good, Byron, 155

governmentality: and agency, 78; in Communist nations *versus* the United States, 115–16, 188n39; concept of, 10–11, 43, 99; demonstrated in the Women's Museum, 123, 125; and devotion to the nation, 66; exhibit's testament to, 126; as interactive process, 100; interpellation of subjects in, 191n60; and liberation of women, 63–64, 66; normalization of single motherhood, 127; and parental and children's responsibilities, 184n18; pedagogical aspect of, 109; population and labor management policies, 51, 170; shift in focus on *xin con*, 134–35; and single mothers in state's agenda, 98–99, 196n2; state reaction to *xin con*, 8–9; and subjectivity, 11, 85, 109; summary of,

Linh (interviewee): about, 172n8; consultation about pregnancy, 150, 151; on generational differences regarding marriage, 142–43; importance of shared blood, 149; and marriage, 139, 141, 143; on maternal rights, 144; use of term *xin con*, 152–53; view of motherhood, 145

loneliness: as assertion of happy family as norm, 118; and assumptions about being alone, 189n46; and childbearing, 21–22, 25, 111–12; sympathy for single women, 116

love in marriage, 61–65

Lý (interviewee): children and psychological stability, 24–25; desire for biological child, 35; and father's involvement with the child, 88; and law, 185n22; strategies to minimize social condemnation, 93; *xin con* experience of, 80, 81–82

Mai (interviewee): about, 15–16; agency of, 168; decision to *xin con*, 3; family, office, and government support of, 16–17; life differences with her mother, 42–43; self-assessment, 15; sociocultural changes experienced by, 15, 168, 169–70; state support of reproductive agency of, 169; subjectivity of, 168–69

Mai Thi Tu, *Women in Viet Nam*, 66

male migration, 55–56

Manzi Art Space discussion, 134, 155

market economy: and changes in family dynamics, 137–38; effect on research participants, x; and regulatory control of families, 139; Vietnam's integration into, 166

marriage: age and marriageability, 56–61, 67, 103, 177n16, 177n18; and availability of men, 44, 49, 50–51, 67; and desire, 178n2 (ch. 3); factors affecting women's chances of, 57, 61, 67; focus on marrying well, 156; and freedom from patrilineal obligations, 192n12; freedom to remain single, 64–65, 193nn16,17; gay marriage, 166; gendered division of labor in, 20–21, 137; generational differences concerning, 42–43; and love, 61–65, 67; and male migration, 55–56; and the marriage squeeze, 50–51, 176n13; and men's attitudes, 142, 143; as norm for Vietnamese women, 42; and restrictions on mobility and communication, 54; and state-assigned work, 47, 48, 176n14; suitability for, 140–42, 143, 168; traditional Vietnamese values of, 19–20; and women's

social life, 20–21; *xin con* and protection of, 87, 92, 95; *xin con* as testament to, 163. *See also* age and marriageability; Confucian heritage; families; single women; subjectivity, women's; Vietnamese kinship values and practices

maternal desire: as driver of *xin con*, 74, 145–46; and kinship norms, 10; and maternal rights, 105–6, 114; and out-of-wedlock births, 108; strategies to satisfy, 143; universality of, 18, 74, 145, 146, 167

maternal love, 167

maternal rights, 105–6, 114, 143–45, 192n6

maternity care, 92–94, 120

Mẹ Việt Nam (statue), 123–25, 124*fig.*, 126

media: and censorship, xii; films, 37–38, 56, 175n30; influence on Vietnamese life, 137; internet discourse on single motherhood, 156–58, 194n29; single mothers as topic of talk shows, 134, 156, 191n1, 195n39

mental health and childlessness, 22, 24–25

Merli, Maria-Giovanna, 49

microcredit programs, xi, 121–22, 125, 126, 169, 170, 190n54

Military Service Law, 45–46

modernity and state development, 102–3, 136–37

moral values: Confucian, 96; single women's ways of navigating, 85–92; teaching of, 174n22; and women's subjectivity, 155

motherhood: single women's views of, 145; state assistance for, 104; state protections for, 106–7, 192n9; statue valorizing, 123; virtues of, 20–24, 25, 26–29, 96, 173n2. *See also* childbearing; maternal desire; single motherhood; *tình cảm*

National Obstetrics and Gynecology Hospital, 147

neoliberal governments, 101

Nga (interviewee): on children and womanhood, 23; and father's involvement with the child, 88; motivation for having a child, 21; multiple pregnancies of, 94; support from family, 96; *xin con* experience of, 80

Ngọc (interviewee): about, 5–6, 180n16; choice to remain single, 65; on the 1986 Law, 104

Ngọc Văn, 111–12, 115; "Discussion on the Matter of Children Born out of Wedlock," 113

maternity care for, 92; and 1986 law, 185n22; support from family, 96; *xin con* experience of, 80

relational views of the self, 32
reproduction as service to the state, 106–7, 109, 125, 126
reproductive rights, 105–8, 113–14, 116, 138, 183n10, 190n50
reproductive strategies, 85–86, 89, 90, 149–52, 154. *See also* adoption; artificial insemination (AI); in vitro fertilization (IVF); *xin con*
Research Center for Gender, Family, and Environment in Development (RCGFED), 105, 109

sexuality: condemnation of free love, 186n31; and Confucianism, 95; gendered notions of, 157; men's preferences, 179n8; sex as act of sympathy and necessity, 114–15, 158, 188n37; social conventions regarding, 75; Vietnamese proverbs about, 114; Vietnamese references to, 178n2 (Cà Mau); women's desire, 191n58, 193n15
Shohet, Merav, 39, 174n22
single motherhood: advice on, 157; difficulty of, 159–60; as global trend, 163–64; and ideology of marriage, 95–96; increases in, 101; legal status for, 32, 104–5; as new and positive subjectivity, 119–20; normalization of, 118–20; popular discourse on, 155–59; shift in attitude toward, 116; the single mum movement, 155–59; state support for, 120–21, 174n18; as topic of talk shows, 134, 156, 191n1, 195n39
single mothers: concentrations of, 181n25; as the "five withouts," 47; improvement in socioeconomic status of, 9; incomplete families of, 118–19; as innocent victims of war, 111; interest in author's research, 121; interest in marriage, 178n2 (ch. 3); married women's views of, 89; mutual support from, 79; personal transformation of, 121–22; prejudices against, 188n41; self-assessment of, 161; shift in attitude within, 116–17; social life for, 80, 122; as state subjects, 108–9; in Vietnamese Women's Museum exhibit, 125–27, 191n63
single women: abuse of older women, 186n30; age-related pressure to marry, 60–61; arti-

cles about happiness of, 186n30; and cultural changes from 1990s to 2000s, 136–37, 159–60; decision to *xin con*, 7–8, 10; decisions to remain single, 139; living strategies for, 28–29, 173n6; loneliness of, 22; and love in marriage, 64–65, 192n12; openness about intent to get pregnant, 150–51; preservation of men's happiness, 90; and rejection of AI, 147–49; reproductive strategies chosen by, 149–52; social life of, 20, 21; state support for, 190n53; volunteer war work of, 45–46, 47. *See also* loneliness
Sinh (interviewee): about, 56, 59; marriageability of, 65, 67; *xin con* experience of, 83–85
Sino-Vietnamese War (Third Indochina War), 48, 50
Slaughter, M. M., 108
Sóc Sơn District: about, 171n3; author's fieldwork in, ix, xi, xii, xiv; NGO work in, 121; societal change in, xiii; Vietnamese Women's Museum inclusion of single women from, 125–27, 191n63; women who chose *xin con* in the 2000s, 192n11
Sóc Sơn People's Committee, xii
social condemnation, 90, 93–94, 185n22, 193n19. *See also* Law on Marriage and the Family (1959)
social interaction: and feelings of belonging, 25; improvements for single mothers, 120; withdrawal from, 60–61
social media discourse on single motherhood, 156–58, 194n29
social scientists: and new subjectivity for women, 11. *See also* Lê Thi
socialism: attitudes toward state work assignments, 53; and changes to social and family values, 66; and children's rights, 107–8; and love in marriage, 62–63; and women's emancipation, 95; and women's marriageability, 10; and women's social interactions, 21
sperm banks, 179n7, 180n14
Star Partnership Project (Columbia University), ix
state and nation building, 194n24; civil rights, 53–54; and Confucian heritage, 43; decrees eradicating limits on women, 45; deployment of biopower, 101; legal age of marriage in, 58; legal bases for marriage in, 63–64; legend about nation's birth, 65–66; nation building in, 51; privacy

state and nation building (*continued*)
    in women's reproductive lives in, xi;
    recruitment of women during war, 45–46,
    46*fig.*, 182n29; response to *xin con*, 8; state
    support of *xin con*, 4–5, 9, 11; support for
    government workers' maternity care, 92–
    93; support for "new socialist woman,"
    179n6; universal drafting of men for war, 44;
    women's sacrifices for the nation, 145, 163,
    164; youth brigades and, 45, 172n4. *See also*
    Decree #12 "On Childbirth by Scientific
    Methods"; Đổi Mới policies; governmental-
    ity; Law on Marriage and the Family (1986);
    market economy; patriarchal ideologies;
    population management; Women's Union
subjectivity, concept of, 11, 136, 190n52
subjectivity, women's: 1986 Law and new sub-
    jectivity for single mothers, 120, 135–36,
    139, 165–66; choice and use of term *xin con*,
    152–53; coalescence of historical change
    and moral practices in, 155; complexity of
    individuals displayed in Women's Museum,
    126; decisions to remain single, 139; gender
    equality in, 141; independence in decision
    making, 150, 153–54; and multiple expres-
    sions of womanhood, 159; openness about
    decision to get pregnant, 150; shift in
    women's self-assessment, 143; shifts in
    women's subjectivity over time, 11; sum-
    mary of, 167–68
surrogacy, 175n28
Swedish International Development Agency
    (SIDA), 185n21

Tân Minh Women's Union, 125
Thắm (interviewee): about, 7; on children and
    womanhood, 23; and father's involvement
    with the child, 88–89; interest in marriage,
    59, 64, 65; loneliness of, 22; on marriage of
    older women, 26, 177n18; maternity care
    for, 93; use of contract by, 7, 87; *xin con*
    experience of, 80–81
Thanh niên xung phong (youth brigade volun-
    teers), 16, 45, 152, 169, 190
Thế Lan, 104
Thị Mai, 149, 152
Three Delays Campaign, 44, 176n2
Three Readies Movement, 44
Three Responsibilities Movement, 44–45
Three Submissions, 58
tình cảm (affective connection): importance in
    choosing a man, 148, 149, 192n12, 194n24;

mutual support among mothers, 79; shar-
    ing with children, 26, 111; through preg-
    nancy and breastfeeding, 34, 36–37, 39–40;
    through shared blood, 34–36; translation
    of term, 173n3. *See also* loneliness
Tô Thị Anh, 22–23
Tuyết (interviewee): about, 172n8; on adop-
    tion, 149; and choice, 168; decision to have
    a child, 152, 194n25; family consultation
    about pregnancy, 150; love and marriage
    for, 139–40; and marriage, 143; on mater-
    nal rights, 144; view of motherhood, 145

unmarried women, threats to, 16

Vân Thanh, 186n30
Vietnam, socioeconomic and cultural changes
    in, xii–xiii, 73, 136–37, 159–60, 162. *See also*
    state and nation building
Vietnam War. *See* American War
Vietnamese kinship values and practices: and
    adoption inside and outside the family,
    30–32; and asking for sex, 75; biological
    versus adoptive mothers, 174n15; blood
    relations in, 34–36; broadening of, 163;
    "child circulation," 30, 173n10; family names
    (*họ*), 181n22; fictive kinships, 182n28; filial
    piety in, 27, 32, 39, 173n5; flexible kinship
    practices, 85–86; gendered relationships,
    58–59, 177n17; ideology in, 3–5, 10; impor-
    tance of family in, 174n20; intentionality
    in *xin con* and, 77–78; of the Kinh ethnic
    majority, 62; navigation of, 95; nondisrup-
    tion by *xin con*, 7, 91; polygyny, 82; shared
    blood in, 149, 173n7, 175n28; and socializa-
    tion of children, 174n22; transformation
    through *xin con*, 4–5, 6; *xin con* agreements
    to protect, 87–92. *See also* Confucian heri-
    tage; families; marriage; patriarchal ideol-
    ogies; polygamy and polygyny; single
    motherhood; single women; Vietnamese
    men
Vietnamese men: and AI, 146; anonymity
    in *xin con*, 90, 91, 180n21; attitudes and
    behavior of, 142, 143; on extramarital sex,
    191n5; participation in *xin con*, 96; as the
    problem, 155–56, 161; and responsibility for
    children of *xin con*, 88, 180n19, 180nn18,19;
    willingness to participate in *xin con*, 87–88
Vietnamese socialist research: advocacy for
    xin con policies and support, 120–22; fram-
    ing public discourse on *xin con*, 110–11; on

loneliness, 111–12; normalizing single motherhood, 118–20; on sex, gender and the happy family, 112–17; on single mothers, 165

Vietnamese Women's Museum, 122–27, 124*fig.*, 167

Võ Thị Hảo, short story "Người sót lại của rừng cười," 111

Werner, Karen, 102

Winter, Jay, 94, 182n28

Wolf, Margery, 36

womanhood: importance of childbearing to, 23–25; model Vietnamese womanhood, 123, 167; multiple subjectivities in, 159

women: mobility of, 54–56, 66–67, 136–37; mortality rates during war, 49–50; use of cosmetics, 123, 190n58; work during and after the war, 44–48. *See also* marriage; patriarchal ideologies; single women; Vietnamese kinship values and practices; Vietnamese men

Women's Trade Union Association, 120

Women's Union: about, 172n2; classes provided by, 123; and Confucianism, 43; discourse on single motherhood, 158; educational responsibility of, 109, 185n20; goal of, 103–4; land allocation for single mothers, 174n18; Model Vietnamese Family designation, 122; as models for society, 93, 188n42; observation of research by, xi; official newspaper of, 185n26; officials' asking for a child, 165, 181n26, 185n24, 188n42;

public advice in the press, 113; and shift in attitude toward single mothers, 116; on socialism and women's lives, 4; support for single mothers, 8, 9, 110, 120–21, 160–61

xin con: agency in, 76; agreements and contracts in, 7, 81, 87–92; asking as mark of femininity, 75–76; author's initial interest in, ix, 3; as cultural project, 10; as deliberate choice, 78; desensationalizing, 118; dynamic interrelationship of agency, governmentality, and subjectivity in, 11; government policies and emergence of, 51; as intentional reproductive strategy, 7; legitimacy of, 104–5, 113, 158, 162; and the mother-child relationship, 36–37, 39; motivations for, 39, 117; one-child limit, 94, 106; parameters of, 74–77, 78; reasons not to pursue, 178n1 (ch. 3); as response to sacrifices made for the nation, 117; as rooted in Vietnamese social practices, 6, 86–87; shifting meaning of, 135, 136–39, 145, 153–55, 161, 162, 170; social recognition for, 4, 11, 40–41, 100, 122; as transformative, 160–61; and use of term *kiếm con*, 4; women's use of term, 152; and younger women, 117. *See also* agency in *xin con*; extramarital relations; governmentality; single motherhood; subjectivity, women's

Xuân Lan, 158

Yến (interviewee): multiple pregnancies of, 94; *xin con* experience of, 82–83